Ayers Bogley

The

Intellectual Life

of

Colonial

New England

Samuel Eliot Morison

THE
Intellectual Life
OF
Colonial
New England

New York University Press

PREFACE TO THE SECOND EDITION

THE SUBSTANCE of this book was delivered as lectures at the Washington Square center of New York University in November and December 1934, and published in 1935 as *The Puritan Pronaos.*

My inspiration, on the positive side, was an enlightening and suggestive book by Dr. Thomas Goddard Wright, *Literary Culture in Early New England*, published posthumously in 1920. In the untimely death of Dr. Wright the intellectual history of America suffered an irreparable loss. I endeavored to push a little farther down the cultural trail that he opened into the colonial wilderness.

On the negative side, I felt impelled to counteract the disparaging and, for the most part, inaccurate accounts of New England colonial culture that had been published during the previous forty years. It was, I believe, Charles Francis Adams who coined the phrase "glacial period" for the century of New England history between 1640 and 1740. According to him, after the banishment of Anne Hutchinson and the death of John Cotton, "a theological glacier . . . slowly settled down upon Massachusetts"; and for a century and a half "absolutely nothing" was produced in the Bay Colony in the way of literature, except Cotton Mather's *Magnalia*.[1] Everyone loves a literary label, which saves one from the labor of thinking; so the "glacial period" quickly became popular, and Brooks Adams, James Truslow Adams, and a host of others used it as a cover to their ig-

---

[1] *Massachusetts, Its Historians and History* (1895), pp. 57, 59, 67.

norance of, or lack of interest in, what went on in the New England mind for a century or more. And it is curious how the recession of this "glacier" always seems to coincide with the rise of the Adams family.

Now, all my studies of early New England go to prove that there was no "glacial period"; that interest in literature and scholarship grew rather than diminished during the entire course of the seventeenth century; that the dominant Puritan clergy, far from being indifferent to culture and hostile to science, as the Adams school briskly asserted, did everything possible under the circumstances in which they lived to stimulate, promote, and even produce intellectual activity. Moreover, it was largely the clergy who persuaded a poor and struggling people to set up schools and a college which continued to serve the community in later centuries.

Indeed, the intellectual life of this period might well be called the "Little Flowering" or "Early Flowering" of New England. It bears much the same relation to the great "Flowering" of the nineteenth century so admirably described by Van Wyck Brooks, as the Carolingian period does to the full flowering of medieval culture in the thirteenth century.

Samuel Eliot Morison

December 1955

CONTENTS

ABBREVIATIONS IN FOOTNOTES

A.A.S. . . . . . . *Proceedings of the American Antiquarian Society*, Worcester, 1812-.

C.S.M. . . . . . . *Publications of the Colonial Society of Massachusetts, Boston,* 1895-.

M.H.S. . . . . . . Massachusetts Historical Society. *Coll. M.H.S.* are the printed *Collections* of this Society, 1792-. *Proc. M.H.S.* are the *Proceedings*, 1859-. Numerical prefixes indicate numbers of series.

Conn. Col. Recs. . . *Public Records of the Colony of Connecticut*, 15 vols., covering the period 1636-1776 (1850-1890).

Mass. Bay Recs. . . . *Records of the Governor and Company of the Massachusetts Bay in New England*, 5 vols. in 6, N. B. Shurtleff, editor, Boston, 1853-1854.

N.E.Q. . . . . . . *The New England Quarterly*, 1928-.

The

Intellectual Life

of

Colonial

New England

I. THE ENGLISH AND RELIGIOUS BACKGROUND

IN THIS book I propose to describe, so far as time permits, and in describing to comment on, the intellectual life of New England in the seventeenth century. It might equally be called a course on the intellectual implications of English puritanism, for in that century there was not room for much in New England outside the stimulating if restrictive embrace of puritanism. There are, to be sure, a few exceptions. William Morrell's poem on New England in Latin hexameters was (like George Sandys' translation of Ovid's *Metamorphoses*) the work of an Englishman who made a brief sojourn in America. Thomas Morton's bibulous circle at Merrymount produced some bawdy verse, a good drinking song, and an amusing tract against the puritans which entered into our literary tradition, inspiring a bad novel of the nineteenth century and a worse opera of the twentieth. Yet it was but a gay episode, in no way affecting the life or mind of the people. The descriptions of New England by nonpuritans like Captain John Smith and John Josselyn belong to English rather than American literature. New England was not only puritan, but a fair test of what values there were in English puritanism: for in New England the puritans had it pretty much their own way. The colonies that they founded were their own colonies, from which anyone who objected violently or even vociferously to the puritan way of life was forthwith expelled. The English government let them almost completely alone, excepting for the short-lived experiment of the Dominion of New England at the close of the century.

All the contents of this book are, in a sense, a test of English puritanism. The colonists in New England (and, for that matter, in Virginia or Canada) were severely handicapped in their struggle to keep up civilized standards. For the most part they were leading a tough pioneer life; their audience was small, their contacts with the centers of learning and culture in Europe were tenuous; their chances of publication were slight. But the puritans of New England did have it their own way as to the shape, the form, and the content of their intellectual life. Their tastes, desires, and prejudices dictated what would be read, studied, written, and published. Everyone knows that those tastes were in a sense narrow—for instance, they proscribed the drama. What is not sufficiently known or appreciated is this: puritanism not only did not prevent, but stimulated an interest in the classics, belles-lettres, poetry, and scientific research. Neither pioneer hardships nor other restrictions were ever so great as to prevent the burgeoning of a genuine intellectual life in that series of little beachheads on the edge of the wilderness, which was seventeenth-century New England.

By intellectual life I do not mean literature alone. Products of the printing press naturally bulk large among the palpable intellectual remains of any modern era; and, as historians (or some of them) dislike speculation about things impalpable, they are easily tempted to confine their attention to printed literature, or even to a few typical writers. My purpose is to depict the life of puritan New England in aspects other than its economic and political. But within so brief a compass I cannot touch architecture, or the minor arts that the early New Englanders cultivated to good purpose.

Purposely I have completely neglected in this book the works of New England's founders who were educated in old England, and who passed an appreciable part of their lives in the Old Country before emigrating. Some of these men—William Bradford, John Cotton, John Wilson, Thomas Shepard, Thomas Hooker, and Roger Williams—wrote prose superior by any standard to that of the later, native-born writers.[1] And for that very reason, they are the much better known and far more has been written about them. My intention is, first, to describe the institutions (school and college) and facilities (libraries, printing, and bookselling) that fostered intellectual life, and then to describe what the native-born, or American-educated, New Englanders made of these opportunities.

Most writers have emphasized the institutional and material aspects of New England colonial history. This is natural, since the institutions the puritans founded, Church, Commonwealth, Town, College, were so firmly established as to outlast the purposes for which they were intended. Church and College and Commonwealth have been patched and altered again and again, without losing all their original character—much as an old mansion of New York City is cut up into flats and offices, yet retains somewhat of of its original dignity. Others have confined their attention

[1] What Moses Coit Tyler wrote about these figures in his *History of American Literature* (1879), vol. I, has never been surpassed. I have written about the Winthrops, Shepard, Nathaniel Ward, and John Eliot in *Builders of the Bay Colony* (1930), and have edited a new edition of Bradford, *Of Plymouth Plantation* (1952). Perry Miller has made a fresh interpretation of Williams, with selections from his writings, in *Roger Williams* (1953) of the Makers of the American Tradition Series.

to the material side of colonial New England: farming, fishing, shipping, trading. All these activities in a sense fed the intellectual life just as modern finance and industry feed medical research, scholarship, and other objects of social value. It is not, however, my purpose to describe the old bottles that were ultimately to be filled with new wine, or the sources of wealth which paid for the wine. Rather do I seek the flavor of the old wine for which the bottles were originally blown. For the wine of New England is not a series of successive vintages, each distinct from the other, like the wines of France; it is more like the mother-wine in those great casks of port and sherry that one sees in the *bodegas* of Portugal and Spain, from which a certain amount is drawn off every year, and replaced by an equal volume of the new. Thus the change is gradual, and the mother-wine of 1656 still gives bouquet and flavor to what is drawn in 1956.

Our vintners have been a pretty close corporation. New blood and wine they have sought and obtained as the price of survival; but it is they—this hierarchy of parsons, professors, and artists—who have determined what should be selected and what rejected. The newcomers who began to arrive in appreciable numbers over a century ago, and who now rule all the cities and most of the public institutions of New England, have contributed very little to the main currents of New England intellectual life, although they manage to make some native intellectuals very unhappy. Our imported ideas have come from England, France, and Germany, rather than from the nations of our immigrant peoples.

New England differed from the other English colonies

in that it was founded largely for the purpose of trying an experiment in Christian living. This statement is self-evident to anyone who has read extensively in the literature of the times, both puritan writings and writings of their enemies. It has, of course, been challenged by people so superior in intellect that they can give you the essence of an era without the labor of reading the sources. We have all been told that the dynamic motive of settling New England was economic, though expressed in a religious jargon. Doubtless the idea of bettering their condition in life was present in a very large number of early New Englanders: the spirit of adventure must also claim a share; but no one who has delved deeply into the origin and history of the New England colonies can, by any fair application of the rules of evidence, deny that the dynamic force in settling New England was English puritanism desiring to realize itself. The leaders, whom the people followed, proposed like Milton to make over a portion of the earth in the spirit of Christian philosophy: a new church and state, family and school, ethic and conduct. They might and did differ among themselves as to the realization of these high and holy aims; but a new City of God was their aim.

Until 1630, New England was anybody's country; the little band of Pilgrims who landed at Plymouth Rock ten years earlier were too few and isolated to have leavened any large lump of people hostile or indifferent to their point of view. But once the Massachusetts Bay Colony was founded, the fate of New England was sealed. In ten years' time, fifteen or twenty thousand people came over under puritan leaders; and three new colonies, Connecticut, Rhode Island, and New Haven, had been founded to contest with Massachusetts Bay in rivalry for divine favor and godly living.

Who were these puritans, and what did they propose to do? They were a party in the Church of England that arose in Elizabeth's reign with the purpose of carrying out the Protestant reformation to its logical conclusion, to base the English Church both in doctrine and discipline on the firm foundation of Sacred Scripture; or in the words of Cartwright, to restore the primitive, apostolic church 'pure and unspotted' by human accretions or inventions. Religion should permeate every phase of living. Man belonged to God alone: his only purpose in life was to enhance God's glory and do God's will, and every variety of human activity, every sort of human conduct, presumably unpleasing to God, must be discouraged if not suppressed.

English puritanism, though essentially a religious movement, had its political and economic aspects. In their search for the original pattern of the Christian church in the apostolic age, the puritan leaders did not agree. They were divided into the Presbyterians, who thought that the primitive church was governed by a series of representative assemblies or synods; and the Congregationalists, who insisted that there never had been a unified church, only churches: each individual congregation should be a democracy of the 'visible saints,' of those admitted to full communion upon satisfactory evidence that they were God's elect. New England was founded by Congregationalists, the more democratic wing; and the latent democratic principle in their polity proved, humorously enough, an exceptionally heavy cross for the autocratically inclined parsons to carry. But whether Congregational or Presbyterian in its polity, puritanism appealed to the average Englishman's anticlericalism. It gave the layman a larger part in the local church than he had enjoyed since the Roman emperors became Christian.

Puritanism also had its economic side. I do not hold to the thesis of Max Weber and Troeltsch, that puritanism arose as a justification for usury; *i.e.*, for taking interest on loans. In New England, certainly, the Church was no respecter of persons, and the spectacle of Robert Keayne, the profiteering merchant of Boston, having to stand up in meeting and take a tongue-lashing from the Reverend John Cotton for infringing the puritan code of business ethics, would have warmed the heart of any modern radical. The Weber thesis, as restated by R. H. Tawney, accords better with the facts as observed in New England. Puritanism was unascetic; it came to terms with this world. Under the medieval church you could only approach perfection (short of Heaven) by withdrawing from this world and entering the priesthood or a monastic order. But puritanism taught that a man could serve God quite as effectually in his chosen calling as by entering the sacred ministry; that a farmer or merchant who conducted his business according to Christian ethics was more agreeable in the sight of God than one who withdrew from the world and escaped his social responsibilities by a celibate or monastic life. This doctrine of the calling, that you could serve God by nobly fulfilling a function determined by the conditions of this world, and thus prove your right to an easy place in the next world, was probably the main reason why puritanism appealed to the rising middle class, the nascent capitalists of the sixteenth and seventeenth centuries. Puritanism was essentially a middle-class movement. It was far too exigent in its moral demands ever to be popular with earthy-minded peasants, or with the nobility and the very rich, who saw no point in having money if you could not spend it as you liked.

In its attitude toward love, puritanism had more in common with Judaism than with medieval Christianity or Jesuit piety. Puritanism did not hold with asceticism or celibacy. The clergy married young and often; their church offered no monastic retreat for men who were too much troubled by women. Milton's invocation 'Hail, wedded love!' in *Paradise Lost* expresses the puritan ideal very neatly; and William Ames, the puritan casuist, implies in his *de Conscientia* that women have a right to expect something more from their husbands than mere duty. 'Increase and multiply,' the oldest of God's commands, was one that the puritans particularly enjoyed obeying—or some of us would not be here. Continence was a moral ideal on which due weight was laid; abstinence was not a superior virtue confounded with chastity but was in conflict with the purpose of creation. Married men who came out to New England were bluntly told to send for their wives or return to them. It was easier to obtain a divorce in New England in the seventeenth century than in old England; for the puritans, having laid such store on wedded love, wished every marriage to be a success.

On its intellectual side, which mainly concerns us, puritanism was an enemy to that genial glorification of the natural man with all his instincts and appetites that characterized the Renaissance and the great Elizabethans. Shakespeare's

What a piece of work is man! how noble in reason! how infinite
in faculties! in form and moving how express and admirable! in
action how like an angel! in apprehension how like a god!

is the antithesis of puritanism, which taught that natural
man was wholly vile, corrupt, and prone to evil; that he
could do no good without God's assistance; that he thor-
oughly deserved to broil in hell for all eternity, and would
do so if he did not grasp the hand of grace proffered him
by a merciful God through Jesus Christ.

Predestination, one of the cardinal doctrines of Calvinism, was not stressed by the New England puritans;
Michael Wigglesworth does indeed touch on it when he
consigns the *reprobate* infants (not the *unbaptized* infants
as is commonly said) to the 'easiest room in hell'; but after
reading some hundreds of puritan sermons, English and
New English, I feel qualified to deny that the New England
puritans were predestinarian Calvinists. John Cotton indeed
was wont to 'sweeten his mouth with a bit of Calvin' before retiring (rather a sour bedtime confection, one would
think), but in general the New England puritans quoted
their revered Ames and Perkins and the church fathers
much more than they did Calvin; and John Harvard had
more volumes in his library by St. Thomas Aquinas than
by St. John of Geneva. The puritan sermons assume (when
they do not directly teach) that by virtue of the Covenant
of Grace, and through the efforts of the churches, salvation
lay within reach of every person who made an effort;
Christ helped those who helped themselves. Fatalism is
completely wanting in the New England view of religion
or of life. The karma of Buddhism implied a blind, mean-
ingless universe; a poor joke that God played on humanity

in one of his idle or sardonic humors. But the puritans, like the Jews, regarded this earth and humanity as a divine enterprise, the management of which was God's major interest; they were God's people and their God was a living God, always thought of as intensely concerned with the actions and characters of people and nations.[2] Each individual was a necessary item in a significant and divinely ordered cosmos. God has a personal interest in me, and has appointed work for me to do. If I am incapable of receiving his grace, it is unfortunate; but if that is God's will, who am I to complain? Yet while there's life, there's hope; and at any time before death my risen Lord may whisper in my heart that I am of the blessed ones elected by his Father to salvation.

It is generally supposed that puritanism hampered intellectual and artistic activity; and there is some truth in this charge. Puritanism banned three forms in which the English excelled: the drama, religious music, and erotic poetry. Just why it banned the drama is still a matter of debate among the professors. Was it that the drama was supposed to lead to immorality, or because it amused people too much? Or simply because a number of the church fathers, like Chrysostom, had thundered against the pagan drama of their day? Whatever the reason, the puritan war on the theatre was hideously successful. There is no stranger phenomenon in literature than the swift rise of the English drama to a high zenith between 1580 and 1611, with Marlowe and Shakespeare; and its equally swift decline a few years after the death of Shakespeare. But it was not the puritans alone who killed the theatre. Their theological

[2] B. H. Streeter, *The Buddha and the Christ* (1932), p. 51 *et passim*.

enemies, Bishop Laud and the high churchmen, were equally responsible. James I liked a good show as much as anyone and, as long as he reigned, the English theatre had court patronage; but Bishop Laud took charge of the conscience of Charles I, and discouraged the King from patronizing the drama as an object unworthy of a Christian monarch's support. Deprived both of middle-class and court patronage, the English theatre had no audience left but the sort that attends burlesque shows today; and the English theatre became not much better than burlesque shows. It was the puritans, to be sure, who closed the theatres; but one imagines that by 1642 the managers welcomed the closure, as it saved them from losing more money.

Although puritanism had nothing against music as such, the puritans injured music by taking it out of the churches. Religious exercises were stripped down to the bare rudiments of the days when early Christians met in secret, and would not have dared to play the organ, even if an organ had been available. Consequently instrumental music, like the other beautiful incidents with which the medieval church had enriched religious expression, was done away with for want of scriptural sanction, and because it was supposed to make the worshiper dreamy. To secular music (as Dr. Percy Scholes has shown in his recent work) the puritans had no objection; Oliver Cromwell kept an orchestra at his court, and the first Italian opera to be played in England was produced under his Protectorate, and by puritans.[3] A few musical instruments were brought to New

[3] Percy A. Scholes, *The Puritans and Music in England and New England* (Oxford University Press, 1934).

England, and more were ordered in the latter part of the century. There was 'no law agin' it,' but music was not a form of activity that the English puritans cared much about, or were willing to make an effort to maintain in the New World.

I do not propose to hide the puritans behind the excuse that there was no room or opportunity for these things in a pioneer community. The German Moravians who came to Pennsylvania in the early eighteenth century maintained high musical standards because they believed that music was worth making some effort to keep up. And the puritans transplanted high educational standards for the same reason. Hard as colonial Americans worked, they, or some of them, had a certain leisure and surplus to devote to things of the spirit; and it depended entirely on their set of values what things of the spirit, if any, they chose to cultivate.

While the puritan wrote off certain cultural activities such as the drama, and failed to do much for others, such as music, he was stimulated by his faith to an intellectual activity that was conspicuously absent in other English colonies. The alternative to a puritanically controlled intellectual life, in new settlements, was intellectual vacuity; the emphasis was on acquiring an estate. The 'best people' were engaged in growing tobacco or sugar cane, or trading with the natives; there was no incentive to lead a life of the spirit, no market for books, or audience for a play. At about the same time as the founding of New England, four other important English colonies—Virginia, Bermuda, Maryland, Barbados—and some lesser island plantations were established. Virginia by 1660 had a population almost equal to that of the whole of New England, and for wealth,

Barbados was not far behind; neither was a puritan colony. But both colonies were singularly barren in literary production,[4] although it may be that some hitherto hidden corpus of poetry, like that of Edward Taylor, or some prose manuscript of great merit, like Robert Beverley's *History of Virginia* (1705), may turn up. And where is the devotional poetry we might expect from Maryland, a Catholic colony? Why did not the scenic beauties of 'still-vext Bermoothes,' which at second hand lend such grace to Shakespeare's *Tempest,* inspire some native Bermudian to song, or prose?

Even in Mexico and Peru, where an enormously wealthy governing class existed almost a century before New England was founded, and whither learned ecclesiastics were constantly emigrating, nearly a century elapsed before a native intellectual life developed. The seventeenth century was the great age of Mexican and Peruvian literature; Don Pedro de Peralta Rocha Barnuevo y Benavídes, the savant of Lima, was almost contemporary with Cotton Mather—and Don Pedro was very much the same sort of indiscriminate and omniscient pedant as Don Cotton. [5] But New England, within ten years of the founding of Massachusetts Bay, had a vigorous intellectual life of its own, expressed institutionally in a college, a school system, and

[4] An exception may be made of the singularly beautiful epitaph on Nathaniel Bacon, beginning "Death, why so cruel!" which is reprinted in C. M. Andrews, ed., *Narratives of the Insurrection,* p. 75; and of a play called "Ye Bare and Ye Cubb" which, according to A. H. Quinn, *History of the American Drama* (1944), p. 5, was performed by three citizens of Accomac County, Virginia, on August 27, 1665; the text, unfortunately, has not survived.

[5] Irving A. Leonard, "A Great Savant of Colonial Peru," *Philological Quarterly,* XII (1933), 54-72; note especially the estimate of him on p. 63.

a printing press; applied in a native sermon literature, poetry, and history. What is more, this life did not perish with the founders: it deepened and quickened as the century grew older, developing a scientific side. For in puritanism, New England had a great emotional stimulus to certain forms of intellectual life.

A humanist New England would doubtless have provided a pleasanter dwelling place, and a more sweet and wholesome stream to swell the American flood than a puritan New England. But there was no such alternative. Humanism is a tender plant, depending on a stable and leisured society, and on a nice adjustment of human relations, that cannot bear transplanting. As already noted, in a new country the natural alternative to intellectual puritanism is intellectual vacuity; and for a very good reason, that the mere physical labor of getting a living in a virgin country is so great as to exhaust and stultify the human spirit unless it have some great emotional drive. That, I take it, explains why in the nonpuritan colonies the humanist tradition of Elizabethan England shriveled; and why those colonies had to wait a century or more before they had any intellectual life worthy of the name. In South Carolina, we are told, the French planters of the end of the seventeenth century brought their Montaignes, and Montaigne is perhaps the best representative in old-world literature of a kindly, reflective, and disciplined humanism; yet the soil was unpropitious, and the tradition perished. Puritanism, on the contrary, throve under conditions of vigor, hardship, and isolation; hence the New England colonies were able almost immediately to create and support a distinct way of life that showed an unexpected vigor and virility long after English puritanism had been diluted or overwhelmed. The intellectual alternatives for New England, then, were not puritanism *or* humanism, but puritanism *or* overwhelming materialism, such as we find in typical newly settled regions whether English, French, Dutch, or Spanish.

Again we have a paradox. Puritanism in New England preserved far more of the humanist tradition than did non-puritanism in the other English colonies. The grammar schools and the college fostered a love of *literae humaniores:* Cicero, Virgil, Terence, and Ovid; Homer, Hesiod, and Theocritus. It was no small feat to keep alive the traditions of classical antiquity in a region that had never known the grandeur that was Rome, the glory that was Greece. The New England schools and colleges did just that; and handed down a priceless classical tradition, which has been mangled and trampled under foot by the professional educators and progressive pedagogues of the last hundred years. The classics flourished in New England under puritanism, and began to decay when puritanism withered.

The reason why the puritans nourished classicism while rejecting other aspects of Renaissance humanism was their concern for the education of posterity. Massachusetts Bay, New Haven, Connecticut, and Rhode Island were ruled both in church and state by men who had attended the British universities and the English grammar schools. A careful combing of lists of emigrants reveals that at least one hundred and thirty university alumni came to New England before 1646. This does not seem a very impressive total; but the entire population of New England in 1645 was not greater than 25,000, and probably less, which means that there was on the average one university-trained man to every forty or fifty families. In addition there was a large but indeterminate number of men who had a sound classical education in the English grammar schools, and therefore saw eye-to-eye with the university men on intellectual matters. These Oxford and Cambridge alumni, moreover, had an influence all out of proportion to their numbers. They were not concentrated in the sea-ports, but scattered all over the country, on the frontier and in country villages. Although they did not monopolize the political ruling class, since most of them were parsons, and as such ineligible to office, they did constitute an intellectual ruling class. Their standards were accepted by the community, and maintained in the college that they founded, largely for the purpose of perpetuating all that they understood by civilization. The intellectual life of New England was determined by the top layers of society; it was no proletarian cult welling up from the common people. *Accepted* by the community, not *imposed* on it, I say; for men of education were the chosen leaders of the puritan emigration. Deprived ministers or discontented country gentry gathered groups of neighbors, friends, and parishioners, emigrated in the same ship, and settled in the same place. They were the shepherds to whom the people looked for guidance and inspiration, on whose spoken words they hung, and whose written words they perused eagerly.

For the sources of New England intellectual life we must look to the English universities, and especially to the University of Cambridge. From the Middle Ages to the eighteenth century the main, almost the exclusive, scholarly preoccupation of the English universities was theology in both its aspects. The one was ecclesiastical polity, the form that the church should assume (including its relations to the state); the other was theology proper, or divinity—the philosophical aspect of Christianity, the relation of man and nature to God and the nature of God himself. There was next to no mathematical or scientific interest in the English universities until the Restoration; Barrow and Newton, who came after our time, were the first to give Cambridge her scientific reputation. Practically all the scientific discoveries of the seventeenth century were made outside the universities, which resisted each advance by a conservative adherence to Aristotelian physics and Ptolemaic astronomy. Medicine was not yet a university subject; young Englishmen studied it as apprentices to physicians or in Continental universities; nor was law. Englishmen read law at the Inns of Court. Universities did not foster creative literature; the great figures in Elizabethan literature were either men like Shakespeare who had merely a grammar-school education, or like Kit Marlowe and Milton, who regarded their college careers as a waste of time. Nor did the universities do much to foster creative scholarship outside the important branch of theology; the deep and fruitful labors of Renaissance humanists in collecting and editing texts of ancient classics went on outside university walls. The Bodleian Library was opened only in 1602, and a much longer time elapsed before Cambridge had a university library worthy of the name. Neither at Oxford nor at Cambridge in 1630 was there any teacher to compare with the Italian humanists of the

quattrocento, or with the French school of classical
scholars such as Scaliger, Casaubon, Lipsius, and Salmasius, or with Dutch university professors such as Heinsius
and Grotius.[6] The most that can be said is that university
training in the liberal arts gave a solid background to men
who already had the spark of creative genius in them—men
such as Bacon, Spenser, Ben Jonson, and Donne.

The University of Cambridge as they knew it, not as
it has since become, was the standard which the New
England puritans attempted, however imperfectly, to attain. The names of her greatest masters, Ames and Perkins,
Preston and Chaderton, were often on their lips, and
always in their hearts. The beauty and serenity of the
cloistered life there they looked back upon with an aching
affection, when endeavoring in a frontier society of poverty and struggle to build up what they called their 'poor
colledge in the wilderness.' And the intellectual life of
Cambridge set the pace for the intellectual life of New
England.

The English universities, in 1630 as in 1230, were regarded primarily as feeders to the church. Every holder of
a college fellowship had to be in holy orders, the ambitious
young men looked forward to becoming prelates; most
of the students who took degrees intended to be clergymen. It is true that the English universities had, at the
time of the Renaissance, opened their doors to young
gentlemen of the leisured or the newly rich class, and
provided for them a relatively easy course in ancient litera-

---

[6] An exception should be made of Hebrew scholarship. Excellent and
scholarly work in the Oriental languages was done at Oxford and Cambridge
by men like Pococke and Tremellius and Lightfoot; the first two presidents
of Harvard were primarily Orientalists.

ture and history that led to no degree; and that this practice had so far become a tradition as to influence the New England college. But this class of young gentlemen, for the most part, had decidedly nonintellectual interests; they did not become tutors or professors or resident scholars; and their influence on the intellectual life of the university, like that of similar frivolous young men in our colleges today, was practically nil.

The one great, absorbing intellectual interest in the Oxford and Cambridge and Dublin from which the founders of New England came was that very ecclesiastical controversy that drove them forth, in Lowell's words, 'to pitch new states as Old-World men pitch tents.' The contest between the Catholic and Protestant points of view, between men who wished to save what was left of the medieval church in the Anglican church, or restore what had been lost, and men who wished to strip off every medieval garment that could not be proved scriptural; the contest between the Arminian theology adumbrated by Archbishop Laud and Launcelot Andrewes and the quasi-Calvinist or 'Federal' theology expounded by Preston and Ames filled the British universities with contention and clamor. It is difficult to make a modern man appreciate the seventeenth-century interest in theology. Man's relation to God was a matter of great pith and moment to people in that era, and they needed no more compulsion to hear sermons than people now need compulsion to read newspapers. For one Englishman who had seen a play and for ten who had read one, there were literally hundreds who read theological literature, and thousands who listened intently to sermons. Theology was the leading topic of conversation around the campfires in Cromwell's army. Richard Baxter records that on a visit to the army in 1643 he found everyone talking about forms of prayer, infant baptism, free grace, free will, antinomianism, Arminianism, and liberty of conscience. The Reverend Mr. Baxter was so alarmed by the heterogeneity of religious opinion in the army that he gave up his quiet parish for an army chaplaincy in order to tell Cromwell's Ironsides what was what, and put the soldiers on the right track to salvation.

No subject of popular interest today, even economics, can compare in pervasiveness with the theology of the seventeenth century. Perhaps we can faintly grasp what theology meant to the people in those days if we imagine all parsons, priests, and rabbis turned out of our modern places of worship, and their places taken by economists who every Sabbath brought you the latest news from Washington, D. C., and told you just how you could escape taxes, or get a share of the divine (federal) bounty.

The puritans were the extreme wing of the Protestant party in the English universities, and the losing wing. They came to New England because they had lost every bout since 1570, when their great champion Cartwright was expelled from his chair of divinity at Cambridge. Until the reign of James I they thought that at least their theology was safe, since the Thirty-nine Articles of the Church of England were predominantly Calvinist; but James I discerned the antimonarchical implications of puritanism, high-church theologians began to interpret the Thirty-nine Articles in a reactionary manner, and through court influence puritans were expelled or excluded from posts of honor and emolument in the universities as in the government. This state of things, coming to a head in the years 1629-1634 with persecution, started the great puritan migration to New England. The educated men who organized and led this exodus brought with them a deep and lively interest in religion. The religious point of view dominated the intellectual life of New England for over a century, almost until the contest with England began.

A secondary intellectual interest in the Oxford and Cambridge of 1600 was poetry. All English schoolboys and college students were trained to write Latin and Greek verse; and at every marriage, birth, or death in the Royal Family, the choice wits of Oxford and Cambridge got out *epithalamia, gaudia,* or *threnodia* celebrating the happy or lamentable event in hexameters or elegiacs. It was an era of religious poetry, mostly by university-trained men— Spenser, Milton, Donne, Quarles, George Herbert, and, later, Cowley and Dryden. This tradition and, to a surprising extent, the amorous poetical fashion of Elizabeth's reign, crossed to New England together with other things of which the stricter puritans did not approve. For New England puritanism, like the Anglican Church of the Restoration, was a *via media;* a middle course between what Cotton [7] Mather called the 'Rigid and High-flown Presbyterians' and the rigid sectaries and separatists. It never formally separated from the Church of England, as Roger Williams passionately believed it should. And New England puritanism had to make terms with humanity because it was in a responsible position. It has often been observed that political responsibility sobers down a fanatic, although of late examples to the contrary

[7] *Magnalia Christi Americana* (1702), book vii, 4-5.

are numerous. When the emigrant puritans found themselves in a position of power in the New England colonies, they were neither so rigid nor so fanatical as one would suppose from the pamphlets they had written when out of power; and so in England itself when the Civil War brought the puritans on top.

It is not, then, correct to judge the puritans, as many writers have done, by the fanatical pamphlets of William Prynne, the Martin Marprelate tracts, and the writings of Richard Baxter. When in power they soon learned that no layman, however sincerely religious, could be expected to give all his waking moments to thoughts of God; that he must be given opportunity for earning a living, and for reasonable recreation, or, as they called it, 'seasonable merriment.' There was much opportunity for love and laughter in colonial New England, though not as much as there should have been. Thus, the puritans forbade the observance of Christmas, because of the pagan revelry that merry England had inflicted on the day of Christ's Nativity; but they established Thanksgiving Day which took its place; and now we have both Thanksgiving Day and Christmas. They abolished May Day, which in Elizabethan England was far from being the innocent schoolchildren's holiday that it is now; but instead they got two holidays in spring and early summer: election day and the college commencement, which soon took on the character of a Flemish kermis. They attempted to regulate the liquor traffic; but they never attempted or even suggested a complete prohibition of all alcoholic beverages. Indeed, it might be agreed that puritan restrictions on purely physical enjoyment tended to stimulate intellectual life; that a good many people who in England would have lingered in a tavern, carousing and singing songs, stayed at home and wrote prose and poetry, or argued over the fine points of the last sermon and picked flaws in their parson's theology!

One must also keep in mind the small and thinly populated area of which we are speaking. The estimates of the United States Census Bureau give the New England colonies 17,800 people in 1640; 106,000 at the end of the century. As a basis of comparison, Virginia and Maryland combined had about the same population as New England from 1660 to the close of the century. Boston, the largest town in the English colonies, had about 7,000 people by 1690. It would be absurd to expect so thinly populated and isolated a province to produce poets of the caliber of Milton and Dryden, or prose writers equal to Lord Clarendon and John Locke. We must remember what is to be reasonably expected of a community of 25,000 to 100,000 people, agricultural for the most part, having no leisure class, or ready means of wealth, or method of conserving inherited property. New England was a poor country, even by the standards of the day, struggling with a niggardly nature for livelihood, subject to the constant tendency of the frontier to reduce humanity to a dead level of ambition and intellect. Under such circumstances we should not expect anything very great, original, or creative; for no new colony, since those of ancient Greece, has been able, during the period of adjustment to a new environment, to equal the intellectual achievement of its mother country. I am inviting you to accompany me in a survey of a small group of people striving manfully, even heroically, to achieve an ideal—an ideal not merely religious, though permeated by religion; an ideal of transmitting a civilization, and of planting in the New World the very vines whose fruit they had enjoyed in the Old. As New Englanders themselves were wont to say, 'Despise not the day of small things.'

II. THE BEGINNINGS OF HIGHER EDUCATION[1]

IN NO way is the high intellectual ambition of the New England puritans so clearly evident as in their founding a college for higher education in 1636 and maintaining it throughout the seventeenth century. Stephen d'Irsay, a recent French historian of universities, remarks on 'the energy, one may say the heroic energy, of those who in the midst of material daily cares on the very frontiers of civilization, struggled to establish only fifteen years after the landing of the Pilgrim Fathers, on the still wild coasts of New England, Harvard University.'[2]

No other commonwealth of the English-speaking world, even our western states, attempted to provide for higher learning so soon after its foundation. The Virginia Company of London did indeed propose to establish a college for the education of the Indians as early as 1618, and whispered the name of a university; money was collected for it, and land laid out; but the funds were dissipated on other objects. That enterprise, moreover, was English, not colonial in origin; and after the Virginia Company had been dissolved, the Virginians themselves made no efforts for almost seventy years to carry out the design. Mexico and Peru did indeed acquire universities far grander than the New England college as early as

---

[1] For references to this chapter, the reader is referred to my *Founding of Harvard College* (1935), and its sequel, *Harvard College in the Seventeenth Century* (2 vols., 1936). The early records of the College are printed in *C.S.M.*, XV, XVI, and XXXI.

[2] *Histoire des Universités* (Paris, 1933), I, 13.

1553, within a generation of the Spanish conquest. But these were the most wealthy communities in the world at that time, with a mighty monarch and a powerful church behind them.

Our earliest colonial 'colledge, the best Thing that ever *New-England* thought upon,' as Cotton Mather exclaimed,[3] is the ancestor of most of the colleges and universities in the United States today. There are indeed two other lines of academic descent in this country; the Anglican, through the College of William and Mary (1693), and the Roman Catholic, deriving from the same common ancestor (the University of Paris) as the New England colleges, but reinvigorated by the Society of Jesus in the sixteenth century. Other influences, Scotch and Continental, have entered the main stream from time to time; but the stream itself flows from the English Cambridge through Harvard before subdividing. The founding, and still more the maintaining, of Harvard College at a certain degree of excellence through the puritan century had a far-reaching influence on the intellectual life of the United States.

This college was founded by a vote of the General Court or Legislature of Massachusetts in October 1636, appropriating £400 'towards a schoale or colledge.' For over a year the project marked time, while the authorities dealt with the Pequot Indians (which was comparatively easy), and wrestled with a clever woman, Mistress Anne Hutchinson (which was more difficult). All through the Christian era there had been an undercurrent of hostility of Christian fanatics to classical learning, and to the uni-

[3] *Magnalia* (1702), book iv, 126.

versities that fostered it. 'What has Christ to do with Apollo?' Should not a Christian education begin with the Sacred Scripture, not with pagan poets and philosophers? But the intellectual leaders of the Christian world illogically went on teaching their pupils rhetoric out of Cicero, poetry out of Ovid, and philosophy out of Aristotle. This attitude of suspicion and hostility to the classical tradition was natural to puritans, with their insistence on scriptural sanction for everything; for when a plain man had been moved by the beauty and wisdom of the Bible, he was apt to feel that all other letters were a vanity and snare to the soul. After all, Christ and his apostles were not university graduates. In the radical fringe of the puritan movement, to which Mistress Anne Hutchinson belonged, hostility to universities and to learned ministers was an article of faith. Sincere fanatics called the universities 'stews of Anti-Christ,' 'houses of lies,' that 'stink before God with the most loathsome abomination.' [4] There was a peculiar danger of this attitude prevailing in a new country, where social and economic conditions fostered crude materialism, pietistic conceit, and complacent ignorance.

In 1637, when the 'Antinomians' had been defeated at the polls and their gifted prophetess banished to Rhode Island, the Bay Colony authorities got on with the college. A Board of Overseers consisting of magistrates and ministers was appointed, an acre lot with a dwelling house purchased in Cambridge, a professor hired, and the first freshman class induced to begin their studies in the summer of 1638. On September 14 John Harvard died, leaving

---

[4] Quoted by President Chauncy in his *Gods Mercy Shewed to his People* (Cambridge, 1655), p. 35, a reply to several pamphlets from the other side.

his library of about four hundred volumes and half his estate (under £800) to the college, which was then named for him.

The beginnings of the college were not happy. Nathaniel Eaton, the first head, had every qualification on paper for a successful president; but he used the rod more freely than college students were willing to put up with even in those rough days, and his wife, who did the catering, served them with mouldy bread, spoiled beef, and sour beer—when there was beer. After Master Eaton had (as Governor Winthrop recorded) beaten his chief assistant with a walnut cudgel 'big enough to have killed a horse,' there was an investigation. Eaton was dismissed and left the country, carrying with him a considerable slice of John Harvard's legacy.

In 1640 the college made a fresh start under Henry Dunster, a remarkable young Cambridge graduate. President Dunster recalled Eaton's pupils to the scene of their freshman floggings, and, assuming the entire teaching burden himself, managed to get them through a liberal arts course in two more years. It is still uncertain whether the college under Eaton was of English university status or a mere boarding school of secondary grade; but Dunster insisted on the higher standard, and in 1652 had the course for the bachelor's degree lengthened to four years. From the first graduating class two promising young men were appointed tutors, others succeeded; and in 1650 the General Court incorporated the president, treasurer, and five fellows as the President and Fellows of Harvard College. Under that charter Harvard University is still governed today, although the original liberal arts college has mush-roomed out into a congeries of graduate schools.

By 1650, then, the college was firmly established. Under her young and energetic president a program similar to that of the English universities was adopted, a new building erected, and corporate autonomy granted by the state. Now, what was the purpose of all this effort? The usual explanation is that Harvard and the other colonial colleges were intended to educate ministers. This is only a half-truth. The dynamic motive, to be sure, was to train up a learned ministry to take the place of Oxford and Cambridge graduates in New England, as they died off. Without that motive there would have been no college, at least not so early. But the purpose of the founders was much broader than that; and the curriculum they established was not a divinity curriculum. 'After God had carried us safe to *New England*,' states the opening paragraph of the first account of Harvard College,[5] 'and wee had builded our houses, provided necessaries for our livelihood, rear'd convenient places for Gods worship, and setled the Civill Government: One of the next things we longed for, and looked after was to advance *Learning* and perpetuate it to Posterity; dreading to leave an illiterate Ministry to the Churches, when our present Ministers shall lie in the Dust.'

It would be a mistake to lay too much emphasis on the final clause. 'To advance *Learning*' echoes Bacon's famous work. And the charter of 1650 declares the purpose of the

[5] *New Englands First Fruits* (1643), reprinted in Morison, *The Founding of Harvard College* (1935), pp. 420-47.

college to be 'The advancement of all good literature, artes and Sciences,' 'the advancement and education of youth in all manner of good literature Artes and Sciences,' and 'all other necessary provisions that may conduce to the education of the English and Indian youth of this Country in knowledge: and godliness.' No mention whatever of training ministers! 'Good literature' is a literal translation of the Ciceronian *bonae literae,* which we use more often in the French equivalent, *belles-lettres.* 'Artes and Sciences' meant the famous Seven Arts and Three Philosophies that had come down through the Middle Ages. As early as 1647 President Dunster tried to obtain some of the 'other necessary provisions.' He asked for means to purchase suitable books, 'especially in law, physicke, philosophy, and mathematics' for the use of the scholars, 'whose various inclinations to all professions might thereby be incouraged and furthered.' And the Reverend Jonathan Mitchell, senior fellow of the college, asked for funds to establish chairs of history, languages, law, mathematics, and medicine, to train up 'choise and able schoolmasters,' 'able eminent and approved physicians,' and education 'to accomplish persons for the magistracy and other civill offices.' It was long before these things were obtained, but the ambition for a real university was present from the start. We may then conclude, without exaggeration or overemphasis, that the purpose of the first New England college was higher education in the broadest sense, not a specialized training in Protestant theology. A religious spirit, of course, permeated the institution. *Veritas,* the first college motto, no doubt meant to it, as to Dante,[6] the

6 *Paradiso,* iv. 124-127.

divine truth; *In Christi gloriam* was inscribed on the first college seal, and the college laws enjoined all students 'to lay Christ in the bottom, as the only foundation of all knowledge and Learning.' But these slogans and injunctions, emphasizing a continuity of purpose with the medieval universities, were not conceived of as limiting the scope of learning; rather did they express the spirit in which knowledge should be acquired and learning advanced.

As to the means and methods by which these high ends should be carried out, the founders were perfectly clear. Excellence was their keynote from the start. Nothing mean or second-rate would satisfy them, or please God. No prudent considerations of economy must limit their ambition for learning. Emmanuel Downing, writing from England, thought that it would be enough at first to hire some minister to read a weekly lecture on 'logick, greke or hebrew,' and let the students shift for themselves—'you need not stay till you have Colledges to lodge schollars.' There was ample precedent for this, in the great universities of the Continent, which no longer attempted to house their students. But, as Cotton Mather observed, 'the Government of *New-England*, was for having their Students brought up in a more *Collegiate* Way of Living.' [7] To the English mind, university learning apart from college life was not worth having; and the humblest resident tutor was accounted a more suitable teacher than the most talented community lecturer. Book learning alone might be got by lectures and reading; but it was only by living as members of the same collegiate community, in constant

[7] *Magnalia* (1702), book iv, 126. Upsala was the example Mather gave of a great nonresidential university.

association with one another and their tutors, that the young men could be really educated. Hence President Dunster trained his own tutors, and devoted some of his best efforts to completing the college building which had been begun as early as 1638.

Generous in proportion, the 'Old College,' as this building was called, had a dining hall on the ground floor that seated fifty at a pinch, a 'Long Chamber' overhead that served as freshman dormitory, a library, and five square chambers where, as in the English colleges, the students slept two-a-bed and four to a chamber, a tutor or graduate student being placed in each group to keep the rest in order. Tiny studies let into the corners of the chambers afforded the only opportunity for privacy. To a considerable extent the decencies and amenities of English college life were observed: high table in hall, where the fellows dined with fellow commoners, students who paid an extra fee for that privilege; a modest array of silver beer bowls and a great silver 'salt,' pewter plates for the fellows and wooden trenchers for the students; and a college brewhouse where the only beverage served at meals was brewed. And at commencement the stately ceremonial of the English universities was observed, with some of the raffish accompaniment that academic solemnities always suggest to young men.

Academic rank was a matter of great importance to the English, and its translation to the New World has always attracted the attention of historians. One of the standard texts used in teachers' colleges, by Professor Knight of the University of North Carolina, has no space for the curriculum, the standards, the literary production, or even the organization of our colonial colleges, but devotes five pages to an account of 'social distinctions' which is both inaccurate and irrelevant.[8]

Harvard and Yale freshmen were placed in what was called an Order of Seniority. This ranking, in the seventeenth and early eighteenth centuries, was based on scholastic merit, as tested by the student's preparation and his performance during the first term or two in college. Around 1720 the practice grew up of placing sons of royal governors and councilors at the top and sons of college graduates next, irrespective of their mental quality. Degradation in this order was commonly used by the faculty as a punishment, and that caused so much trouble that the system was given up by Harvard and Yale in 1768.[9]

Naturally the colonial colleges were not democratic, as the community was not; but from the first there were scholarships and ways of earning money to enable poor boys with the necessary intellectual qualifications to graduate. The most highly prized of these jobs at early Harvard was that of butler; for he kept the keys to the buttery and dispensed the beer for breakfast, dinner, and supper.

No college that is properly run can be self-supporting.

[8] Edgar W. Knight, *Education in the United States* (1929); repeated without change in 1951 edition, pp. 78-82. Dr. Knight also devotes two pages to denouncing the lack of democracy in the English colonies, and this is followed by a section entitled "Enslaved to Superstition." This is the sort of thing that has been fed to our budding teachers in courses on the History of Education for the past quarter-century.

[9] For the seventeenth century, see my article "Precedence at Harvard College," in *A.A.S.*, n.s., XLII (1932), 371-431, and *Harvard College in the Seventeenth Century* (1936), I, 62-64. For the eighteenth century, see article by C. K. Shipton in *Harvard Alumni Bulletin*, December 11, 1954, pp. 258-63, and addenda, *ibid.*, March 12, 1955, p. 417.

Tuition fees never cover the cost of a college course, and there is no reason why they should, since every educated man and woman is an investment for the community. Tuition at Harvard was raised to £2 in 1655, and has since continued in the same direction, upward. The average cost of board, including beer, was £10 a year around 1650, and the total expense of four years in college from £50 to £75.

Our first steward's accounts, begun while New England was still pulling out of the depression of the 1640's and before she had resumed specie payments, show an amazing variety of farm products and other goods with which the students discharged their debts to the college. The most popular commodities were wheat and malt, which the college steward could always use for baking and brewing; but apparently any kind of grain, livestock, meat, or farm produce would do. Even firewood, lumber, tallow, wax, turnips, and live goats were accepted by the long-suffering steward. Sons of merchants drew on their fathers' stock to meet their college dues. Sir Henry Mildmay, the regicide, sent over 'a runlett of sack' to his dull-witted son, who had been transferred from Emmanuel to Harvard in the hope of keeping him out of trouble. William Mildmay's prudent tutor would not allow him to consume the sack, but used it to establish a credit of £4 5s. on the college books. Isaac Allerton of Plymouth discharged a term debt to the college by providing the sack for commencement, 1650, and his classmates paid for it at 2s. a quart. Samuel Willard, future theologian and vice-president of the college, brought from his home '17 quartes of hott watters' which wiped out a debt of £1 14s.; and Samuel Hooker brought all the way from Hartford 14s. 2d. worth of rose water, of all things. This suggests that the custom still practiced in some of the English colleges of handing around a basin of rose water after dinner, as a sort of community finger bowl, was in vogue at puritan Harvard. One student, son of a trader, paid almost his entire cost of college education in boots and shoes, which the steward had to find customers for, but eventually had 30s. worth left on his hands—or feet.

Historians of education may more profitably note the low cost and general availability of a college education in the seventeenth century than dwell on imaginary social distinctions among those who got in. A quarter's tuition at Harvard under President Dunster was more than covered by a bushel and a half of wheat. Gershom Bulkeley was kept in college an entire year by a side of beef, a 'small side of backen,' five bushels of wheat, 14 of corn, 15½ of apples, and a cask of butter. Joe Farnsworth's father sent him a 'lyttell browne Cowe,' which, with four bushels of barley malt, paid his board and study rent for six months. Zach Brigden obtains food and drink for a term by the proceeds of one fat hog; his tuition, rent, and other expenses are paid partly by waiting on table, and the balance discharged by six bushels of malt and a bushel of parsnips. Taking into account the decreased labor cost of producing farm products, it would seem that the cost of a college education, in terms of farm labor, has risen ten to fifteen fold in three centuries.

Cheap as a college education was in comparison with our standards, the problem of financial support was serious for early presidents. The New England people were forced to

tax themselves for things that in England were provided
by endowments for religion and education. In England,
ministers' salaries and the expenses of maintaining churches
came out of tithes and a variety of pious funds; in New
England the towns had to build and maintain the meeting-
house and provide the minister's salary. At Oxford and
Cambridge the colleges were all well endowed with lands,
from the rents of which a large number of scholarships and
fellowships were provided; and in the grammar schools
that prepared boys for the universities, there were hundreds of free places, paying a scholar's board and lodging
as well as tuition. But education in New England had to
be supported by a 'pay as you go' policy. The Colony's
£400 grant and John Harvard's legacy (all that Eaton left)
were consumed in building. Quite early New Englanders
began to present the college with land; but land was a drug
on the New England market, as in every new country, and
fetched very little rent. After 1654 the Bay Colony paid
the president's salary (£100 to £150), and granted the college the tolls of the Boston-Charlestown ferry, which
brought in about £50 annually. Including student's fees,
the college had to be run on an annual budget of around
£250 in mid-century; and most of this was in 'country pay'
—farm produce. It was only by a series of expedients,
which called for much sacrifice from the people, that the
college was kept alive.

In 1644 the New England Confederation put the college
under its patronage, and requested every family in New
England to give annually a quarter bushel of wheat, or a
shilling in money, or the equivalent in wampum, 'for the
mayntenance of poore Schollers at the Colledg at Cam-

bridg.' Each colony undertook to gather the 'Colledge Corn' as these contributions were called, and forward them to Boston; New Haven and Connecticut were quite as forward in the matter as Massachusetts Bay. During that critical period, the plain farmers of New England, with their pecks of wheat, strings of wampum, and pine-tree shillings, supported the entire teaching staff (except the president), and provided ten or twelve scholarships as well. In 1662 the people of Portsmouth, New Hampshire, bound themselves to send £60 to the college annually for a space of seven years. This promise was faithfully redeemed in local products of pine boards and pipe staves; the college treasurer had to turn lumber merchant and find customers for the 'Piscataqua benevolence.'

Later in the century, when the 'Old College' threatened to tumble down, a subscription list was circulated in Massachusetts for a new building. In 1674 the frame was raised; but before the 'Old Harvard Hall' was completed King Philip's War broke out. It was impossible to collect all the money, as many of the original subscribers had been ruined or killed; but new ones were found, and the hall was completed in 1677 at a cost of about £2,000.

This note of devotion and sacrifice to the cause of learning, first heard in the New England of the 1640's, has been heard wheresoever the Yankee native has taken up a new abode. New Englanders have not been accustomed to wait for a millionaire to found a college, or for the state to provide a university. They have turned to and done it themselves. Yale was started by a group of ministers, who robbed their own precious libraries for the college library, and by shillings and sixpences squeezed out of slender family budgets at New Haven, Saybrook, and Hartford. Amherst College was not built by the fabulous Lord Jeffrey, but from the savings, sacrifice, and voluntary labor of local clergymen and farmers. Mary Lyon collected the wherewithal to build the first women's college, Mount Holyoke, in denominations of ten cents to five dollars. Mr. Anson G. Phelps took a leading part in founding New York University, eager to grant young men of the great city the same facilities for higher education enjoyed by the farmers' lads throughout New England. Schools and colleges were the first and the longest-lived fruits of the fathers' principles; of their stouthearted insistence that learning they would have, whatever it might cost.

One unfortunate result of the poverty of Harvard in early years was inability to keep her teachers. If money had been available, the college would have had three or four teaching and one or two research fellows; but the funds were barely sufficient to support two or three tutors, young graduates who were so ill paid that at the first opportunity they slipped off into other occupations, mainly the ministry. It was not until the last twenty years of the century, when income from benefactions reached the stupendous sum of £75 to £100 per annum, that the college could keep a permanent teaching force. But if tutors were young and inexperienced, they were that much nearer the pupils among whom they lived; and there was constant interchange of good fellowship, with a wholesome ingredient of horseplay. This intimacy extended even to vacations. We find one tutor taking a mathematically inclined student on a surveying expedition to the wilds of New Hampshire, and two others accompanying their pu-

pils on a trip to New York; one which, like many subsequent visits of New England collegians to the metropolis,
had unexpected thrills.

It was the summer of the exciting year 1689. Tutors
Leverett and Brattle with their charges happened to arrive
at a time when Jacob Leisler was in a state of jumpy nerves,
expecting Sir Edmund Andros, whom he had ousted from
the government, to come back at him with force. Informed
by a busybody that strangers who did not answer a watch-
man's challenge (it was probably in Dutch) had arrived,
Leisler leaped to the conclusion that the Harvard party was
Governor Andros and Lieutenant-Governor Nicholson in
disguise, with their bodyguard. He promptly had the lot
conducted to the Battery and locked up in the fort for the
night. Wild rumors spread about nervous Manhattan to the
effect that Sir Edmund had landed a small army to surprise
the fort. Five hundred militia turned out to defend the city.
Dutchmen and Englishmen suspected of hankering for
Andros' return were seized and confined with the college
contingent, and the whole town roared with excitement.
Next morning arrived a letter from Boston telling who the
visitors were, and they were released. Let us hope that
Manhattan hospitality more than compensated for the
night in jail.

I might easily amuse you by similar tales of colonial student life; but it is time to say something about the contribution that the college made to the intellectual life of New
England. This can best be judged by the subjects studied,
the books read, and the methods pursued. We have far less
data than we would like on the seventeenth-century curriculum, but quite enough to tear up the usual picture pre-

sented by secondary writers on our colonial colleges, of a few score pallid and pious youths 'boning up' Calvinist theology, with an occasional exercise in Hebrew irregular verbs. The New England colonial colleges trained ministers, but they were not theological seminaries. Less than half the alumni of seventeenth-century Harvard entered the sacred calling. All students, whether or not candidates for the pulpit, took a prescribed course in six of the traditional Seven Arts (Grammar, Logic, Rhetoric, Arithmetic, Geometry, and Astronomy), in the Three Philosophies (Metaphysics, Ethics, and Natural Science), and in Greek, Hebrew, and Ancient History. Latin was supposed to have been mastered in grammar school; it was the language of instruction, and of most of the textbooks. It was a very similar program to that which many founders of New England had studied at Old Cambridge, containing the same three elements: the medieval arts and philosophies, founded largely on the works of Aristotle; the more serious Renaissance study of Greek and Hebrew; and the lighter Renaissance study of classical belles-lettres. All these subjects were considered essential to a gentleman's education. The professional study of theology began only after taking the bachelor's degree. Undergraduates were given only as much divinity as was supposed to be requisite for an educated Christian layman; and that of course was a great deal, according to our standards. It included the careful study and analysis of the Bible in the original tongues, a short handbook of Protestant divinity (Ames's *Medulla* or Wolleb's *Abridgement of Christian Divinity*), taking notes on two long sermons every Lord's Day, and being quizzed on them subsequently.

The bachelor's course was intended to be, and was, a liberal education for the times, having no practical or professional value, equally suitable for a future divine, physician, or ruler. President Oakes addressed one of his graduating classes as 'gentlemen, educated like gentlemen.' It was intended to introduce young men to the best thought and literature of past ages, not to make them receptive to the thought of their own time. Nevertheless, Harvard boys began very early to pluck Aristotle's beard, and to welcome the 'neoterics,' or exponents of the new experimental philosophy.

The college was founded, as we have seen, 'to advance *Learning* and perpetuate it to Posterity.' But the first few generations had no means or opportunity to *advance* learning in the Baconian sense. They were too much engrossed in endeavoring to *transmit* their cultural inheritance to posterity.

Logic was the basic subject in the curriculum. It was at once an introduction to philosophy and a means of training students in the art of thinking. The most esteemed writer on this subject was Peter Ramus, the great French logician who was murdered in the St. Bartholomew's Eve massacre. His *Dialectica* and *Institutiones Logicae* were in constant use, and their effect on New England methods of reasoning was deep and lasting.[10]

Two ends and objects of their education were constantly held up to students in the puritan century: the attainment of a greater knowledge of God, through knowledge of his word and works; and Εὐπραξία. This word from the Nico-

[10] Perry Miller has pointed out the importance of Ramean logic in *The New England Mind: The Seventeenth Century* (1939).

machaean Ethics of Aristotle, sometimes Englished as *eu-praxia*, is variously translated 'good conduct,' 'right action,' and 'true welfare.' As Aristotle used it, it is more nearly equivalent to what we mean by 'doing the right thing at the right time.' One of the theses frequently debated at commencement was 'Εὐπραξία is the object and goal of the Arts.' Indeed so often did Harvard students have *eupraxia* thrown up at them, that one witty graduate in 1666 published some Latin verses to the effect that if the tutors would observe the principles themselves when praising it, their pupils might be able to hand a little of it back.[11]

Authorities on the history of education have too readily assumed that colonial students were forced to study Hebrew and Greek simply in order to read the Bible. As regards Hebrew, that may well have been the real reason, though the *good* one assigned in an early commencement thesis was that Hebrew is the mother of languages. This theory, that Hebrew was the archetype of all western tongues, was common in the Renaissance; the great English Hebraist, John Selden, among others, believed it. A smattering of that language was then supposed to be part of a classical education in England; Sir Humphrey Gilbert had it on the program for his proposed academy for young gentlemen of the court; and even in the late eighteenth century President Samuel Johnson of Columbia declared that Hebrew was part of a 'gentleman's education.' Wilhelm Schickard, professor at the University of Tübingen, prepared especially for his pupils a Hebrew text with the attractive title (in Latin), *The Hebrew Sun-dial, or, Advice as to how the Elements of that Holy Language may be Suf-*

[11] *N.E.Q.*, VI, 537-38.

ficiently apprehended by College Students in a Space of Twenty-four hours. Harvard students must have been very 'dumb,' for it took them not twenty-four hours, but almost one day a week for four years to master enough Hebrew, Syriac, and Aramaic to satisfy their exigent instructors. Presidents Dunster and Chauncy were both good Hebrew scholars; the one corresponded with Christian Ravis, a German Hebraist resident in London, putting him right on sundry points; and Chauncy's knowledge of Hebrew is mentioned with respect by Archbishop Ussher, the learned Primate of Ireland. The College Library acquired from English Hebraists an excellent collection of Targums, Talmuds, and works of Rabbinical exegesis; hence the advanced divinity students were well equipped for Old Testament criticism.

As for Greek, we know naught of President Dunster's attainments in that literature, but President Chauncy had been one of the best known Hellenists of his day in Cambridge. He was one of the two Greek lecturers at Trinity College when the poet George Herbert was the other. A part, doubtless, of the reason for studying Greek in college was to perfect the student's knowledge of the New Testament already begun in school. One of the college entrance requirements in 1655 was 'to be able to construe and Grammatically to resolve ordinary Greeke, as in the Greeke Testament, Isocrates, and the minor poets, or such like' and the Greek Testament was read in at least one of the New England grammar schools (the Boston Latin School), perhaps in all. A whole day of each week, on President Dunster's program, was devoted to advanced Greek grammar, composition, versification, and the reading of Greek texts.

Of these, two very edifying authors are mentioned in the earliest program: Nonnus of Alexandria, who wrote a metrical paraphrase of the Gospel according to St. John which was much admired in the Renaissance, and James Duport, a Cantabrigian of John Harvard's day, who translated the Psalms and the Song of Solomon into Greek verse, and published a volume of Excerpts from Homer.

Fortunately we are not limited for knowledge of what college students of the seventeenth century read to books mentioned in the programs, or we would be forced to conclude that their intellectual fare was meager indeed. By carefully combing a few of the older New England libraries, over two hundred books have been found with dated signatures of seventeenth-century college students, proving that the books were owned by them in college.[12] And of these some of the most interesting are the Greek books. An entering freshman in 1676 purchased Canter's edition of Sophocles' Tragedies; and had he wished, he could have consulted Melanchthon's edition of Euripides and the Genevan Aristophanes of 1607 in the College Library. We have two copies, with marks of undergraduate ownership, of Jean Crespin's Collection of the Georgic, Bucolic, and Gnomic Greek poets. This closely printed little book of near a thousand pages contains Hesiod's *Works and Days*, *Shield of Heracles*, and *Theogony;* the gnomic poems of Theognis of Megara, Phocylides, and Pythagoras; Simonides of Ceos and a host of minor poets; the *Bucolics* and *Idylls* of Theocritus, Bion, Moschus, and others; and even a

[12] A complete list of these, edited by Professor Arthur O. Norton, who found most of them, is printed in *C.S.M.*, XXVIII, 361-438.

selection of choice morsels from the poets of the Middle and New Comedy—all well annotated. And, what was more important to undergraduates, it was provided with a Latin translation on each page opposite the Greek.

The college authorities had evidently made a search for edifying works to read. The ethics of Hesiod would have appealed to the most solemn puritan. Yet whatever the reason may have been for placing Hesiod's *Works and Days* on the curriculum, no more admirable introduction to Greek literature could have been devised for the boys from New England farms and seaports. Hesiod was the original 'Old Farmer' of the almanacs; his adages on husbandry found response in his readers' experience. New England farmers, like Boeotian swains of the eighth century B.C., marked the seasons by Arcturus rising brilliant from the ocean stream at dusk, followed by the Pleiades 'like a swarm of fireflies,' by Sirius parching hayfields on hot August nights, and by the Belt of Orion, flashing in the winter sky.

Theognis of Megara was filled with maxims of practical morality, as well as Byronic complaints on the degeneracy of his age; the reading of his, and the more martial elegies of Simonides of Ceos, probably did much to foster the popularity of elegiac poetry among early Harvard graduates. Simonides, moreover, was impregnated with that Hellenic and puritan self-restraint so roundly condemned by moralists of the pseudo-Freudian school under the name 'inhibition.' Yet the college students were not confined to morally edifying works. The lyric and bucolic *flores* in the Crespin collection, notably Theocritus, Bion, and Moschus, can hardly have been turned to moral advantage by the most ingenious tutor—and what a vista the *Idylls* of Theocritus opened up for any young man of taste! As for epic poetry, it is difficult to say how early or how extensively Homer was read at Harvard. A member of the Class of 1675 owned a *Clavis Homerica*, a book of short selections printed at Rotterdam in 1673; but whether or not this was all that his classmates had, one cannot tell. The earliest surviving copy of an *Iliad* used by a Harvard student was the Cambridge edition of 1672, which a member of the Class of 1684 acquired as a freshman; the book had seven subsequent student owners.

If Hesiod, Simonides, Theocritus, Homer, and Sophocles are not a humanist program, what are they?

A better test perhaps of the quality of intellectual life in the college is to discover what books outside the curriculum the students bought and read. That the college inculcated a taste for letters is certain. A dozen dated *ex libris* of seventeenth-century college students have come down to us, proving that no small number of undergraduates began to accumulate libraries of their own.[13] The interesting will of Joseph Browne of Charlestown, who died in 1678 when twelve years out of college, leaves £100 in books to his 'honored father . . . for all that care and cost which he hath been at' for his education; £30 in books to each of three brothers, and £20 in books to a sister; Bryan Walton's great Polyglot Bible to a clerical friend; and to his former tutor a most fitting combination legacy: a copper still with a pewter worm belonging to it, Dr. Pearson's

[13] There is a list of the known examples in *A.A.S.*, n.s., XLIII (1935), 315-16.

book on the Apostles' Creed, and 'My Negroe Boy Dick.' [14]
Another student who died in 1676, just before taking his
master's degree, left a library of about eighty titles, only
ten or twelve of which were religious, the most part
being medical; his works on general literature included
Horace, Homer, Hesiod, and Plutarch, Bacon's *Advancement of Learning*, and Browne's *Religio Medici; Don
Quixote* in Skelton's translation, and perhaps another work
of Cervantes.[15]

Students with literary tastes, in the days when books
were hard to come by, kept 'commonplace' or notebooks
into which they copied out verses or prose extracts that
particularly appealed to them. After long search, I have
succeeded in discovering only three such books that were
kept by college students in the seventeenth century, between 1650 and 1680. All three show such a close similarity
in tastes as to admit of generalization. None can be regarded as exceptional or furtive, for all were kept by their
owners after they grew up, and left to their children. One
was made by John Leverett, afterwards tutor and president
of the college; another by Elnathan, son of President
Chauncy; and a third by Seaborn Cotton, who later became a minister and used the blank leaves of his notebook
for church records. It is amusing, and somewhat of a shock
to the common notions of puritans, to find record of births
and marriages in the Hampton (N. H.) church, following a
highly erotic extract from Sir Philip Sidney's *Arcadia*.[16]

---

[14] J. L. Sibley, *Harvard Graduates*, II, 208.

[15] Alcock's library, in *C.S.M.*, XXVIII, 350-57.

[16] John Leverett's is in the M.H.S.; Elnathan Chauncy's, owned by a de-
scendant, is described in *C.S.M.*, XXVIII, 1-24; Cotton's, in the New England
Historic Genealogical Society, is described in *C.S.M.*, XXXII, 307-418.

The future President Leverett, who appreciated Abraham Cowley, copied several stanzas from his "Elegie upon Anacreon" and "The Mistress," such as

> *Now by my Love, the greatest Oath that is,*
> *None loves you half so well as I:*
> *I do not ask your Love for this;*
> *But for Heavens sake believe me, or I die.*

Seaborn Cotton had access to a very earthy anthology printed in London in 1640, called *The Witts Recreations*. From it he copies one of the familiar Shakespearian lyrics:

> *Take, oh take those lips away,*
> *That so sweetly were for-sworne;*
> *And those eyes like breake of day.*
> *Lights that doe mislead the morne:*

Elnathan Chauncy had access to Herrick's *Hesperides*, from which he copies most of "Gather ye rosebuds while ye may," the whole of "A willow garland thou did'st send," and other lyrics. Both young men, as befitted scholars, appreciated the more bookish type of love poetry, that had some play of wit on the subjects they were studying.[17] Seaborn quotes from his facetious anthology:

ON WOMEN

> *Woman's the center, and the lines be men,*
> *The circles love, how doe they differ then?*
> *Circles draw many lines into the center,*
> *But love gives leave to onely one to enter.*

[17] In quoting these students' quotations, I have not reproduced their erratic spelling and punctuation and frequent mistakes, but have collated every verse selection with an old edition of the author, such as the student himself might have read.

Elnathan quotes the whole of Cleveland's "Song of Mark Anthony" that brings in all the Seven Arts; and from Beaumont's "Psyche or Loves Mysterie" such verses as this:

> *Are not the Eyes those universale Glasses*
> *In which the World doth fairly copied lie?*
> *Man for a Microcosme by favour passes,*
> *But in a blinde and duskie Mystery.*

Some of the books quoted by these three young men were old enough to have been brought over by their fathers, but quite a number were published in London in the 1640's and later. Beaumont's poems that attracted Elnathan came out in 1648, and Cleveland's "Song of Mark Anthony" first appeared in his *Character of a London-Diurnall* (1647)—a strange work to be circulating in a puritan college. Elnathan went through the entire book. He passed over the satires on the puritans, except one on Oliver Cromwell which was too good to omit; he copies the lines on Oliver's nose, but leaves out his name. Cromwell, apparently, was Elnathan's contemporary hero. From an elegy that I have been unable to identify he quotes:

> *The sun himself looks heavy and puts on*
> *in spight of light a sad privation*
> *since Cromwels dead, whose glorious breath*
> *was too too pretious to be stolne by death*

All three youths were fond of poems addressed 'To My Mistress.' John worked through Cowley's book of like title; Seaborn has four poems to his mistress from *The Witts Recreations*, of which one may serve as sample:

> *Sweetest faire be not too cruell,*
> *Blot not beauty with disdaine,*

> *Let not those bright eyes adde fewell*
> *To a burning heart in vaine,*
> *Least men justly when I dye*
> *Deem you the candle, mee the fly.*

But of the several collegiate mistresses, this one, whom Elnathan discovered in William Warner's "Albion's England," is the loveliest:

> *My Mistresse is a Paragon, the fayrest Fayre alive,*
> *Atrides and Æacides for fair lesse faire did strive,*
> *Her colour fresh as damaske Rose, her breath as Violet,*
> *Her bodie white as Ivory, as smooth as polisht Jet,*
> *As soft as Downe, and were she downe, Jove might come*
>   *downe and kiss*
> *A Love so fresh, so sweet, so white so smooth, so soft as*
>   *this.*

There are many prose quotations as well; epigrams and aphorisms, such as the deathbed advice of the Prince de Condé to the Duc d'Enghien: 'Never to revenge a private injury, and freely to hazard his life for the Publick Good,' and 'Truth and the rational soule are twins,' culled by Elnathan from Walter Charleton's translation of Van Helmont's *Ternary of Paradoxes*. Other prose extracts are of an obscenely vituperative sort, recalling Mark Twain's "Conversation by the Social Fireside in the Time of the Tudors." The future President Leverett, for instance, saves this choice paraphrase from Fuller's *Worthies of England*:

If any Speaketh against mee, saith Sir Walter Raleigh, to my face, my tongue shall give him an answer, but my backside is good enough to return to whom abuseth mee behind my backe.

Elnathan selects from Thomas Vaughan's splenetic attack on Dr. Henry More:

> Let not your Thoughts feed now on the Phlegmatic, indigested Vomits of Aristotle.
> Could thy *Alma Mater* teach thee nothing but *Anticks?*
> I will pick your *bones,* and bestow you afterwards on *Cambridge* for a *Fool's Anatomie.*

And from John Bulwer's *Anthropometamorphosis: or, The Artificiale Changling* (1653):

> *Venus-Morris-Dancers* frisking often to the tune of their own Codpiece-musique. . . . Castrati whose voices scandelize their breeches. Abscissionem Testiculorum is the surest remedy that can be devised for Cupids Colts.

And there are a few satires on women, especially the bawdy counterparts or parodies that poets liked to write on their own love lyrics. Chauncy, for instance, copies Cleveland's counterpart to the "Song of Mark Anthony," and Cotton, Sidney's "Verses upon brave Mopsa":

> *Like great god Saturne faire, and like faire Venus chaste:*
> *As smooth as Pan, as Juno mild, like Goddesse Iris fac'd.*

But for the most part these boys are in search of beauty and amorous sentiment. Seaborn quotes the whole, and Elnathan a few lines, of a well-known English ballad "The Two Faithful Lovers," beginning:

> Man. *Farewel, my heart's delight,*
> *Ladies adiue,*
> *I must now take my flight,*
> *what e'ere ensue;*

> *My Country-men I do see,*
> *They cannot yet agree;*
> *Since 'twill no better be,*
> > England *farewel.*

Maid. *O be not so unkind,*
> > *heart, love and joy,*
> *To leave me here behind,*
> > *breeds my annoy:*
> *O have a patient heart,*
> *I'll help to bear the smart,*
> *E'er I from thee will part,*
> > *my turtle-dove.*[18]

Elnathan's taste is more classical than that of his fellows. He has over twenty closely written pages of quotations from Spenser, covering most of his poems except *The Faerie Queene*, and almost the whole of *The Shepheards Calender*. This for June:

> *But friendly Faeries, met with many Graces,*
> *And lightfoote Nymphs can chase the lingring night,*
> *With heydeguyes, and trimly trodden traces,*
> *Whilst sisters nine, which dwell on* Parnasse *hight,*
> *Do make them musick, for their more delight:*
> *And Pan himselfe to kisse their crystall faces,*
> *Will pipe and daunce, when Phoebe shineth bright:*
> *Such pierlesse pleasures have we in these places.*

From the *Prothalamion*:

> *Calme was the day, and through the trembling ayre,*
> *Sweet-breathing Zephyrus did softly play*

---

[18] Quoted as printed in J. W. Ebsworth, *The Bagford Ballads*, II, 471-74. Chauncy's copy shows variations consistent with the metre (such as 'Ere ye and I depart'), which suggest that he had heard the ballad sung, and wrote it down from memory.

There, in a Meadow, by the Rivers side,
A flock of Nymphes I chaunced to espy,
All lovely daughters of the Flood thereby,
With goodly greenish locks, all loose untyed.

Love's tragedy is not forgotten; Elnathan copies the lament for Dido from the November eclogue, concluding:

Dido is gone afore (whose turne shall be the next?)
There lives she with the blessed Gods in blisse:
There drinks the Nectar with Ambrosia mixt,
And joyes enjoyes, that mortall men doe misse.
The honour now of highest God she is,
   That whilome was poore shepheards pride:
While heere on earth she did abide,
   O happy herse.
Cease now my song, my woe now wasted is,
   O joyfull verse.

From the *Daphnaïda*:

O that so faire a flowre so soone should fade,
And through untimely tempest fall away.

She fell away in her first ages spring,
Whilst yet her leafe was greene, and fresh her rind,
And whilst her branch faire blossomes forthe did bring,
She fell away against all course of kind:
For age to die is right, but youth is wrong;
She fell away like fruite blowne downe with wind.

Such were the intellectual recreations of our earliest college students. The humanist tradition, one of the noblest inheritances of the English race, went hand in hand with conquering puritanism into the clearings of the New England wilderness. The glory that was Greece shone down a path that the Roman legions had never traced; and 'light-foote Nymphs' played hide-and-seek in college yard with homespun lads who would pass the remainder of their days ministering to rural communities.

III. THE ELEMENTARY SCHOOLS

Only a small proportion of the New England people was directly touched by higher education. The total number of college students in the seventeenth century was less than six hundred,[1] of whom 465 graduated. The intricacies of Latin grammar were a *pons asinorum* which only a few could cross; and even with scholarships and exhibitions to help the poor, there were not many fathers who could afford to see a boy through the four years of college.

A good deal of what the college students learned percolated through to the people in sermons and other writings of the graduates, and from college-educated schoolmasters; and in return the schools gave college graduates jobs and prepared boys for college; so there was constant action and reaction between them. But the schools must have influenced the intellectual life of the people as a whole much more than the college. Yet on no subject in colonial history is it more difficult to find accurate information and unbiased appraisal. New England schools have been approached from almost every point of view but the historical; and with altogether too much emotion. One class of writers becomes almost dithyrambic in describing the colonial school system; and we have extravagant claims such as this: 'In popular education New England not only led the continent but the world, there being a school house, often several, in each town. Every native adult in Massachusetts

[1] Total graduates, classes of 1642-1701, 465; total nongraduates recorded, 97; probably there were 20 to 30 more who are not recorded.

and Connecticut was able to read and write.'[2] The New England historians, in general, praised their colonial schools to such a degree that a natural reaction set in; and the general tendency in manuals and monographs on the history of education during the present century has been to decry the New England school system as a mere device to enforce the puritan creed, devoid of real educational value and pretentious rather than practical. The late Charles M. Andrews wrote that the schools laws 'were more honored in the breach than in the observance,' that 'even when honestly carried out, they produced but slender results,' and that grammar schools were not only 'rare,' but 'did not reach a very high level.'[3] A typical statement of the nineteen twenties, in Professor Knight's history of American education, is that the Massachusetts School Act of 1647, 'instead of being a foundation stone upon which the American school system has been constructed . . . seems rather to have been an effort to restrict the influence of Catholics and adherents to the English Church and to impose the Puritan creed upon this first generation of native-born New Englanders.'[4]

Who these intrusive Romans and Anglicans, hitherto unknown to history, may have been, he does not specify. It seems to be an axiom with Professor Knight, as with many other professional educators of today, that schools inspired

[2] E. B. Andrews, *History of the United States* (1894), I, 128.
[3] *The Fathers of New England* (1919), pp. 84-85; *Colonial Folkways* (1919), p. 132.
[4] E. W. Knight, *Education in the United States* (1929), p. 85; repeated without change in 1951 edition. Cf. Charles and Mary Beard, *The Rise of American Civilization* (1927), I, 179, who repeat Andrews' 'honored in the breach.'

by the spirit of religion, or conducted by ecclesiastics, are worthless. If that is true, we must condemn all schools and universities of the first sixteen Christian centuries; and all Catholic, Rabbinical, and church schools of our own day, in the same breath with those of colonial New England. Supposing that the schools of New England were just as religious in purpose as the parochial schools and Jesuit colleges of today, by what pedagogical or philosophical principle is a knowledge of the elements and of Latin grammar and literature rendered socially negligible when inculcated by teachers with a definitely religious purpose and outlook?

If secularization be progress, the New Englanders took an important step in advance by placing their schools under the control of the communities and commonwealths, and by insisting that the schoolteachers be laymen. If diffusion of education be progress, New England again deserves credit for making her education in many places free as well as public. But the free school was no new idea to the English-speaking world in 1630. England in 1660 was better provided with secondary schools, many of them free in part, than at any time prior to the Education Act of 1870; and the puritans were more keen on education than any other group of the English people. Emigration enabled them to carry out in education, as in religion, the system that they thought best.

The best schools in England were the grammar schools, which took a boy between the ages of six and eight, and taught him Latin grammar and literature and a little Greek until he was fit to enter Oxford or Cambridge at the age of fourteen to sixteen. The Protestant Reformation gave an immense impetus to the founding of grammar schools, especially in the reigns of Edward VI and Elizabeth, until by 1600 'every boy, even in the remotest part of the country, could find a place of education in his own neighborhood competent at any rate to fit him to enter college.'[5] Almost every market town had an endowed grammar school; in London alone there were eleven, and the existence of over 360 has been ascertained in the country as a whole.[6] All but about fifty were controlled by boards of trustees, or by corporations such as the livery companies and the university colleges; the rest were controlled by municipalities. All had scholarships, covering board and lodging as well as tuition, for those whose parents could not afford to pay; and many were altogether free, supported by endowments or municipal grants.[7] The masters were commonly men in holy orders, and the approval of the bishop or other clerical authority was required for their appointment. Religious exercises were as frequent and pervasive as in the New England schools, even including what seems to us the cruel requirement of repeating sermons. One of the important free grammar schools in the West Country of England from which many New Englanders came was the Free School at Dorchester, whose school-

[5] J. and J. A. Venn, *Alumni Cantabrigienses*, I, xv. Dr. John Venn reached this striking conclusion through a careful examination of the matriculation and college records at Cambridge, which disclosed the existence of dozens of grammar schools in 1600 that later were allowed to close.

[6] J. Howard Brown, *Elizabethan School Days* (Oxford, 1933), p. 7. The ratio to population was then about one boy in grammar school to 375 people.

[7] Nearly all had entrance fees running from 4d. to 10s. and several required the payment of 2s. to 20s. a year for fuel, cleaning, etc. Brown, *op. cit.*, pp. 13-14. For a good example of a free school, the Perse School at Cambridge, see Charles H. Cooper, *Annals of Cambridge*, III, 95-101.

master was the local rector, the same Master John White who did so much to organize the Massachusetts Bay Company. A contemporary diarist proves that the seeds of democratic ideas in education were already sown in England before the puritan migration. At a meeting of the burgesses of Dorchester, one faction argued that the Free School should be free for all, 'whereas the deed being produced showed that the Founder meant it should be Free onely for poore mens children. Sir Francis Ashley was present at the debat, and showed them their errours, yet they were very unmannerly, and in an insolent manner cried out, "a free schole!" "a free schole!" '[8]

When the Civil War impaired the value of endowments, the Long Parliament came to the rescue of the English grammar schools with an ambitious program of state aid, beginning in 1649.[9] Under the puritan ascendancy much was done to improve the grammar schools and make them more available for the common people; but the restoration of the monarchy in 1660 marks a distinct decline in standards and facilities of primary and secondary education. Free schools were attacked by high Anglicans and Tories as dangerous to the monarchy and to the social hierarchy, as

diverting those, whom Nature or Fortune had determin'd to the Plough, the Oar, or other Handicrafts, from their proper design, to the study of Liberal Arts, and even Divinity it self. . . . Nay, great contention hath bin needful to convince Towns, after many years, to admit such foundations, tho fairly endow'd, as any wayes beneficial to the Neighborhood; with so much the more reason may the Gentry require that *such as would have the liberal Arts*

[8] Whiteway Diary, quoted in F. Rose-Troup, *John White* (1931), p. 38.

[9] J. E. G. de Montmorency, *State Intervention in English Education* (Cambridge University Press, 1902), pp. 101 ff.

and Sciences should pay for them: without censure *keep their blood unmixt with mean conversation.* . . .[10]

The overthrow of the puritan regime in England dealt the cause of free, public education a blow from which it did not recover until the nineteenth century. After all we have been told of the 'blight' of puritanism on education, and the 'class' or 'caste' nature of the early New England schools, it is interesting to observe that Foster Watson, a leading authority on the history of secondary education in England, ascribes the decline of free grammar schools in England to the prevalence of utilitarianism over humanism, and the survival of the free grammar school in New England to the persistence of humanism among puritans.[11] The puritan version of humanism may have been somewhat emasculated, compared with that of Elizabethan England; but such as it was, it gave more in educational values to the common people than the England of Charles II regarded as safe or socially desirable.

By the same token, the puritans did far more than the Anglicans for elementary education. That was the weak point of English education in 1600. Ordinarily, a boy's parents had to teach him themselves to read and write English before he could enter a grammar school, or else send him to a private dame school. This worked such a hardship that many illiterate lads were admitted to the grammar schools, where they managed to pick up enough of the elements to qualify them for studying Latin. This condition of affairs

[10] Christopher Wase, *Considerations Concerning Free-Schools* (Oxford, 1678), pp. 1, 13.

[11] *The Old Grammar Schools* (Cambridge University Press, 1916), pp. 128 ff.

was promptly wrestled with by the puritan colonies; and within thirty years three of them—Massachusetts, Connecticut, and New Haven—'had passed a remarkable series of educational acts and established agencies for education which, in comparison with other colonies at the same date, were truly extraordinary.' 'Indeed,' says Professor Jernegan of Chicago, whom I quote, 'we may say that by this date (1660) several essential principles of elementary and secondary education had been formulated and the foundation of the American public school laid.' [12]

Although ambition for popular education was probably no stronger in early New England than in early Virginia, the system of settlement in New England rendered accomplishment far easier. Englishmen in Virginia tended to dispersion; in New England, to concentration. In Virginia there was nothing resembling a town until the eighteenth century, and no village except Jamestown; New England was a chain of seaport and river towns, each vying with the other in shipping and commerce, and a back country of vigorous village communities. In the 'Old Dominion' the individual plantation, in New England the village or seaport, was the economic and social unit. Consequently, in Virginia the difficulties of establishing schools for day scholars were almost insuperable; while in New England the village school was as easy to set up and maintain as the village church, or the town meeting, when the entire population dwelt in a relatively compact group; every child could walk to school. In the next century, when increase of population forced the building of farmsteads in outlying

[12] M. W. Jernegan, *Laboring and Dependent Classes in Colonial America, 1607-1783* (1931), p. 63.

parts, several miles distant from the village center, the village school system no longer served; and the 'moving school,' or rather the itinerant schoolmaster, was invented in order to prevent children who lived in the outskirts from growing up illiterate. This meant a dispersion of educational effort, and the breakdown of the town grammar school.

For want of records there is still much obscurity in the educational history of colonial New England. Our forbears left us meticulous records about establishing churches, which to them were of transcendent importance; but their schools, especially the elementary schools, they seem to have taken largely for granted, even more so than the weather. From old annotated almanacs we can gather far more data on the New England weather of the seventeenth century than from all available sources on the school system. Hence it is not unnatural that some historians have assumed that the one was as bad as the other!

Still, we have definite evidence that a number of the leading towns took measures to establish schools even before they were required to do so by legislation. Boston hired a schoolmaster in 1635, and took up a private subscription for his maintenance the next year. Charlestown in 1636 voted to hire an English university graduate 'to keepe a schoole for a twelve monthe,' voted him £40 a year out of town rates, and appointed a school committee. Dorchester established a school in 1639, and chose a master to teach 'English, latin and other tongues,' leaving it to the selectmen to decide whether 'maydes shalbe taught with the boyes or not.' Unfortunately, we do not know what they decided, but we infer that the 'maydes' lost out. The owners of an island within the Dorchester jurisdiction were so public-spirited as to convey it to the town, in order that the community might rent it out for school support. Ipswich established a school with seven free scholarships in 1642, and voted £11 for that purpose; but the majority of the pupils were expected to pay. Dedham in 1643 set aside land for 'a fre Schoole,' but did not manage to get it going for several years.[13] At about the same time, a university graduate set up a school in Cambridge; but it was some years before the town gave him assistance, and meanwhile President Dunster raised money to build a stone schoolhouse on a piece of his first wife's land. New Haven, only three years after the colony was founded, took measures to establish a free school, and two years later engaged New England's most famous schoolmaster, Ezekiel Cheever. Hartford was only a few months behind New Haven. Roxbury created a board of 'feoffees,' like the trustees of an incorporated English school, to take care of education in that town, and raise the money. And there are a few other towns in which similar definite action is recorded before 1647.[14]

LAWS AND MOTIVES

From these slender data, it is evident that the New England towns were feeling their way along lines familiar to them in the Old Country. Various ways and means were tried, from the incorporated grammar school supported by endowments and contributions to a free town school for all

[13] The printed *Records of the Town of Dedham* are more full on school matters than those of any other town, hence it has been well 'publicized.'
[14] Jernegan, *op. cit.*, pp. 71-83.

grades, supported by taxation. Circumstances turned most towns toward the public school. Land rents, the standard investment for English school funds, was bound to fail in a country where land was abundant, and immigrants did not care to become tenants. How far these pioneer schools took care of elementary education we do not know; but the colony certainly thought that children were being neglected. Hence the first New England school legislation, the Massachusetts Act of 1642, which put the responsibility for elementary education on heads of families. Parents and masters of indented servants were required to teach their children or servants 'to read and understand the principles of religion and the capital lawes of the country,' [15] and to see to it that they were kept constantly employed in some useful occupation. Obviously the motives of this law were a mixture of the educational, religious, and social. Precautions must be taken lest children grow up ignorant and idle, a charge on the community. Idleness, 'waste of precious time' in the time-honored phrase, was to the puritans a deadly sin. 'An hours Idleness is a sin, as well as an hours Drunkenness,' wrote Hugh Peter; for time was given man by God to improve, not to waste.[16] As re-enacted in the revision of the Bay Colony laws of 1648, this act has already become more definitely educational in purpose: the preamble begins 'Forasmuch as the good education of children is of singular behoof and benefit to any Common-wealth.' And a New Haven law of about the same time is equally explicit: 'For the better trayning up of youth of this towne,

---

[15] The 'capital lawes' had reference to the broadside with that title, printed the same year at the Cambridge press. It took the place of the customary list of 'seven deadly sins' in the English primers.

[16] Hugh Peter, *A Dying Fathers Last Legacy* (London, 1660), p. 35.

that through God's Blessinge they may be fitted for pub-
lique service hereafter, either in church or commonweale.'
Connecticut copied the Massachusetts act with its preamble almost verbatim in her first code of laws, two years
later; and Plymouth Colony followed suit at a considerable
distance of time, in 1677.[17]

It seems, then, a fair inference from these earliest educational acts of four New England colonies that the motives
were not to exploit the labor of the poor and helpless, or
to impose 'on all children the creed of the Puritan sect,' as
the popular survey by Charles and Mary Beard declares.[18]
When a small, homogeneous group of men in a colonial
legislature declares that education is of singular benefit to
the commonwealth, and that it fits children for future
service in church or state; and when they enforce these injunctions by suitable administrative regulations, pains, and
penalties (as these acts did), it may be supposed without
undue charity that they mean what they say, and that
education was conceived of as a training for citizenship and
service in a civilized state, rather than as a vehicle for sec-
tarian propaganda, or 'caste' dominance.[19] We shall find
more data pointing the same way, in the grammar-school
curriculum.

Unwary authors have ignored this earliest legislation,
and drawn their inferences from the Massachusetts Act of
1647, which opens with the oft-quoted preamble:

It being one chief project of that old deluder, Satan, to keep
men from the knowledge of the Scriptures, as in former times

---

[17] *Plymouth Colony Records*, XI, 246-47.
[18] *The Rise of American Civilization* (1927), I, 179.
[19] Merle E. Curti, *The Social Ideas of American Educators* (1935), p. 24.

keeping them in an unknown tongue, so in these later times by perswading from the use of Tongues, that so at least the true sense and meaning of the Originall might be clowded with false glosses of Saint-seeming-deceivers; and that Learning may not be buried in the graves of our fore-fathers in Church and Commonwealth, the Lord assisting our indeavours: [20]

It is then enacted that every Massachusetts town of fifty families shall forthwith appoint a common schoolmaster 'to teach all such children as shall resort to him to write and read,' his wages to be paid either by the parents or the town, as the town shall elect; and that towns of a hundred families or more 'shal set upon a Grammer-School, the masters thereof being able to instruct youth so far as they may be fitted for the Universitie.' ·

This 'old deluder Satan' law has become just such an obstacle to a proper understanding of education in New England, as Governor Berkeley's 'Thank God there are no free schools in Virginia' speech has been to an appreciation of Virginia's educational efforts. Both belong to that class of historic sayings that are so striking and amusing as to get into every textbook, however brief, and to give a completely wrong impression. Virginia actually had free

[20] *Laws and Liberties of Massachusetts* (1929 reprint of 1648 ed.), p. 47. Cf. John Knox's *Buke of Discipline* of 1566: 'Seing that God hath determined that his Churche heir in earth, shallbe tawght not be angellis but by men; and seing that men ar born ignorant of all godlynes; and seing, also, how God ceassith to illuminat men miraculuslie, suddanlie changeing thame, as that he did his Apostlis and utheris in the Primitive Churche: off necessitie it is that your Honouris be most cairfull for the virtuous educatioun, and godlie upbringing of the youth of this Realme . . . Off necessitie thairfore we judge it, that everie severall Churche have a Scholmaister appointed, suche a one as is able, at least, to teache Grammer and the Latine toung, yf the Toun be of any reputatioun. . . .' John Knox, *Works* (ed. 1846-1864), II, 209. It is not suggested that the General Court of Massachusetts was familiar with the *Buke;* it is a case of two groups of puritans doing the same thing for the same reason.

schools, several of them; and Massachusetts had many other reasons for setting up schools than to out-smart Satan. The 'old deluder' preamble was doubtless affixed to the law by some colonial Solon in order to add a religious sanction to a social obligation which poor people in the towns were loath to assume. A few years' experience had shown that laissez-faire in education was a failure. Parents could not be depended on to do their duty, hence towns must be forced by law to make proper provision for teaching the young.

This Massachusetts Act of 1647 for the compulsory provision of common schools and grammar schools was also copied by Connecticut in her code of 1650.[21] New Haven, a small colony with few towns but with great public spirit, probably found such a law unnecessary, and continued to rely on the principles of the earlier legislation placing responsibility on parents. After New Haven had been annexed to Connecticut, and a county organization adopted, the law as respects grammar schools was changed to provide that such a school be maintained in each of the four counties.[22] The earlier legislation in Connecticut and Massachusetts did not lapse with the compulsory school law; parents and masters were now given the option of teaching children and servants their letters at home or sending them to school. New Hampshire was under the jurisdiction of Massachusetts from 1641 to 1679, and Maine under Massachusetts after 1652. Thus by 1672 all the settled territory of New England, with the exception of Rhode Island, was under a system of compulsory education.[23]

[21] *Conn. Col. Recs.*, I, 554-555.
[22] *Connecticut Laws of 1672* (1865 reprint), p. 63.
[23] Jernegan, *op. cit.*, p. 99.

Rhode Island, the colony of religious liberty, democracy, and intense individualism, had no school system or compulsory education laws throughout the colonial period; but toward the end of the century communities of wealthy merchants and planters provided tutors or private schools for their own children at Newport and on the Narragansett shore. Only one boy from Rhode Island, so far as we know, attended college in the entire seventeenth century. He did not manage to enter until the age of twenty-one, and he was allowed by the authorities to graduate in three years, on the plea of his age, and his petition to the effect that a great part of his life 'hath been Spent in a land of darknesse prophanenesse Sabbath breaking and Atheisme.'[24] It was not until mid-eighteenth century that Rhode Island had an intellectual life worthy of the acute and original minds of her founders. If want of schools was not responsible for this cultural chasm, what was?

We should all like to know to what extent the education laws of New England were enforced. There are only two ways of testing that: from the town and court records, and from the state of literacy in the latter part of the century. Town records are fragmentary; of existing county court records only those of Essex County, Massachusetts, and ten years of Suffolk have been printed; and the data from which conclusions as to literacy can be compiled are far from satisfactory. Moreover, we have no reliable statistics of population to tell us which towns had over fifty or over one hundred families, making them liable to support common, or both common and grammar schools.

[24] J. L. Sibley, *Harvard Graduates*, IV, 486. It is only fair to say that this referred to Block Island, not Rhode Island proper.

At least this is clear, that the system did not operate anything like a hundred per cent perfect. In towns of less than fifty families, the selectmen were supposed to see that parents taught their children to read; and Professor Jernegan gives several instances of parents being fined for failure in this respect. But how about frontier settlements, where there was no town organization, or outlying villages of a township? One such place, the village of Poquanock in the township of Fairfield, Connecticut, petitions the General Court in 1678 that, being distant four miles from the town, and 'seeing it very difficult to get our Children Educated at School' they have hired a schoolmaster who is now teaching forty-seven children; hence they beg permission to cease paying school rates to the town of Fairfield.[25]

Boston offers a curious problem. The Grammar (Boston Latin) School was the only public school down to 1684, when a writing school was established; and it is probable that only children who already read were admitted to that.[26] The only other of which we have any record is a private writing school opened in 1666.[27] Apparently the children in the largest town of New England were dependent for elementary instruction on their parents, or on dame schools for which we have no record; they must have learned to read somehow, since there is no evidence of un-

[25] Connecticut Archives, Hartford, *College and Schools*, I, 6. Cf. Schenck, *History of Fairfield*, I, 206. For another and similar instance in Massachusetts thirty years later, see J. L. Sibley, *Harvard Graduates*, IV, 232, and *Essex Institute Historical Collections*, X, part i, 78-79. Muddy River Village (Brookline) was voted a separate school by Boston in 1700 as a sop to prevent it from seceding.

[26] Robert F. Seybolt, *The Public Schools of Colonial Boston* (1935), p. 21. Cf. his "Schoolmasters of Colonial Boston," *C.S.M.*, XXVII, 130-56.

[27] *Report of the Boston Record Commissioners*, VII, 32.

usual illiteracy in the town. And a Boston bookseller's stock in 1700 includes no less than eleven dozen spellers and sixty-one dozen primers. [28] In Cambridge, too, there is no record of elementary schools until 1680, when it is recorded, 'For English, our schooldame is goodwife Healy; at present but nine scholars. Edward Hall, English schoolmaster, at present but three scholars.' [29]

In Essex County, Massachusetts, the county for which we have the fullest records, three towns (Salem, Ipswich, and Newbury) had a school before 1640, another (Amesbury) before 1650, three more (Beverly, Rowley, and Haverhill) by 1660, one (Marblehead) in 1675, and only four more (Lynn, Manchester, Gloucester, and Topsfield) before the end of the century. Some of these may have been grammar schools—that of Ipswich certainly was. During the forty-four years for which the county court records are printed, only six towns were presented for not having the statutory schools; and of these only one was fined; the others were let off on satisfying the court that they either had engaged a schoolmaster, or were about to do so. One of the six towns, Haverhill, was presented thrice; this was a frontier settlement which suffered during the Indian wars, and the repeated presentment of it indicates that Indian raids were not considered a proper excuse for closing school.

The Connecticut Valley and the Long Island Sound settlements were, if anything, more prompt than the Bay towns in establishing schools. Springfield appropriated land for a school as early as 1653; Northampton and Hadley had schools in 1664 and 1665, shortly after they were founded; Hartford in 1642; New Haven as early as 1638 and Guilford about 1646; Windsor and Wethersfield in the next decade.

After New Hampshire and Maine came under the Bay jurisdiction, the school laws of Massachusetts began to be enforced in those areas. The Maine Court Records contain this item for 1673:

Wee present the Town of Yorke for not provideing a schoole and schoolemaster for the aeducation of Youth according to Law.

Captain Raynes as a Select man promiseth to use all means to procure a schoolemaister—which the Town hath provided.[30]

The Massachusetts and Connecticut school laws certainly placed too heavy a burden on small farming communities; it is surprising that we do not find more evidence of dissatisfaction with the system, or resentment at school taxes. Probably more existed than the direct evidence indicates. For instance, an election-day preacher declared, 'too many of our unlearned seem to be possessed with prejudice' against schools and their cost.[31] Note that it is the *unlearned* who object; not, as in the early nineteenth century, the privileged classes. Educational ideas in New England percolated from the top down, and did not rise from the bottom up. It took about a century for the college graduates and ruling class generally to 'sell' the ideal of

[30] *Province and Court Records of Maine* (ed. C. T. Libby), II, 264. Cf. 262, 306, 309.

[31] Joseph Belcher, *The Singular Happiness* (Boston, 1701), p. 42; cf. *Dedham Pulpit: or, Sermons by the Pastors of the First Church* (Boston, 1840), p. 136.

tax-supported public education to the community; and a second century elapsed before this principle spread to any extent outside New England. In the seventeenth century, the ruling class was trying to enforce an extraordinarily high standard on a poor and hard-working country population, who wanted the labor of their children on the farm or in fishing, and could hardly appreciate the social and civic reasons for universal education.[32] An early complaint of popular failure to accept these high standards is in President Chauncy's commencement sermon of 1655, entitled *Gods Mercy Shewed to His People in giving them a Faithful Ministry and Schools of Learning.* He lists several degrees of unthankfulness for these blessings, on the part of 'coveteous earthwormes' who slight the privilege of having 'schools to teach their children, and keep them out of harmes way, or teach them to write and read, and cast accounts, but these despise the Angels bread, and account it but light stuff in comparison of other things. . . .' They are to be compared with Jeshurun, who waxed fat, and kicked. But there is a lower class of ingrates, declares Chauncy:

There be many in the country that account it their happiness to live in the wast howling wilderness, without any ministry, or schooles, and means of education for their posterity, they have

[32] In the Connecticut law of May 8, 1690, (*Conn. Col. Recs.*, IV, 31), it is stated, 'This Court considering the necessity many parents or masters may be under to improve their children and servants in labour for a great part of the yeare, doe order that if the towne schooles in the severall townes, as distinct from the free schoole, be, according to law allready established, kept up six moneths in each yeare to teach to read and wright the English tongue, the sayd townes so keeping their respective schooles six moneths in every yeare shall not be presentable or fineable by law for not haveing a schoole according to law, notwithstanding any former law or order to the contrary.'

much liberty (they think) by this want, they are not troubled with strict sabbaths, but they may follow their worldly business at any time, and their children may drudge for them at plough, or hough, or such like servil imployments, that themselves may be eased. . . . Thier practice about their children is litle better than the mercyless unnaturall and prophaness of the Israelites, Psal. 106. 36 *That sacrificed their sonns and their daughters unto Devils.*

In 1672 the Reverend Thomas Shepard of Charlestown declared: 'There is a great decay in Inferiour Schools, it were well if that also were examined, and the Cause thereof removed, and the Foundations laid for Free-Schools, where poor Scholars might be there educated by some Publick Stock.' [33] This certainly sounds as though the elementary-school system had broken down, before King Philip's War. Yet in the ten years 1671-1680 only two of the ten towns of Suffolk County were presented for not having the statutory schoolmaster; and they promptly satisfied the court that the information was mistaken.[34] And such complaints of decay in schools are rare. The next one that I have noted after Shepard is by Cotton Mather in 1690. He speaks of 'the too general Want of Education in the Rising Generation; which if not prevented, will gradually but speedily dispose us, to that sort of Criolian [35] Degeneracy, observed to deprave the Children of the most noble and worthy Europeans, when transplanted into America.' [36] Creole degeneracy! The General Court of Connecticut, the same year, declared that there were many

---

[33] *Eye-Salve* (Cambridge, 1673), quoted in Sibley, *Harvard Graduates*, I, 330.

[34] *C.S.M.*, XXIX.

[35] Mather and other Englishmen of his day called all European colonists, not merely Spaniards, Creoles.

[36] *The Way to Prosperity* (Boston, 1690), pp. 33-34.

people in that colony 'unable to read the English tongue,' and in 1701 the Massachusetts legislature complained that the compulsory school law was 'shamefully neglected by divers towns.' [37]

The New England schools as a rule required the payment of a small tuition fee from all parents who could afford it, the Boston Latin School being a notable exception. The usual fee in the seventeenth century was 3d. a week for the elementary, and 4d. a week for the grammar grades; 6s. and 8s. respectively for a six months' school year. This was supposed to supplement the meager salary that the schoolmaster had from the town. So long as this fee was waived for poor children, as appears to have been done in most of the towns that have full records, it is not likely that anyone was denied an education from mere poverty. But there was no obligation on the part of parents to send children to school at any time in the colonial period. The parents' duty was limited to seeing that their offspring learned to read, somehow. This could be done either at the elementary dame school, at a private school, or at home. There was no parental obligation to see that a child learned to write or cipher.[38]

We have been told by one class of writers that the New England schools were no good because they were religious; another group decries the system because it was undemo-

[37] *Conn. Col. Recs.*, IV, 30; *The Acts and Resolves of the Province of the Massachusetts Bay*, I, 470; Increase Mather reported to Lieutenant-Governor Stoughton in 1700 that the standard of learning in the College was suffering from inadequate preparation in grammar schools. *Mather Papers*, Harvard University Archives.

[38] Dedham seems to have gone somewhat beyond the minimum in requiring that children who did not attend school 'be sufitiantly taught to read and wright.' *Early Records of the Town of Dedham*, IV, 164.

cratic. To which it is sufficient answer to say that the English mind had not conceived of completely secular education before 1700, and that the colonies at that time were equally far from political democracy. The New England school system was not intended to be democratic, since democracy was not the polity of any New England colony in the seventeenth century except Rhode Island, which had no school system. But it was democratic in comparison with eighteenth-century England or Virginia; and at least made schooling available and cheap through the grammar grades and gave poor scholars a chance to work their way through college, helped out by an occasional ill-favored cow from the parental farm. Democracy in education, as used by modern educators, generally means a free education for all, with studies suited even to defective intellects, up to the age of sixteen or later. Of course nothing approaching such all-inclusiveness existed in the seventeenth century, anywhere. Girls were unprovided for after learning the three R's, and a boy who could not master Latin grammar was out of luck—he simply had to leave school, unless his parents could afford to send him to a private school or to one of the few writing schools.

In the seventeenth century there were very few private schools in New England.[39] It is only in Boston that we have evidence of any considerable number of children attending them; and there the private schoolmasters had to be licensed by the selectmen. In 1666, for instance, one Mr. Jones was forbidden 'to keep schoole any longer'; but the next year Mr. Will Howard was licensed 'to keep a

[39] References to statements and quotations in this section will be found in Robert F. Seybolt, *The Private Schools of Colonial Boston* (1935).

wrighting schoole, to teach children to writte and to keep accounts.' Samuel Sewall's Diary for the last decade of the century has several references to his sons and daughters being sent to private dame schools.

From about 1687 there was also a private grammar school in Boston to compete with the public grammar school. It was being kept by Joseph Dassett, a young college graduate, in 1692, and at his death the following year was taken over by Peter Burr, the future Chief Justice of Connecticut. Master Burr charged £2 tuition a year, and taught English and Latin both to boys and to girls. A second private schoolmaster, who began preparing boys for college as early as 1690, was Edward Mills, also a college graduate. And there was a French school for children of the Huguenot congregation, from about 1687. Possibly a careful search of the records in other places, such as Professor Seybolt has made for Boston, would disclose other private schools; but it is clear that, until the eighteenth century, they had little importance in comparison with the public schools. Early in the next century, with the rapid development of commerce, of handicraft, and in the art of living, a demand sprang up for vocational instruction and modern language for boys; and for dancing, music, French, fancy needlework, and other polite accomplishments for girls. Advertisements in the Boston newspapers show that this demand was promptly met, with the establishment of schools for young people of both sexes. Most of them offered to prepare boys for seafaring and business, by teaching such subjects as French, mathematics, accounting, and navigation, which the Latin grammar schools did not cover.

THE NEW ENGLAND PRIMER

What books were used in the elementary schools? Doubtless every child began with a hornbook. This was merely a printed alphabet sheet with a few words of one syllable and the Lord's Prayer, mounted in a wooden frame, with a sheet of horn to protect the surface.[40] These had been used in English schools since time immemorial. We know that they were used in New England, for Samuel Sewall the diarist has left us a pleasant picture of little Joseph toddling off to his first day of school at the age of two years and eight months, in charge of cousin Jane Tappan, aged sixteen, who carried his hornbook.[41]

The other books used in the elementary schools were a spelling book, a primer, and a catechism. Among the earliest books printed in New England were a Speller (1643) and a Catechism, a reprint of the Reverend John Cotton's *Milk for Babes, Drawn out of the Breasts of both Testaments Chiefly, for the Spirituall Nourishment of Boston Babes in either England.*[42]

No doubt other catechisms were used as well, for England was full of them; Hugh Peter wrote in 1661 that over a hundred different ones were circulating.

We do not know what primer was used in the earliest New England schools. Until very recent times, a primer or first reader has always combined religious with secular

[40] G. E. Littlefield, *Early Schools and School-Books of New England* (Boston: Club of Odd Volumes, 1904), pp. 110-117.

[41] Sewall, *Diary*, I, 344 (April 27, 1691).

[42] Title from the first edition, London, 1646, 13 pp. The earliest American edition, *Spiritual Milk for Boston Babes,* is Cambridge, 1656. No copy of the Speller has survived.

instruction; hence it was inevitable that the puritans should compile a primer to suit themselves. The alphabet in the famous *New England Primer*,[43] from

> *In Adam's Fall*
> *We sinned all*

to

> *Zaccheus he*
> *Did climb the Tree*
> *His Lord to see*

was definitely religious, and the inevitable illustration was a crude woodcut of the martyrdom of John Rogers. Society has ever sought, and probably always will seek, to impose its creed on very young children. Church schools today use church catechisms; American public schools salute the flag; Soviet schools have their communist catechisms. One of the first things the Protestant reformers attended to was getting out Protestant primers—Melanchthon's of 1519 is the earliest. Henry VIII authorized no less than three official primers, marking successive stages in his quarrel with Rome; and the puritans, as they drew away from the Church of England, naturally got out primers of their own. Why their schools should be singled out for scorn because they used a primer with religious bias is difficult to understand, unless our historians of education imagine that the *New England Primer* was the first of all primers. In any event, the *New England Primer*

[43] Paul Leicester Ford, *The New-England Primer* (1897) is still the best account of this book, although his brother Worthington C. Ford provided some important new facts in *Bibliographical Essays, A Tribute to Wilberforce Eames* (1924), and the bibliography has been greatly enlarged in Charles F. Heartman, *The New England Primer issued prior to 1830, a Bibliographical Checklist* (3d ed., 1934).

cannot have been so very bad, since it outlasted the Century of Enlightenment, and was reprinted and used in New York and Pennsylvania almost as extensively as in New England.

Nothing definite has been discovered about the primers used in New England schools before 1680.[44] Apparently the local press was unable to keep up with the demand, for Thomas Shepard, in his election sermon of 1672, complains of imported Anglican primers with images of Christ, the Virgin, and the Saints, as 'among the artifices of Satan' that lay in wait for Boston babes:

> In the very primmers for children whereby they may even suck in poison in their tender years, . . . sold in some shops, or brought over among us: things that will take with children, but though they may seem minute, yet will surely prove of dangerous consequence at length to those tender years, and may become an Introduction to Popery it self. I wish such things might get crushed in the eggs . . . *principiis obsta:* watch against it.[45]

The long-felt want of a special primer for New England was finally filled toward the close of the century, when John Gaines, an obscure London printer, entered a title in the Stationer's Register for 1683, *The New England Primer or Milk for Babes*. By 1685 this edition was sold out, and not a copy was to be found in London. Benjamin Harris, a London bookseller who emigrated to Boston in 1686 and there established a book and coffee shop, took up

[44] Except that a unique copy, now at Edinburgh, of John Eliot's Indian Primer of 1669 permits us to infer that the primers then used in New England schools contained the alphabet, the Lord's Prayer, the Apostle's Creed, the Ten Commandments, the Westminster catechisms, and the names and order of the books of the Bible.

[45] Thomas Shepard, *Eye-Salve* (Cambridge, 1673), p. 31.

the idea; and in the New England Almanac for 1691 is advertised the "Second Impression of the *New England Primer* Enlarged." From that time on, edition after edition of the *New England Primer* was printed; but so ephemeral are old schoolbooks, so quickly lost or soon worn out, and so soon replaced by new, that the earliest dated one known to exist today is a copy of the Boston edition of 1727. It was printed in New York as early as 1750, and we have a documentary evidence that between 1749 and 1766 Benjamin Franklin and his partner printed at Philadelphia 37,000 copies of the *New England Primer*. Yet only a single copy of one of these editions has come to light. Prior to 1830, when the *Primer* began to be replaced by First Readers, it had been produced in places as remote from New England as Baltimore and Pittsburgh and Chillicothe, Ohio; Charles F. Heartman, the principal authority on the bibliography of this great little book, estimates that over six million copies in all were printed.

LITERACY

The fairest test of the school system of seventeenth-century New England is the literacy of the people. And of this it is difficult to arrive at any satisfactory conclusion for want of anything resembling a census. Still, there are sufficient data to invalidate some of the wild statements current, to the effect that everybody in New England could read and write, or that comparatively few could do so.

Literacy was lowest among women, since little provision was made for their education outside the home. George H. Martin, one of the most careful writers on New England education, concluded from a painstaking count of names in the manuscript court records of three Massachusetts counties, that only about forty per cent of the women could sign their names, the rest signing by mark.[46] Dr. William Kilpatrick, in preparing his monograph on the Dutch schools of New Netherland, counted the signatures and marks on the deeds of Suffolk County, Massachusetts, for two periods including four hundred and fifty-six names. In 1653-1656, eighty-nine per cent of the men and forty-two per cent of the women signed their names; in 1681-1697 the proportion of male literates was the same, and that of the women had risen to sixty-two per cent.[47] A careful compilation by Dr. Shipton of over twenty-seven

[46] *The Evolution of the Massachusetts Public School System* (1904), p. 75. J. Truslow Adams, however, declares that around 1716 'almost all women' signed by mark (*Provincial Society*, p. 133). Mr. Adams probably obtained this notion from Harlan Updegraff, *Origin of the Moving School in Massachusetts* (1907), p. 115, where it is remarked that 'about 1700, many men and almost all women signed legal documents by their marks,' an astonishing statement to anyone who has worked in the legal documents of that period. Adams cites two pieces of evidence for his gloomy conclusions. One (from Updegraff), contains 13 names, and is a release by squatters in the poor fishing town of Manchester, 8 of whom signed by mark. The other is the town of Natick, where in 1698 'only one child in seventy could read.' Adams admits that this particular showing of illiteracy was 'probably an exceptionally bad case.' But he fails to inform his readers that Natick was an Indian town, without a single white inhabitant at that time!

[47] William H. Kilpatrick, *The Dutch Schools of New Netherland...* (1912), p. 229. Cf. the statistics collected by P. A. Bruce, in *Institutional History of Virginia*, I, 452-57.

	Number of Signatures	Number Signing by Mark	Per Cent Literate
Virginian jury entries, 17th century .	1,166	994	54
Virginian deeds and depositions, 1641-1700, men	7,439	5,006	60
Virginian deeds and depositions, 1641-1700, women	756	2,310	25

hundred names from petitions, addresses, and other documents in the Massachusetts and Connecticut Archives yields the following result: [48]

Date of Documents	Number of Signatures	Number Signing by Mark	Per Cent Literate
Massachusetts, 1640-1660 . . .	670	47	93
Massachusetts, 1661-1680 . . .	642	14	98
Massachusetts, 1681-1700 . . .	428	23	95
Connecticut, 1640-1679	442	26	94
Connecticut, 1680-1700	547	28	95
Total, 1640-1700	2,729	138	95

Geographical Groups	Per Cent Literate
Seaports and earliest settled towns	99
Connecticut Valley towns of Massachusetts	97
Interior and frontier towns, mostly Essex County . . .	90
Connecticut Colony	94.5
Plymouth Colony (62 signatures)	81

The poorest people, indented servants and the like, had slight opportunity to sign deeds or petitions; hence any accurate estimate of total illiteracy is impossible to attain. Still, it is striking that Dr. Kilpatrick's compilation from deeds, and Dr. Shipton's from petitions and similar documents should produce almost the same result: 89 and 95 per cent, respectively.

[48] For purposes of this compilation, he discarded documents with less than six signatures, petitions signed by selectmen or small groups 'for the rest of the inhabitants,' or by ministers, magistrates, and church members only. Where there was evidence that several or all the signatures were in one hand, they were not included in the count unless the doubtful names included marks. The only document containing any large percentage of marks was a petition from Salisbury, dated 1654, in which 20 out of 39 signed by mark. There are no women's names on these documents.

It must also be remembered that these literacy tests apply to writing as well as reading; and the compulsory school laws extend to reading only. It was the custom in the New England schools, following medieval and English practice, to teach children first to read, with a hornbook or primer. Writing and ciphering were begun only after they were able to read the primer or the Bible to satisfaction; and these subjects, as in Old England, were often taught by writing masters, or in special schools called writing schools, that paralleled the grammar schools up to a certain point. Consequently it is certain that very many, perhaps a major part, of the colonists, not only in New England but in the Middle Colonies and Virginia, who were unable to write their names could read the King James Bible and other simple English texts.

IV. THE PUBLIC GRAMMAR SCHOOLS

LET US now turn to secondary schools—the grammar schools, as New England secondary schools were called in the seventeenth and eighteenth centuries, after their English models.[1] There were about three hundred and sixty grammar schools in England in 1600, the great majority of them far from being noble and wealthy foundations like Eton and Westminster, but one-teacher schools maintained partly by modest endowments, partly by municipal funds, and mostly under municipal regulation. Typical of scores of these grammar schools was the one at Wakefield in Yorkshire, the master of which in the latter part of the sixteenth century was Edward Maude, father of Daniel Maude who became master of the grammar school at Boston, Massachusetts, in 1636.

By statutes adopted in 1607, the schoolmaster at Wakefield was required to be an M. A. of Cambridge or Oxford 'well reputed of for his knowledge, religion and life,' but he must not be a minister or regular preacher. He was required to take an oath to 'abhor all popishe superstition and renounce all forraine jurisdiction of the church of Rome and the now pope.' Saturday afternoon was devoted to religious instruction, and every Sunday the master accompanied the boys to church and saw that they took notes on the sermon, upon which they must be examined

[1] Dr. C. K. Shipton, who helped me with thorough and skillful research for this and the previous chapter, has an article, "Secondary Education in the Puritan Colonies," in *N.E.Q.*, VII (1934), 646-61, which is the best account that has yet appeared.

the next Wednesday morning—a cruelly long interval for a schoolboy to remember a sermon! The master was to teach 'grammar and the Latin and Greeke tongues, reading unto them the most classick authors, as in Latin these or some of them, Terence, Tully, Caesar's commentaryes, Titus Livius, Ovid, Virgil, Horace; in Greeke, Isocrates, Demosthenes, Hesiode or Homer. For . . . Latin, Lylyes Grammar; for the Greeke that grammar which in the Universitie of Cambridge ys most usually read in the greater number of colleges.' The master received £26 13s. 4d. a year, and his assistant, £12. Admission requirements were 'to be able in tollerable sorte to reade English and be promoted to the accidence' (the beginning Latin book). Admission fees were 12d. for those of the town, but the 'sonne of a daytaile man [2] or one of like povertie' was to pay no admission fee. 'Everie foreigner whatsoever,' *i.e.,* every out-of-town boy, was to pay 2s. School hours were 6.00 to 11.00 a.m. and 1.00 to 6.00 p.m. from October to March; and from sunrise to 6.00 p.m., with two hours' nooning, from March to October.[3] There was to be a fortnight's holiday at midsummer, and three weeks at Christmas.[4]

---

[2] A day laborer.

[3] A very similar schedule of hours is found in the Dorchester, Massachusetts, regulations for their grammar school in 1645 (*4th Report of the Boston Record Commissioners,* pp. 54-57), and in the Watertown, Massachusetts, regulations of 1677 (*Watertown Records,* I, 129).

[4] William Page, ed., *History of Yorkshire,* I, 442-443. A fine collection of documents on Yorkshire grammar schools, edited by Arthur F. Leach, is in the *Yorkshire Archaeological Society Records,* vols. XXVII, XXXIII. From these it appears that the Wakefield school was representative. In such considerable towns as Ripon, the grammar school had only one master and one usher at a time in the seventeenth century, and the masters changed frequently. See also Nicholas Carlisle, *Concise Description of the Endowed*

Although every Elizabethan grammar school had individual features, there is a striking sameness in the curricula, which consisted exclusively of Latin and Greek. For the most part, an English grammar scholar spent seven years in school without a scrap of mathematics, geography, history, or any modern language. The object of the curriculum was to make him completely at home in reading, writing, and speaking Latin as a living language and to give him a good start in Greek; nothing else mattered. Such was what the founders of New England understood to be the proper secondary education of a boy.

Massachusetts Bay in 1647 required every town of a hundred families to establish a grammar school, and the law was re-enacted in 1692, when Massachusetts became a royal province.[5] Connecticut adopted the hundred-family law in her code of 1650. After New Haven Colony was annexed to Connecticut this law was changed so as to require but one grammar school in each of the four counties.[6] This requirement was halved by a law of 1690, passed in the midst of King William's War; but re-

---

Grammar Schools in England and Wales. In vol. I, 158, is the curriculum of 1583 for the Grammar School at St. Bees, strikingly similar to that of the Boston Latin School in 1712. In the list of schoolmasters of the grammar school of Boston, Lincolnshire, one finds (I, 790) in 1619 Thomas James, who became the first pastor of Charlestown, Massachusetts. The average term of the masters in this school from 1608 to 1652 was less than four years. There are many such suggestive connections between the English grammar schools and those of New England; the subject merits a thorough investigation.

[5] *The Acts and Resolves of the Province of the Massachusetts Bay*, I, 63.

[6] *Connecticut Laws of 1672* (1865 reprint), p. 63. It is not likely that more than four towns had over a hundred families at that time. The *Century of Population Growth* estimate gives the Colony a total population of 14,000 in 1679, and 22 towns; Hartford, New Haven, and New London were very much larger than the other 19 towns; and several thousand people lived in unorganized plantations.

established in 1700.[7] Plymouth followed the other two Bible commonwealths in providing for grammar schools, in 1673. These New England grammar schools, so far as we have any record of them, were very close copies of the English. They kept long hours throughout the greater part of the year, took boys at the age of seven or eight, and in seven years' time prepared them for the college, whose entrance requirements were about the same as those of Oxford and Cambridge.[8]

What was the purpose of establishing schools of this kind, so unsuitable, according to our notions, for a newly settled country? What justified the heavy expense to a poor and struggling people? We find a few hints in contemporary documents. In the Dorchester regulations of 1645 the master is required to instruct his pupils 'both in humane learning, and good litterature,' which meant the humanities, and the ancient classics.[9] Plymouth, in providing encouragement for grammar schools in 1673, refers to 'littrature for the good and benefit of posteritie.'[10] The Massachusetts School Law of 1647 requires that grammar

[7] *Conn. Col. Recs.*, IV, 30-31, 331.

[8] Oxford and Cambridge had no official entrance requirements in the seventeenth century, but a college would not as a rule accept a boy until he had been through grammar school, or could satisfy a college tutor that he was ready to use Latin as the language of instruction. Presumably a certain acquaintance with Greek was required, as at Harvard.

[9] See New English Dictionary, under 'humane'; *literae humaniores* is the Latin equivalent. The phrase 'good literature,' very common in English educational literature of the Renaissance and later, is a translation of the Ciceronian *bonae literae*, and means the studies suitable for a liberal as distinct from a vocational or professional education. President Chauncy observes in his *Gods Mercy Shewed to his People* (1655), p. 35, that 'humane learning' had two currently accepted meanings: ancient as distinct from Christian literature, or the liberal arts as distinct from theology.

[10] *Plymouth Colony Records*, V, 108.

schoolmasters be 'able to instruct youth so far as they may be fitted for the Universitie.' And *New Englands First Fruits* (1643) describes the Cambridge Grammar School as founded 'for the training up of young Schollars, and fitting of them for *Academicall Learning*, that still as they are judged ripe, they may be received into the Colledge.' There was no incompatibility then, as there may well be today, between a good general education and college preparation; and in the colonies as in England there was no alternative to the classics for boys who did not continue their education in the university. We do not know what proportion of New England grammar-school graduates entered the college. I would guess less than half; for down to 1690, the college classes were so small as to allow for only one or at most two students, on an average, from each of the existing New England grammar schools.

These schools were not in any peculiar sense religious or puritanical. Saturday afternoons were probably spent on catechism, as in England, and schools were opened and closed with prayer; [11] doubtless there was quizzing on the Lord's Day sermons, and in some cases the boys were all marched to hear the week-day sermon or 'lecture.' But even these regulations, as we have seen, were copied from the English grammar schools under Anglican control. Almost invariably it was required in English schools that the master be a conforming member of the Church of England. An Act of Massachusetts Bay, passed in 1654, at the time when President Dunster's religious aberrations were startling the colony, enjoined selectmen 'not to admitt or

[11] Dorchester regulations, *4th Report of the Boston Record Commissioners*, pp. 54-57.

suffer any such to be continewed in the office or place of teaching . . . that have manifested themselves unsound in the faith or scandalous in theire lives.' [12] It was not until 1701 that a provincial law required grammar schoolmasters to be approved by the ministers of the town, and of the two next adjacent towns, or any two of them,[13] and the same law ruled out town ministers from themselves qualifying as grammar schoolmasters. The intent of the licensing provision was probably quite as much to ensure proper scholarly qualifications in the teacher as to keep out Anglicans and dissenters.

Grammar schools, like common schools, were controlled by the towns. Professor Thomas Jefferson Wertenbaker has declared that New England schools 'in one sense were church schools, supported out of church funds.' [14] One would like to know in *what* sense they were church schools, since the churches and the ministers had nothing to do officially with the selection of teachers, the payment of salaries, the choice of books, or the supervision of schools.[15] Not a penny of church money was used for the schools; their support came entirely from secular sources: taxation, tuition fees, and a few dwindling rents of land.

The penalty on a town of the requisite size which failed

[12] *Mass. Bay Recs.*, IV, part i, 182-83.
[13] *The Acts and Resolves of the Province of the Massachusetts Bay*, I, 470.
[14] *The First Americans* (1927), p. 245.
[15] 'No appointments of teachers were made without the full approbation of the ministers,' *ibid.* No formal approval, as we have seen, was required in Massachusetts until 1701; although doubtless the ministers possessed the same informal veto on school appointments that various pressure groups exercise on New England school appointments today. Professor Wertenbaker returns to the charge in his *The Puritan Oligarchy* (1947), p. 143.

to provide grammar instruction was a fine of £5 or £10, payable to the nearest town that conformed to the law. This was an ingenious provision, for the rivalry of New England towns was such that to pay money to the next town was humiliating, as well as expensive. As the law was construed by the courts in Massachusetts, it did not require a special master for grammar grades; a town could qualify if it maintained a schoolmaster of sufficient capacity to teach Latin and prepare boys for college, if required. If no grammar scholars appeared, the master took care of the younger pupils. For instance, Josiah Cotton taught six years at Marblehead just after he graduated from college in 1698; he had but two Latin grammar students, one of them the minister's son.[16] The schoolmaster at Taunton had the same experience, at the same date,[17] and a few years later when the town of Gloucester engaged Joshua Moody he agreed to teach all the common branches and 'lattine, if scholars appear.'[18] In 1681, when Andover was presented for want of a grammar school the Reverend Francis Dane, an alumnus of the University of Cambridge, appeared in court and declared, 'I thought it my duty to signify that for these thirty & two yeers I have taught any Schollers that they Sent to me to learne to write, and some in their Grammar'[19] and apparently that let the town out. In places too small for a grammar school the minister was apt to fit boys for college; at Newbury, for instance, the

---

[16] Diary, quoted in S. Roads, *The History and Traditions of Marblehead* (1880), pp. 38-39. Marblehead was a fishing town without puritan traditions.

[17] S. H. Emery, *History of Taunton* (1893), p. 280.

[18] J. J. Babson, *History of the Town of Gloucester* (1860), p. 233.

[19] *Essex County Records*, VIII, 100. 'Grammar,' as used in the seventeenth century never means English grammar, which was not taught.

Reverend Thomas Parker, who had studied at two British and two Dutch universities, conducted in his parsonage a free grammar school that was famous in its day; Samuel Sewall the diarist was one of his pupils. The town was fined £5 in 1658 'for want of a lattin scoole,' [20] but from that time until Parker's death his parsonage school was allowed by the courts to fill the requirements; thereafter a 'lattin schoolmaster' was maintained continuously.[21] The normal effect of the hundred-family law, then, was to force towns to hire a college graduate as schoolmaster, in order that any town boy wanting Latin might have it; and the usual practice was to employ a pious youth fresh from the college, at a salary of £20 or £30, until he obtained a parish. Hadley, for instance, had thirty-one teachers in forty-five years, all but two college graduates; of eleven successive teachers at Newbury, only one lacked the A. B.; Dedham had twenty-seven teachers in sixty years, all but the first three being fresh from Harvard.[22] Thirty pounds a year was a good salary for a young man in the seventeenth century; and the use of college graduates 'without previous experience of teaching,' although frowned upon by teachers' colleges today, probably tended to keep up town-school standards, and to encourage ambitious lads to win a college education themselves.

The experience of the town of Woburn may be cited to show that the Massachusetts law was being enforced near

[20] Joshua Coffin, *A Sketch of Newbury, Newburyport and West Newbury* (1845), p. 62.

[21] *Ibid.*, pp. 117, 120, 121, 148, 156, 158, 161, 169.

[22] Samuel Sewall, *The History of Woburn* (1868), p. 586; S. Judd, *History of Hadley* (1905), pp. 58-59; Carlos Slafter, "Schools and Teachers of Dedham," *Dedham Historical Register*, I, 86ff; J. J. Currier, *History of Newbury* (1902), pp. 395ff.

the end of the century, and that the community was more eager to start grammar schools than parents were ready to patronize them. In 1685, the town having passed the hundred-family mark, the selectmen appointed Mr. Samuel Carter, an elderly college graduate and town resident, to keep grammar school for a year, at a salary of £5; but for Latin no scholars appeared. Next year the master (who probably farmed for a living) was promised £5 if he had one or more Latin scholars, or £1 10s. if he had none. Mr. Carter collected the thirty shillings for doing nothing, while a school dame was paid ten shillings for doing all the teaching in the town elementary school. Nothing more was done about a grammar school until 1690, when Mr. Carter was re-engaged on the same terms, and enjoyed the same unruffled school year. In 1694, Mr. Carter having died, Mr. Jabez Fox, minister of the town and a college graduate, agreed to 'instruct any children that belong to this town of Woobourne, to wright, and in the gramer' for one year. The same engagement was renewed in 1699. The following year, a committee of three was chosen in town meeting to engage 'some suitable person to keep a grammar school in the town, and occasionally to assist the Rev. Mr. Fox in the ministry.' Nothing was done; and three months later Woburn was presented at court for failing to comply with the law, and fined £10. The town then empowered a committee to make 'as easy terms as they can' with 'Sir Fox [John Fox, A. B. 1698, the minister's son] or any other gentleman' to keep grammar school for four months; and Sir Fox agreed to do so for £9. When the four months were up he demanded and obtained a salary of £28 for the next year, 1701; there must therefore have been some scholars, but not many; for the following year, 1702, Master Fox (as he now was called, having taken his M. A. at the College) obtained £18, with a promise that 'in case he should have more worke in that place than he had the last year, he should have forty shillings more.' The indications are that most of Master Fox's 'worke' was of an elementary nature, since the town voted that those who sent children or servants to school with him should pay 3d. a week per child, if they could afford it. He continued to qualify as grammar schoolmaster until 1703, when he became the town minister in succession to his father.

The town then applied to the college for a successor. It must have been an era of prosperity, for the college had no unemployed graduates to suggest. The town then engaged a classmate of young Fox, Dudley Bradstreet, who was teaching school at Andover, to connive with them in evading the law. They reported to the court that he had been engaged as grammar schoolmaster. One day he walked over to Woburn and formally opened school. No scholars appeared, Master Bradstreet returned to Andover with eighteen shillings in his pocket, and no school was held. This farming community (which fifty years later gave birth to Benjamin Thompson, Count Rumford) made no demand for grammar schooling at the turn of the century; hence the town had the choice between paying a college graduate to do elementary-school teaching, and hiring a cheap schoolma'am and risking court censure and the £10 fine.[23]

---

[23] Sewall, *Woburn*, pp. 52-53, 209-15; Sibley, *Harvard Graduates*, II, 196; IV, 394-95, 404.

There has been a good deal of facile generalization about the 'degeneracy' or 'collapse' of the New England school system toward the end of the century. So far as my observation of the sources goes, the dangerous period was in the early 1670's, just before King Philip's War. Both in 1672 and 1673 the ministers who preached the Massachusetts election sermon complained 'that the Schools languish, and are in a low Condition in the Countrey.'[24] Grammar instruction lapsed at both New Haven and Hartford in 1673, and at Watertown in 1675.[25] Yet this was perhaps the most prosperous period of the century for New England, when Benjamin Tompson, poet-schoolmaster of Charlestown and Braintree, complained of the luxuries coming in from Europe and the West Indies.[26]

The college, too, came nearer extinction at this period than at any time since 1639. There was no graduating class in 1672, only four graduates the next year, and two in 1674. Dr. Leonard Hoar, chosen president with great expectations in 1672, proved so unpopular with students and tutors that they deserted the college in the winter of 1674-1675, and forced him out. Probably there was action and reaction here; grammar schools had no pupils because the college was under a cloud, and the college fell into a low state because the grammar schools sent it no pupils. But the deeper cause probably lay in prosperity. Trade with Europe and the West Indies was booming; likely lads preferred a berth in the forecastle or cabin of a Yankee

[24] Sibley, I, 177, 330.
[25] See notes 35 and 41, below.
[26] See Chapter IX, below.

vessel to spending seven years in grammar school and four more in college.

King Philip's War took a heavy toll of life and property in New England. About one man in ten of fighting age was killed; the frontier of settlement was flung back so far that another forty years barely sufficed to recover what was lost; and the people, without help from England or credit for loans, were crushed by heavy taxation. Yet after the war was over, in 1677, education in New England seems to have taken a brace; and except in Connecticut, where the Act of 1690 (passed in the midst of another war) reduced the required number of grammar schools from four to two, I can see little evidence in the records but that of slow and steady advance until the very end of the century, when we find a new series of complaints against the burden of supporting the schools.

A considerable number of new grammar schools were established after the war. Benjamin Tompson, the poet, became schoolmaster of Braintree in 1679; he was not hired to teach Latin, but apparently did so, for in 1696 the inhabitants, on the ground that he had 'many years kept a grammar school' in the town, raised his salary £10.[27] Nearby Hingham had had a grammar master since 1670. Newbury hired one in 1676, when Thomas Parker became too feeble to maintain his free preparatory school. Concord began a grammar school before 1680;[28] Northampton engaged schoolmaster Warham Mather in 1688, with an addition of £20 to his regular salary of £40, to

[27] Sibley, II, 104-107; *Records of Braintree* (1886), pp. 18ff.
[28] L. Shattuck, *Concord*, p. 220.

bring scholars 'up to Learning to fit them for the colledge so that they may be fit the Service of God in the church or otherwise in the publick.' [29]

New Plymouth, oldest and poorest of the New England colonies, founded by a group of puritans not particularly interested in education, first showed ambition for a secondary school in 1670. The General Court passed a law appropriating the profits from seine-fishing at Cape Cod toward free schools 'for the training up of youth in literature for the good and benefitt of posterity.' In accordance with this vote a school was established at Plymouth Town, and the master's salary paid by the town; but there is no evidence of grammar instruction before 1699, when it was voted that 'Every scollar that Coms to wrigh or syfer or to lern latten shall pay 3 pence per weke,' the balance of school expenses to be levied by rate on the inhabitants. In 1677 the Colony voted to distribute the fishing profits at the rate of £5 to each town that set up a grammar school, the town to raise the rest. Duxbury seems to have qualified the same year; Rehoboth had one in 1678.[30] But the honor for scholastic ambition in the Pilgrim colony rests with the Baptist town of Swansea, which voted in 1673 to set up a school 'for the teaching of grammar, rhetoric, and arithmetic, and the tongues of Latin, Greek, and Hebrew; also to read English and to write.' Herein one may indeed trace church influence; for the leader in Swansea, the Baptist minister John Myles, an

---

[29] J. R. Trumbull, *Northampton*, I, 193, 386, 389-90. Mather, a college graduate, also had to instruct the younger children, 'readers at 3d. pur weeke and writers at 4d. pur weeke.'

[30] *Plymouth Town Records*, I, 270; *Plymouth Colony Records*, V, 107-8, 259; XI, 247.

alumnus of Oxford University ejected from his Welsh parish, was the first schoolmaster.[31]

Connecticut, in 1677, adopted the Massachusetts system of fining the four shire towns that should have kept a 'Lattin Schoole' and did not, £10 for benefit of the next town that would. In 1687 it distributed some surplus revenues to the counties for their schools. But three years later it decided to give up trying to coerce or cajole the two poorer counties into doing their duty, and concentrated on the Hopkins Grammar Schools of Hartford and New Haven, granting their masters £60 each in 'country pay' (commodities), half out of the colony treasury, and half out of the revenue from Governor Hopkins' bequest.[32] A bill was introduced in 1691 to establish two more grammar schools,[33] but it did not pass.

So the average grammar school of seventeenth-century New England consisted of a young man qualified to prepare students for college, who took any Latin scholars that happened along, but for the most part was occupied in giving small children a grounding in the elements. A few exceptional towns had a proper grammar school on the English model, with a permanent master and sometimes an usher or assistant as well who had no duties other than teaching the grammar grades. So far as I can ascertain from existing records, the only towns that had grammar schools of any description for any appreciable length of time in the seventeenth century were Boston (1636), Cambridge

[31] O. O. Wright, compiler, *History of Swansea, 1667-1917* (1917), p. 57; *Dictionary of American Biography*, XIII, 376.

[32] *Conn. Col. Recs.*, II, 312; III, 224-25; IV, 31.

[33] Connecticut Archives, *College and Schools*, I, 7.

(1642), Roxbury (1646),[34] Watertown (1651),[35] Charlestown (1636),[36] Dorchester (1639),[37] Salem (1637),[38] Ips-

[34] The 'Free School' founded in 1646, and placed under the control and
responsibility of a board of feoffees, is said by the local historian, Francis
Drake (p. 197), to have become a grammar school only in 1674, when a
certain legacy became available. Roxbury, however, sent more students to
Harvard before 1674 than any other town except Boston, Cambridge, and
Ipswich; hence it may be inferred that the Free School prepared for
college before that date. Cf. Cotton Mather, *Magnalia* (1702), book iii,
187; C. K. Dilliway, *History of the Grammar School at Roxbury* (1860).

[35] Schoolhouse built, and Mr. Richard Norcross engaged 'for the teaching of Chilldren to Reed and write and soe much of Lattin, according to
an Order of Courtt, as allso if any of the said towne, have any maidens,
that have a desire to learne to write that the said Richard, should attend
them for the Learning off them; as allso that he teace such as desire to Cast
accompt . . . ,' *Watertown Records,* I, 21 (Jan. 6, 1650/51). He was allowed
to charge 3d. a week for English and 4d. for Latin scholars, and had £30
from the town, and a schoolhouse built by the town (*idem,* 18, 26); in 1667
the school was made 'Free to all the setteled Inhabitance,' what out-of-town
scholars paid to be deducted from Mr. Norcross's salary (*idem,* 91). Norcross continued until 1675, when the grammar department, as we might call
it, was temporarily given up; he was taken on again in 1679 for £20.
Watertown was presented for want of a grammar school in 1680 (Ms.
Court Records, Middlesex County). In 1693 the tuition for Latin scholars
was raised to 6d. The Watertown Records are uncommonly full and de-
tailed on schools.

[36] The first schoolmaster in 1636, William Wetherell, was a Cambridge
graduate, but there is no indication that the Free School had grammar
grades until 1666, when Ezekiel Cheever became the master. In 1671, when
engaging Benjamin Tompson, the Town stipulated 'that he shall prepare
such youths as are capable of it for the college, with learning answerable.'
R. Frothingham, *Charlestown,* pp. 157, 177.

[37] William Dana Orcutt, *Good Old Dorchester,* pp. 290-300; Town
Records (*4th Report of the Boston Record Commissioners*), pp. 54-57. In
1655 Ichabod Wiswall, who had just left college without a degree, was
engaged for three years to instruct in 'Ennglish Latine and Greeke'
(*idem,* 73) for £25 per annum. After he left, there was a succession of young
masters, mostly college graduates; Dorchester was a regular feeder to
Harvard.

[38] The Reverend John Fiske was the teacher in 1637, and Edward Norris
in 1640; both were English university graduates and were prepared to
teach Latin grammar; but Salem sent very few boys to college before the
last quarter of the century. In renewing a contract with Daniel Epes in
1677, the town required him to 'Learn and Instruct all Such Schollers as

wich (1651),[39] New Haven (1637),[40] and Hartford (1643).[41]

Of these eleven grammar schools, only four seem to have had an unbroken existence from the first ten or fifteen years of the colony's existence. These were the grammar schools of Dorchester, Roxbury, Cambridge, and Boston. The Cambridge Grammar School (unlike some of the grammar schools of Oxford and Old Cambridge) had no

---

shall bee Sent to him, from any person or persons In the towne, in the English, Latten and Greek tongue Soe as to fitt them for the university.' Sidney Perley, *The History of Salem*, II, 94.

[39] A grammar school was started in 1636, but did not succeed. In 1650 the town granted 'The Neck' to 'the Grammar School,' appointed a board of trustees, and built a schoolhouse. Ezekiel Cheever was succeeded in 1662 by Thomas Andrews. Down to 1672, Ipswich sent only a few less students to college than Boston.

[40] Ezekiel Cheever, who began teaching in 1637, and his successor, Bowers, both complained of having too much time taken up with abecedarians (E. E. Atwater, *History of the Colony of New Haven*, pp. 262, 265, 267). A colony grammar school was established in 1660, with a Harvard alumnus as teacher, given up in 1662, and re-established in 1664. This school gradually merged into the Hopkins Grammar School, endowed under the will of Governor Edward Hopkins; the master, a college graduate, received £30 a year from the town. In 1668 the master had eight Latin scholars, and was expecting five more (Sibley, *Harvard Graduates*, II, 160); but grammar instruction lapsed about 1673, and was not renewed until 1684; thereafter it was continuous. The school was free to all boys from New Haven County. Leonard W. Bacon, *Historic Discourse on the 200th Anniversary of Hopkins Grammar School* (1860), pp. 55-60; *Commemoration Exercises of 250th Anniversary of Hopkins Grammar School* (1910), pp. 25-27.

[41] William De Loss Love, *The Colonial History of Hartford*, 1914, pp. 253-54, regards the school established in 1643 as a grammar school, but it did not have a college graduate for teacher until 1655 (p. 259), and if he taught grammar grades they were shortly after given up. In 1666 Hartford received her share of the Hopkins legacy, which, with two other legacies for the same purpose and town grants, enabled her to maintain a grammar school. Yet in April, 1673, Governor Winthrop wrote to a young friend, 'the Schoale heere is broken up, and Mr. Holioke is gone, because he had but 2 or 3 schollers . . . therefore I desire you to be put to schoale to Cambridge or Salem or Ipswich or where . . .' (Winthrop Mss., M.H.S., V, 106; cf. Sibley, *op. cit.*, II, 96).

organic connection with Harvard College but, on account of its situation and the fame of Elijah Corlet (B.A. Oxford and M.A. Cambridge), the master for forty-five years, it attracted boarders from other parts of New England; and from 1672 to the end of the century it sent more boys to the college than any other school.

The 'Free School' or 'Free Grammar School' of Boston, which it will be convenient to term by its modern name, the Boston Latin School, has had a continuous existence from 1636. For all but three of the following seventy-two years, until 1708, it was taught by English university men.[42] For thirty-eight years it had the most famous of all colonial schoolmasters, Ezekiel Cheever—Corderius Americanus, as his pupil Cotton Mather called him, after Calvin's famous schoolmaster at Geneva. Cheever, like Corlet, was a graduate of the Blue Coat School (Christ's Hospital) of London; he entered Emmanuel College, Cambridge, at about the time when John Harvard was graduating, but emigrated with the Eaton and Davenport group to New Haven before taking a degree. As Cotton Mather writes, Cheever 'held the rod for 70 years' in New England—*Primo Neo-portensis; deinde, Ipsuicensis; postea, Carolotenensis; postremo, Bostonensis*—'first at New Haven, then at Ipswich, later at Charlestown, and finally at Boston,' where he rounded off the last thirty-eight years of his life, dying in harness at the age of ninety-two, never missing a day of school.

Cheever's progress from school to school can be traced

[42] Daniel Maude, M.A. Cambridge, 1636-1643; John Woodbridge, alumnus but not graduate of Oxford, 1643-1645; Robert Woodmansey, M.A. Cambridge, 1645-1667; Benjamin Tompson, A.B. Harvard, 1667-1670; Ezekiel Cheever, M.A. Cambridge, 1670-1708.

by the matriculations at Harvard. When he had charge of the Ipswich grammar school, that small town sent only two or three less pupils to the college than did Boston. After he migrated to Charlestown, that place began to send students to Harvard; and it was only after his final terrestrial translation to the Boston Latin School that Boston became one of the principal feeders of the New England college. Ezekiel Cheever meets us at every turn in colonial literature: Hawthorne's *Grandfather's Chair;* in the Diary of President Stiles of Yale, where we are told about his long white beard, the stroking of which was a signal to the boys to 'stand clear'; in the jingling elegy by Cotton Mather, where these parting words are put in the beloved master's mouth:

> Tutors, *be* strict; *but yet be* Gentle *too,*
> *Don't by fierce* Cruelties *fair* Hopes *undo,*
> *Dream not, that they who are to Learning slow,*
> *Will mend by Arguments in* Ferio,
> *Who keeps the* Golden Fleece, *Oh, let him not*
> *A* Dragon *be, tho' he* three tongues *have got.*
> *Why can you not to Learning find the way,*
> *But thro' the Province of Severia?*
> *'Twas* Moderatus, *who taught Origen;*
> *A* youth *which prov'd one of the Best of men.*
> *The lads with* Honour *first and* Reason *Rule;*
> Blowes *are but for the refractory fool.*
> *But, Oh! first teach them their* Great God *to fear;*
> *That you, like me, with joy may meet them here.*[43]

We meet Cheever, too, in the autobiography of John Barnard, one of his seventeenth-century pupils. Johnny

[43] Elizabeth P. Gould, *Ezekiel Cheever, Schoolmaster* (Boston, 1904), p. 84.

entered the Latin School at the age of eight, so playful and mischievous that he hindered his classmates in getting their lessons. Master Cheever soon announced that if any of them failed, Barnard would be beaten. It worked all right, until one boy who didn't like the scapegoat, failed several times on purpose. Johnny then beat him so badly that his parents took him out of school. Barnard looked back with particular satisfaction at having caught his teacher in the wrong on a rule of Latin grammar. After proving the point to him by book, Master Cheever said, 'Thou art a brave boy; I had forgot it.' 'And no wonder,' adds Barnard, 'for he was then above eighty years old.' [44]

The headmasters of the Boston Latin School were annually appointed or reappointed by the town meeting, and paid out of the town treasury. Master Cheever had an annual salary of £60, and for part of his long administration he had an usher, or assistant, whom the town also paid. There was no tuition fee, except for nonresidents; and no other fee, except 6s. a year per pupil for wood to warm the schoolhouse, which was remitted for poor scholars. Apart from that, all the expenses of the school were met by the town.

From 1652, if not earlier, the Boston schoolhouse was located on the street which, since the death of Cheever, has been called School Street. We do not know how large the seventeenth-century schoolhouse was; smaller, no doubt, than the new one built in 1704, which measured forty by twenty-five feet, with eleven-foot stud, and an upper floor. Experts on school construction perhaps can estimate the pupil capacity; but it is not likely that Cheever ever had as

[44] 3 *Coll. M.H.S.*, V, 179-80.

many as one hundred pupils at a time, since thirty years after his death the school numbered but one hundred and thirty-eight.

This Boston Latin School is the only one of whose curriculum we have an exact account. It is dated 1712; [45] but there are several reasons for believing that this curriculum was put into effect by Cheever long before: (1) most of the books are mentioned by Cotton Mather as having been studied by him in the sixteen-seventies; (2) copies of some of them, owned by Latin School boys of the time, are still in existence; [46] and (3) several are mentioned in Boston booksellers' invoices and lists of stock between 1682 and 1700.

The three first years were spent in learning by heart an "Accidence," as beginning Latin books were then called,[47] together with the *Nomenclator*,[48] a Latin-English phrase-book, and vocabulary called *Sententiae Pueriles*.[49] For construing and parsing, the *Distichia* attributed to Dionysius Cato, a collection of maxims popular since the early Christian era, was used.[50] Corderius' *Colloquies* [51] and Aesop's

[45] Printed by Kenneth B. Murdock, "The Teaching of Latin and Greek at the Boston Latin School in 1712," *C.S.M.*, XXVII, 23-25.

[46] See Note II at the end of this chapter for list.

[47] The Boston Accidence is supposed to have been composed by Ezekiel Cheever before 1650, and to have been circulated in ms. copies until 1709, when first printed at Boston as *A Short Introduction to the Latin Tongue* (G. E. Littlefield, *Early Schools and School-Books of New England*, pp. 251-55); but Cheever's authorship of this book has lately been challenged. Michael Perry had no less than seventy-four "Accidences" for sale in 1700 (John Dunton, *Letters from New England*, 1867 ed., pp. 316-19).

[48] There are 11 copies of this in Perry's stock, 1700.

[49] Perry had 43 copies, and an invoice of 1685 (see next chapter) included 100 "Hoole's *Sententiae*."

[50] Eighteen "Catos" on Perry's stock, and 50 in an invoice of 1683/84.

[51] "Hoole's Corderius," 14 copies, in Perry's stock.

Fables [52] were also read, in Latin. Fourth year began Erasmus' *Colloquies*,[53] continued Aesop, studied Latin grammar,[54] and read Ovid *de Tristibus*. Fifth year continued Erasmus and Ovid, including the *Metamorphoses*,[55] and began Cicero's *Epistolae*,[56] Latin prosody, and Latin composition with Garretson's *English Exercises for School-Boys to Translate*. Sixth-year scholars began Cicero *de Officiis*,[57] Lucius Florus, Virgil's *Aeneid*, and Thomas Godwyn's excellent English treatise on Roman history and antiquities, which had been used at the University of Cambridge in John Harvard's day; [58] they continued the *Metamorphoses*, made Latin verse, dialogues, and letters, and began Greek and Rhetoric. During the seventh and last year, the boys, now fourteen to sixteen years old, began Cicero's *Orations*,[59] Justin, Virgil, Horace, Juvenal, and Persius, made Latin dialogues, and turned 'a Psalm or something Divine' into Latin verse, with a Latin theme every fortnight. For Greek, they read Homer, Isocrates, Hesiod, and the New Testament.

All in all, a pretty stiff and thorough classical course,

[52] Fourteen copies in Perry's stock.

[53] Found in almost all the booksellers' lists and private libraries.

[54] Perry's stock includes 45 Latin Grammars.

[55] *Metamorphoses*, 4 copies; *de Tristibus*, 5 copies, in Perry's stock.

[56] A dozen of John Sturm's edition in an invoice of 1683/84; 8 copies of "Tulleys Epistles" in Perry's stock.

[57] Perry has 7 copies, and 7 Virgils; there are 18 *de Officiis* in an invoice of 1683/84.

[58] *Romanae Historiae Anthologia;* cf. Morison, *The Founding of Harvard College*, p. 68; *Harvard in the Seventeenth Century*, p. 264n; and list of Harvard textbooks in *C.S.M.*, XXVIII, 407.

[59] Perry stocks 6 copies, and one Juvenal (Stapleton ed.). I find no Greek authors except Isocrates in the invoices, but 19 Greek Grammars in Perry's stock.

with nothing especially puritan about it. Professor Werten-baker's description of the New England grammar-school course as a mere beginning of Latin seems rather on the cautious side. Beginning, indeed! For seven years the Boston grammar student studied hardly anything but Latin—grammar, literature, prose, composition, and verse-making. We cannot, of course, assume that every New England grammar school had the same high standards as Master Cheever's, but all grammar schoolmasters who had a B.A. degree (and most of them had), were capable of teaching this course, since they had had four years of Greek in college; and Greek was an entrance requirement at Harvard throughout the century.[60] But the fact that most of Cheever's program for the seventh year was repeated at Harvard suggests that the college could not count on the same degree of preparation by all freshmen. Nor can she today.

To conclude, the New England colonies, except Plymouth and Rhode Island, put into effect at an early date, and maintained fairly consistently throughout the century, an ambitious school system. Some schools were completely free, in the modern sense; the others were open to qualified students for a small tuition fee, which was waived for poor scholars. These schools were in no sense church schools, but in every contemporary sense of the word *public*

[60] Occasionally a town prescribed that the schoolmaster should teach Greek, e.g., Hingham in 1670 (F. H. Lincoln, in *History of the Town of Hingham*, p. 84); Reading in 1706 (L. Eaton, *Genealogical History of the Town of Reading*, 1874, p. 129); Salem in 1677 (M. V. B. Perley, *A Short History of the Salem Village Witchcraft Trials*, 1911, p. 94). In others, it is prescribed that the master undertake to 'fit' youth 'for the colledge,' e.g., Northampton in 1688 (Trumbull, *History of Northampton*, I, 390).

schools; and their continued existence through two centuries provided the basis, a century ago, for the American system of free public education for all.

These colonies well and honestly carried out the ambition of their founders to raise up a learned clergy and a lettered people. Amid conditions often of grueling hardship, they maintained the splendid tradition of learning that the Church had fostered through the Middle Ages, and to which the Renaissance and the Reformation had given new life.

NOTE I

Parallel between Elizabethan Curriculum of Westminster School and the Curriculum of the Boston Latin School in 1712 [61]

WESTMINSTER	BOSTON
I YEAR Cato; Vives' *Exerc. Ling. Lat.;* Corderius' *Dialogues & Confab. Puer.*	
II YEAR Terence; Aesop's *Fables* in Latin; *Dialogi Sacri;* Erasmus' *Colloquies*	Cato; Corderius; Aesop's *Fables* in Latin; *Sententiae Pueriles; Accidence; Nomenclator*
III YEAR Terence, Sallust, Cicero's *Epistolae;* Aesop in Latin	
IV YEAR Terence, Sallust, Ovid *de Tristibus,* Cicero *de Officiis;* begin Greek Grammar; Lucian's *Dialogues*	Erasmus' *Colloquies;* Aesop; Ovid *de Tristibus;* Garretson's *Exercises*

[61] John Sargeaunt, *Annals of Westminster School* (London, 1898), p. 38; C.S.M., XXVII, 23-25.

V YEAR	Justin, Cicero *de Amicitia;* Ovid's *Metam.,* Isocrates, Plutarch	Cicero's *Epistolae;* Erasmus; Ovid *de Tristibus* and *Metam.*
VI YEAR	Caesar, Livy, Virgil, Demosthenes, Homer	Cicero's *Epistolae* & *de Officiis;* Lucius Florus; Ovid's *Metam.;* Virgil
VII YEAR		Cicero's *Orationes;* Justin; Greek Testament; Isocrates; Homer; Hesiod; Virgil; Horace; Juvenal; Persius

NOTE II

Books Owned by Pupils in the Boston Latin and Other New England Grammar Schools

In searching our older libraries for books bearing evidence of ownership by Harvard students of the seventeenth century, Professor A. O. Norton and I happened upon several that from their dates must have belonged to such students when in grammar school. Miss Pauline Holmes lists others in the *Harvard Alumni Bulletin* for April 19, 1935. The dates of A.B.'s refer to graduation from Harvard. The abbreviations of location are: A.A.S. for American Antiquarian Society, Worcester; B.P.L. for Boston Public Library; H.C.L. for Harvard College Library.

ALDUS

Phrases Linguae Latinae, ab Aldo Manutio conscriptae. London, 1636.   Norton, p. 418. H.C.L.
Owned by John Whiting (A.B. 1657) of Lynn, in 1651.

AELIAN

Variae Historiae Libri XIII, cum Latine interpretatione. Cologne, 1630.   Prince Library, B.P.L.
Inscribed 'Samuell Sewal his booke 1665: 21: 4.' Sewall graduated from Harvard in 1671. He must have used this book in Thomas Parker's private grammar school at Newbury.

CICERO

Ethicae Ciceronianae libri duo, seu doctrina de Honeste vivendi ratione ex Ciceronis libris et sententiis expressa, et Rameâ methodo digesta, à M. Antonio Buschero. London, 1651.

Prince Library, B.P.L.

Inscribed by Edmund Davie (A.B. 1674) in 1667, and George Alcock (A.B. 1673) in 1668. The former probably prepared at the Boston, and the latter at the Roxbury, grammar school. Other signatures of boys who did not attend college.

JOHN CLARKE

Formulae Oratoriae, in usum Scholarum Concinnatae. London, 1659.   H.C.L.

Inscribed 'John Higginson Tertius 1712/13,' the subfreshman year of that youth.

COMENIUS

Janua Linguarum Reserata. London, 1650.   H.C.L.

Belonged to Elisha Cooke of Boston (A.B. 1657), and in 1650 to his younger brother Elkanah, then aged nine or ten.

Another Edition. London, 1672.   Yale Library

Belonged to Timothy Stevens (A.B. 1687) of Roxbury, in 1681. Both these *Janua*, with others that may have been used in grammar schools, are described in *C.S.M.*, XXI., 184-85.

THOMAS DRAXE

Calliepeia, or a Rich Store-House of Proper, Choyce, and elegant Latine words, and Phrases: Collected (for the most part) out of Tullies Works, by Thomas Drax. London, 1643.   H.C.L.

'Elisha Cooke His Booke 1649.' He graduated from the college in 1657. 'Amos Richardson his Booke 1662.' A Boston boy who did not attend college. Other undated signatures.

ERASMUS

Colloquia, cum annotationibus Arnoldi Montani. Amsterdam, 1658.   Prince Library, B.P.L.

Belonged in 1701 to Joseph Sewall (A.B. 1707), who prepared for college at Peter Burr's private grammar school and the Boston Latin School.

Another edition. Title and first 50 pages missing.

Prince Library, B.P.L.

On p. 95 is the name John Richardson (possibly A.B. 1666; more probably his son John, b. 1677, not a college graduate). On p. 98 begins a list of 'The boys that belongs to the publick grammar school,' over 25 names, apparently written by Henry Messinger (A.B. 1717) who signs his name with 'Ejus Liber 1709.'

Another edition. London, 1711.   A.A.S.

Inscribed in 1716 by Joseph Lynde of Boston, who graduated from college in 1723, and in 1735 by Grindal Rawson (A.B. 1741).

THOMAS FARNABY

Index Rhetoricus et Oratorius, Cui adjiciuntur Formulae Oratoriae, et Index Poeticus. London, 1646.   A.A.S.

Inscribed 'Daniel Greenlefe His Booke 1670' (Greenleaf was A.B. 1699); 'This book was lent with good intent to me Moses Hale' (A.B. 1699); and in the same hand, 'Daniel Greenleaf lent me this book 1692'; 'This book is lent, with true intent to be return'd again. Samuell Moody' (A.B. 1697). All three boys were of Newbury.

CHARLES HOOLE

The Common Rudiments of Latin Grammar, Usually Taught in all Schools. By Charles Hoole, M.A.L.C. Oxon. London, 1657.

H.C.L.

'Elisha Cooke' (probably the one who graduated A.B. in 1697). On the fly-leaf in a childish hand is this inscription of his son Middlecott, who gave the book to the H.C.L. in 1764,

'Middlecott Cooke
Hujus Si cupias Dominum cognoscere Libri
Nomen subscriptum perlege quaeso meū'

Sententiae Pueriles Anglo-Latinae quas olim collegerat, Leonardus Culman; et in Vernaculum Sermonem nuperrime transtulit, Carolus Hoole. Boston in N. E. Printed by B. Green, and J. Allen, for Samuel Phillips at the Brick Shop, 1702.   H.C.L.

This edition of one of the most famous schoolbooks of all time was one of the earliest school texts printed in this country. It was obviously printed for Latin School use, but the earliest dated signature in this copy is that of William Williams, who entered the Boston Latin School in 1748.

LILY

A Short Introduction of Grammar. Cambridge, 1666.
                            Collection of George A. Plimpton.
This book belonged to Governor Thomas Hutchinson at the age of fourteen,
and was inherited from his grandfather John Foster, master of the Dorchester
Grammar School, 1669-1674.

EILHARD LUBIN

Clavis Graecae Linguae. London, 1647.   H.C.L.
Inscribed

> 'Hujus si cupias dominum cognoscere libri.
> Inferius legito et nomen habebis ibi.
> Elisha Cooke
> Jan: (1) 1650'

LYCOSTHENES

Apophthegmata ex probatis Graecae Latinaeque linguae scriptori-
bus. Geneva, 1668.   A.A.S.
Inscribed 'Cottonus Matherus 1673.' Cotton was then at the Boston Latin
School, under Master Cheever.

HUGH ROBINSON

Scholae Wintoniensis Phrases Latinae. London, 1658.   H.C.L.
Acquired, probably in England, in 1659 by Joseph Eastbrook (A.B. 1664). It
has his dated signature in Greek letters. Later owned by his college classmate
Samuel Brackenbury, in 1703 at Latin School by Edward Wigglesworth
(A.B. 1710), and in 1743 by his son of the same name (A.B. 1749).

TERENCE

Plays, in Latin and English (*Andria, Eunuchus, Heantontimoru-*
menos, Adelphi, Hekyra, Phormio). Title page gone.   H.C.L.
Owned in 1686 by Penn Townsend of Boston (A.B. 1693). It also bears the
signatures of his elder brother James (A.B. 1692), his college classmate Isaac
Chauncy, Joseph Sewall (A.B. 1707), and of a number of others who did not
go to college.

V. PRINTING AND BOOKSELLING

I. PRINTING

THE New England puritans were as prompt in setting up a press as in establishing schools and colleges. Printing went on continuously in New England from 1639, the year after the first press arrived. It was not the earliest in America; a German printer had sent out a press to Mexico exactly a century before, with an Italian to operate it,[1] and over two hundred imprints are known to have come from the Mexican presses before New England was founded. But it was easily the first in North America outside Mexico. Virginia had printing continuously only from 1729. Pennsylvania, even more prompt than Massachusetts, had a press four years after her foundation, in 1686; and the first Philadelphia printer, William Bradford, became the first New York printer in 1693, when driven from the City of Brotherly Love for publishing something that the authorities did not like. There was no press in the present Dominion of Canada until 1751, when a Bostonian brought one to Halifax; and none in Quebec during the entire century and a half of French rule. Even more striking, by way of comparison and contrast, is the fact that many cities of England and Scotland came after Cambridge, New England, in establishing printing. Glasgow had no press until the year after Cambridge;[2] and Liverpool, not until about 1750. Measured by the number (not the quality) of imprints, Boston in 1700 was the second publishing center of the

[1] H. R. Wagner, in *Bibliographical Essays, A Tribute to Wilberforce Eames* (Harvard University Press, 1924), p. 249.

[2] James Denholm, *The History of the City of Glasgow* (Glasgow, 1804), p. 417.

English empire, surpassing even Cambridge and Oxford.[3]

Naturally the Cambridge press has attracted an intense interest on the part of American bibliographers and historians of printing, who have tended to overemphasize its importance, and to weave myths about the early printers. Indeed, one school of thought seems to regard Harvard College as a sort of annex or appendage to the printing press. The facts of the foundation may be briefly stated. The Reverend Jose Glover, M.A. (Oxon.), who had been suspended from his Surrey rectory for refusing to read the Book of Sports, set sail for New England in the summer of 1638 on the ship *John* of London, with his wife, five children, numerous servants, a printing press costing £20, a stock of print paper worth £40, a font of type contributed by some English residents of the Netherlands, a Cambridge locksmith named Stephen Day under indenture to serve him and operate the press, goodwife Day, son Matthew Day, and several young Bordmans, sons of Goody Day by a former marriage.

The bringing over of a press at that time was probably connected with events at home. For several decades the English puritans, unable to get their works passed by the censorship in England, had been having them printed in the Netherlands.[4] As part of Archbishop Laud's conformity campaign of the 1630's, diplomatic pressure was brought to bear on the States General, which resulted in breaking up

---

[3] Oxford averaged 23 a year (Falconer Madan, *A Brief Account of the University Press at Oxford*, p. 36); Cambridge produced 14 in 1700 (S. C. Roberts, *A History of the Cambridge University Press*, 1521-1921, p. 177); and Boston had 42 imprints in 1700, not counting separate editions of the same work.

[4] William Brewster, leader of the Pilgrim Fathers, had been one of the English printers in the Netherlands.

some of the English puritan churches in the Netherlands, and making things unpleasant for the printers. Just as the college at Cambridge was originally intended for all puritans, English or American, so the Cambridge press, in all probability, was designed to be the nucleus of a large establishment for producing English puritan tracts, the smuggling of which into England would be a profitable and exciting occupation for Yankee skippers. We find Hugh Peter, for instance, trying to drum up trade for the Cambridge press in Bermuda. 'Wee have a printery here,' he writes to a puritan minister there in December, 1638, 'and thinke to goe to worke with some speciall things'; and if his correspondent has any suitable copy, he 'may send it safely' by the bearer, Captain Pierce, an 'honest godly man of our church.'[5] But the outbreak of Civil War in England opened the English presses to all manner of political and theological heterodoxies. Harvard became a provincial college, and only local business was left for the Cambridge press.

Master Glover was taken ill on the voyage to New England, and died before the ship *John*, the publishing fraternity's *Mayflower*, reached our shores. Mistress Glover, apparently undaunted by her loss, purchased one of the largest houses in Cambridge, together with a small one for the Day family, where the press was set up in the fall of 1638. A broadsheet containing the freemen's oath, and an almanac, were printed in 1639, and the next year Stephen Day produced a work of which the typography was more creditable than the literary quality: *The Whole Book of*

[5] 4 *Coll. M.H.S.*, VI, 98-99; Raymond P. Stearns, Ms. dissertation on Hugh Peter, Harvard College Library.

Psalmes Translated into English Metre, generally known as the *Bay Psalm Book*.

The printing press, like the college, was soon overtaken by the depression occasioned by the English Civil War and stoppage of emigration. Mistress Glover, who had been living in grand style, found her affairs going from bad to worse. She contracted a matrimonial alliance with President Dunster, who thereby added the printing press and five stepchildren to his responsibilities. The press itself was removed to a lean-to in the President's lodge, which the Colony built for the presidential couple in 1645. Mistress Dunster in the meantime had died, and the President married again; but as executor for his first wife and guardian of her children, he continued to manage press, property, and children. Stephen Day, prototype of the versatile Yankee Jack-of-all-trades, did not have enough printing to keep him occupied, and took to prospecting for minerals and promoting ironworks. In the first ten years of the press there are known to have been but twenty-three imprints: [6] ten annual almanacs, five college commencement broadsides, a speller, a catechism, two editions of the *Bay Psalm Book*, a propaganda pamphlet for an Indian war that never came off, and *The Book of the General Laws and Liberties*.[7]

Stephen Day left the conduct of the press to his son Matthew, who died in 1649. President Dunster's choice of the next printer shows that he had an eye for men. Samuel Green of Cambridge was one of those popular, versatile,

[6] *Dictionary of American Biography*, V, 163. To the list there given should be added the second edition (1647) of the Bay Psalm Book.

[7] Reprinted by the Harvard University Press in 1929 from the only known copy, in the Huntington Library.

and energetic characters apt to be found in college towns; sergeant in the militia, college barber, stationer, and odd-job mechanic. He accepted the responsibility with some reluctance, but was quick to learn, and his work during his forty-three years as printer showed much improvement. The first book that he printed was *The Platform of Church Discipline*, which had been adopted by the New England churches' synod at Cambridge. The next year he brought out an almanac, a catechism, and a supplement to the Laws of 1648. And in 1651 he issued a revised *Bay Psalm Book*,[8] intended to replace the rude staves of that New England incunabulum (at which even the elders poked fun) with verses at once more accurate and more polished. 'It was thought,' says Cotton Mather,[9] 'that a little more of Art was to be employ'd upon them: And for that Cause, they were committed unto Mr. *Dunster*, who Revised and Refined this Translation; and (with some Assistance from one Mr. *Richard Lyon*, who being sent over by Sir *Henry Mildmay*, as an Attendant unto his son, then a Student in *Harvard Colledge*, now resided in Mr. *Dunster's* house:) he brought it unto the Condition wherein our Churches ever since have used it.' I have recently had the privilege of examining the only known copy of this work at the New York Public Library. It is a fat little book of over two hundred pages, containing not only metrical translations of the entire psalter, but of selected portions of the Old Testament, such as the Song of Solomon and the Book of Isaiah; and of some of the canticles in the New Testament, including the *Magnificat*,

---

[8] *The Psalmes Hymns And Spiritual Songs of the Old and New Testament, faithfully translated into English metre, for the use, edification, and comfort, of the Saints, in publick, & private, especially in New-England.*

[9] *Magnalia* (1702), book iii, 100.

which the translators call "The song of the blessed virgine Mary." [10] This Dunster psalm book went through edition after edition, in both Englands. No less than twenty-seven are listed by Wilberforce Eames, [11] and there are probably others that have escaped bibliographers. It was used by the dissenters in England, as well as in the New England churches. [12] Dunster and Lyon, by paying due attention, as their preface promised, 'to the gravity of the phrase' and the 'sweetness of the verse,' gave their version a life of over a century. This and other puritan versions of the psalms deserve a careful study by historians of literature, since they were the only songs commonly sung among a large section of the English people, and must have had a moral and aesthetic influence second only to that of the Bible.

The Cambridge press was not the only outlet for the intellectual life of New England. The principal writers, ministers like Cotton, Hooker, Mather, Hooke, and Shepard, naturally preferred to print their works in England, where they could reach a greater audience, and market; but publishing at such a distance brought many inconveniences. Rough notes of a sermon would be sent to a friend in England, who prepared the copy; and after he and the London printer and English proofreaders had all had a whack at it, the sermon sometimes expressed the direct contrary to what the author intended. Anne Bradstreet had very mixed feelings when she saw her first book of poems, *The Tenth Muse*, printed in England through the efforts of her devoted

---

[10] Facsimile in Morison, *The Founding of Harvard College*, p. 349.

[11] In Sabin's *Biblioteca Americana* (under 'Bay Psalm Book'), XVI, 35; also issued separately over Mr. Eames's name.

[12] Thomas Prince's introduction to the edition of *Psalms, Hymns, and Spiritual Songs* (Boston, 1758), which replaced the Dunster version.

brother-in-law; her first glance at the book, chock full of er-
rata, provoked some of her most playful verses:

> *At thy return my blushing was not small,*
> *My rambling brat (in print) should mother call.*
> *I cast thee by as one unfit for light,*
> *Thy visage was so irksome in my sight;*
>
> *   *   *
>
> *I wash'd thy face, but more defects I saw,*
> *And rubbing off a spot, still made a flaw.*
> *I stretcht thy joynts to make thee even feet,*
> *Yet still thou run'st more hobbling than is meet.*

Yet the press did accomplish something. Everyone knows
how nice it is to see your name and your own words in
print; and the fact that you could have a broadside elegy
struck off for a few shillings must have stimulated many to
write who otherwise would not have taken the trouble. The
annual almanacs, moreover, gave the college 'Philomathe-
mats' who prepared the copy, opportunity to fill up the
blank spaces with their own essays and verses.

The most ambitious work done by the press in mid-century was the Indian library, for which John Eliot was largely responsible. After he had printed an Indian primer and
his Algonkian translation of the Book of Genesis, an English
puritan missionary society—generally known as the New
England Company—undertook to finance the entire Indian
Bible. They sent over a new press, enough brevier type to
set up eight pages at a time, and a young printer, Marmaduke Johnson, to help Sergeant Green. The press, in the
meantime, had been transferred to the Indian College, a little brick building constructed in the Harvard Yard for Indian students. There was a brief setback when Marmaduke

Johnson, who had a wife in England, paid his addresses to a Cambridge maid, one of the nineteen children of Sergeant Green, who demanded damages for this 'presumptuous and wicked attempt.' The court tolerantly sentenced Johnson to pay £5 damages, and to return to England and his proper wife *after* the Bible was finished. By the time that was done, the wife had run off with another man, and President Chauncy was able to report that Marmaduke 'though he hath bene in former times loose in his life and conversation, yet this last yeere he hath bene very much reformed.'

Within a year of Johnson's arrival, the New Testament was finished; and the entire Bible of 1200 pages was ready in 1663. This first Bible printed in the New World was a credit to its printers, as well as to the translator.

Although the Bible and Eliot's Indian tracts were the most profitable part of the Cambridge printing business for several years, they did not occupy the two presses to the exclusion of authors in English. During the years 1655-1672 there are known to have been issued from the Cambridge presses about one hundred books and pamphlets, of which fifteen were in the Indian and eighty-five in the English language; and the number of broadsides and leaflets, all record of which is lost, must have been considerable. Almost any day the college students, when passing through the yard, could peer through the windows of the Indian College, watch the Indian 'devil,' James the Printer, sweating at the hand lever, Marmaduke Johnson feeding in sheets of paper and removing them with that neat-fingered deftness of the trained printer, and Sergeant Green sulkily setting up type for the next sheet.

Routine work, such as almanacs, laws of the New England colonies, catechisms, primers, and psalm books, continued; but we also begin to find more creative offshoots of colonial authors, who after 1660 found the English presses much less hospitable than before. Election sermons, for instance: Richard Mather's *Farewell Exhortation to the Church and People of Dorchester* (1657); controversial literature on the Half-Way Covenant; Davenport's (or Cotton's) *Discourse About Civil Government* (1663); Shepard's *Wine for Gospel Wantons: Or, Cautions Against Spirituall Drunkenness* (1668); Samuel Danforth's *Astronomic Description of the late Comet or Blazing Star* (1665); the Funeral Elegy on Governor Winthrop by 'Perciful Lowle,' first and worst of the Lowellian poets; John Cotton's *Spiritual Milk for Babes* (1656), which attained immortality when incorporated in the *New England Primer*. Of current English literature, the Cambridge press reprinted Thomas Vincent's narrative of the great London plague and fire (1668); the Earl of Winchilsea's *True and Exact Relation of the Late Prodigious Earthquake and Eruption of Mount Ætna* (1669); and an English translation of De Brès's *Histoire des Anabaptistes* (1668). The press was also the means of publishing several colonial works in history, biography, and poetry: Nathaniel Morton's *New-Englands Memoriall* (1669), the first history of an English colony to be printed in America; Increase Mather's *Life and Death of that Reverend Man of God, Mr. Richard Mather*, the pioneer American biography (1670); and Michael Wigglesworth's *Day of Doom* (1662). In that epic of intense imagination and terrific implication, Green and Johnson captured a bestseller. The entire edition of eighteen hundred copies was sold out within a year, enabling the reverend author to take a trip to Bermuda; two more editions were called for within the decade; and for a century more it continued to be reprinted and sold in both Englands.

By 1662 the college press had become sufficiently important to stimulate legislation, which begins the long and inglorious history of book censorship in Massachusetts. Following the English and European system of press control, the General Court forbade printing to be done outside Cambridge, and appointed a new licensing board, consisting of President Chauncy and the ministers of Cambridge, Charlestown, and Watertown. We do not know what this board may have prohibited; possibly some plays or romances that Johnson would have liked to try on this virgin market—for he was brought up short for publishing Henry Neville's travel book *The Isle of Pines* (1668) without a license.[13] In one instance, the licensers' permission to print was overridden by the General Court. A translation of the famous *De Imitatione Christi* was already in press, in 1669, when the General Court on 'being informed that there is now in the presse, reprinting, a book, title Imitacions of Christ, or to that purpose, written by Thomas a Kempis, a Popish minister, wherein is conteyned some things that are less safe to be infused among the people of this place,' recommended to the licensers 'the more full revisall thereof, and that in the meane time there be no further progresse in that worke.' The board declined to be responsible for an expurgated version, and the *Imitation of Christ* did not appear

13 Cf. Worthington C. Ford, *The Isle of Pines* (Boston: Club of Odd Volumes, 1920).

in Massachusetts. This incident portended many such clashes, in years to come, between an educated and comparatively liberal university community and a jealous and narrow-minded legislature. The significant thing about it is not the legislative prohibition, but the fact that the Harvard president and his board of puritan parsons wished to print this beautiful Catholic manual of devotion.

After 1675, when the General Court allowed a new press to be set up in Boston, the printing business at Cambridge declined sharply. Five years later two Dutch visitors found nobody in the printing room of the dilapidated Indian College. A glass window had been replaced by a paper sash, and this too was broken; they peered through, and 'saw two presses with six or eight cases of type,' which impressed them not. But the press was not abandoned. That same year (1680), Green brought out *Wusku Wuttestamentum,* the second edition of the New Testament of Eliot's Indian Bible; and the whole Bible reappeared in 1685. Typographically it was inferior to the first edition. Marmaduke Johnson was missed and the type that he had carried off and sold, still more so. In 1681, Green printed for Samuel Sewall, who was then conducting a bookshop in Boston, the first American edition of Bunyan's *Pilgrim's Progress;* and next year he captured another bestseller, Mrs. Rowlandson's account of her captivity in King Philip's War. Thereafter Green's business fell off, in competition with the more active and enterprising printers of Boston; and after publishing Cotton Mather's *Ornaments for the Daughters of Zion* in 1692, the college press went out of business. It had served the community well. Almost every printer and publisher in New England, and many of the great houses of New York,

can trace their ancestry to the little college printery oper-
ated by the Days and the Greens and the young man Marmaduke, 'in former times loose in his life and conversation.'

The most interesting Boston printer of the seventeenth
century was the first, John Foster.[14] This young man, who
died in 1681 at the age of thirty-two, showed in his short
life a versatility that is uncommon among New Englanders
before Benjamin Franklin. The son of a respectable brewer
and militia captain of Dorchester, Foster graduated from
the college in 1667. For five or six years he taught the grammar school at Dorchester for a salary of £25, rising to £30;
and while engaged in that not very leisurely occupation, he
began wood engraving; he has the indisputable honor of
being the first wood engraver in the English Colonies. In
1670 Foster cut the earliest American engraved portrait, a
woodcut of Richard Mather, as frontispiece for the biography of that worthy; and he was also responsible for the excellent woodcut map of New England in Hubbard's *History of King Philip's War* (1677). In the modest inventory
of Foster's possessions at the time of his death a 'Gittarue' is
included,[15] indicating that he owned a guitar, and presumably played it. He was an amateur astronomer, making the
calculations for six New England almanacs,[16] and in one of
them printing an interesting essay, "Of Comets, their Motion, Distance, and Magnitude," which showed acquaint-

---

[14] The best account of Foster's life is in Samuel A. Green, *John Foster*,
published by the M.H.S. (but not in their regular series of *Collections*),
in 1909.

[15] S. A. Green, *op. cit.*, p. 52.

[16] For 1675, 1676, 1678, 1679, 1680, and 1681; that of 1675 was printed by
Samuel Green.

ance with some of the latest astronomical works in Europe.

It was probably under Increase Mather's patronage that Foster set up as the first Boston printer in 1675, 'over against the Sign of the Dove.'[17] During the six remaining years of his life, Foster printed more important works, prose and poetry, of native New Englanders than any other printer of the century. For Roger Williams he printed the Rhode Islander's famous attack on the Quakers, *George Fox Digg'd out of his Burrowes* (1676), a substantial tract of over three hundred pages. Governor Coddington of Rhode Island, who was severely handled by Williams in this book, replied to it in a letter to Governor Leverett of Massachusetts; Foster then printed a reply by Roger Williams. For Increase Mather, Foster printed several sermons, the reports of the Synod of 1679, and two histories of Indian warfare. For William Hubbard he printed an election sermon, and two issues of his ambitious history of the Indian wars: *A Narrative of the Troubles with the Indians in New-England, from the first planting thereof in the year 1607 to this present year 1677*. John Eliot employed Foster for his *Harmony of the Gospels*, an attempt at a Life of Christ. *The Song of Deliverance* by the Reverend John Wilson of Boston[18] (an inferior narrative poem on the defeat of the Spanish Armada) and *New Englands Crisis* by Benjamin Tompson, the homespun epic on King Philip's War, were printed by Foster. A broadside that he put out for the Reverend Thomas Thacher, *Brief Rule To guide the Common-Peo-*

---

[17] As on title page of Mather's *Brief History* (1676).

[18] Reprinted, with facsimile title page, in K. B. Murdock, ed., *Handkerchiefs from Paul* (Harvard University Press, 1927), pp. 23-75. The first edition was London, 1626.

ple of New-England How to order themselves and theirs in the Small Pocks, or Measeles, is the earliest medical publication in this country. But by far the most important of Foster's imprints was the second edition of the poems of Anne Bradstreet.[19]

Samuel Sewall the diarist succeeded John Foster as manager of the Boston press, and obtained the services of Samuel Green, Jr., as printer.[20] The younger Sam died in 1690, and was succeeded by his brother Bartholomew Green, who also had learned his trade at the college press in Cambridge. A third brother, Timothy, opened up a second printing establishment at Boston in 1700.[21]

Under the Dominion of New England, printing dwindled away; but as soon as the Revolution of 1689 was over, normal production was resumed. The Duke of Monmouth's *Abridgment of the English Military Discipline* was reprinted by Samuel Green in 1690 for Benjamin Harris, publisher of the *New England Primer;* and the same enterprising bookseller in 1690 made the first attempt to publish a colonial newspaper. But *Publick Occurrences both Forreign and Domestick* went no further than volume I, number 1, since Governor and Council promptly suppressed it as a menace to our institutions.

Cotton Mather, whose style had been cramped under the Dominion, now got into his stride. Seven of his works, totaling about eight hundred pages of print, appeared in

[19] *Several Poems Compiled with great variety of Wit and Learning, full of Delight . . . By a Gentlewoman* (Boston, 1678).

[20] G. E. Littlefield, *The Early Massachusetts Press* (Boston: The Club of Odd Volumes, 1907), II, 17-18, 25-28.

[21] *Idem*, p. 69. Several other printers' names appear on Boston imprints between 1685 and 1700; but Mr. Littlefield conjectures that they were simply temporary managers of the press that had been Foster's.

1690, and nine more, including the excellent *Life of Eliot*, in 1691. Fortunately, by this time there was a press which could answer Cotton Mather. William Bradford published at Philadelphia in 1692 a tract of which the following is but a portion of the title only:

A Serious appeal to all the more sober, impartial and judicious people in New-England to whose hands this may come, whether Cotton Mather in his late Address, etc. hath not extreamly failed in proving the people call'd Quakers guilty of manifold heresies, blasphemies, and strong delusions, and whether he hath not much rather proved himself extreamly ignorant and greatly possessed with a spirit of perversion, error, prejudice and envious zeal against them in general, and G[eorge] K[eith] in particular. . . .

During the last decade of the century, the Mathers wrote about thirty per cent of all the books printed in Boston and Cambridge. In 1698 appeared Cotton's *Bostonian Ebenezer*, an attempt at a History of Boston; and in 1699 his *Decennium Luctuosum*, an account of the wars and witchcrafts and revolutions of the past decade. Cotton celebrated the last year of the century by no less than seventeen titles.

2 . BOOKSELLERS

Publishers, in the modern sense of the word, did not exist in the English-speaking world until the eighteenth century. The reading public was so small, even in the old country, that there was no need of a publisher to sell an author's works, to advance him royalties, and interpret his personality to the public. A forthputting author dealt directly with the printer, himself assuming the cost and risk; a modest author, if we may believe prefaces and title pages, let himself be persuaded by his friends to put his manuscript in the hands of a bookseller, who paid the printing bills and gave (or promised) the author a lump sum for the privilege. The *New England Primer*, for instance, which ranks with the world's bestsellers, was the venture of Benjamin Harris, bookseller, 'at the sign of the Bible over-against the Blew Anchor' in Boston. But Harris was not the first Boston bookseller. Hezekiah Usher, who is supposed to be a relation of the learned Primate of Ireland, opened the earliest Boston bookshop about the year 1642; and the almanac for 1647, the only one of that decade still preserved intact, was printed for him by Matthew Day. Hezekiah was a prominent and successful merchant of Boston featuring bookselling as but one of numerous lines; and in 1669 he turned over that department to his son John Usher who continued it to the end of the century. In the year 1700 there were at least seven booksellers in Boston;[22] and Salem, New Haven, and possibly other towns as well, had shops that sold books. In addition, hawkers and peddlers went about the country selling broadsheet ballads, chapbooks, pamphlets, and the like, and (when Cotton Mather could so persuade them), working off 'devout and useful books' as well. One James Gray 'that used to go up and down the Country Selling of Books,' left almost £700 in cash of every conceivable denomination, when he died in 1705; good evidence that the people of the interior not only bought books, but paid good hard money for them.[23]

Only a very small portion of the stock of these Boston booksellers consisted of native productions. The rest was

[22] Convenient list in T. G. Wright, *Literary Culture in Early New England*, pp. 115-16; but the principal compilation for this subject is G. E. Littlefield, *Early Boston Booksellers* (Boston: Club of Odd Volumes, 1900).

[23] Wright, *op. cit.*, pp. 126, 192-93.

made up of importations from England, or of private libraries that were placed in their hands for sale by executors, or
duplicates and other books that New Englanders wished to
dispose of. No doubt the majority of each bookseller's stock
consisted of religious works, which formed the majority of
all public and most private libraries in New England at the
time; but such lists of booksellers' stocks as we have are by
no means exclusively theological.

The stock of Michael Perry, bookseller 'over against the
Townhouse' of Boston at the time of his death in 1700,[24]
consists of four distinct parts: religious works, which are in
a strong majority; textbooks for the grammar schools and
the college; practical works on husbandry, navigation, surveying and home doctoring (such as *Salmons Dispensatory*,
Pharmacopia Hagiensis, and Culpeper's *English Physician*);
and miscellaneous histories, poetry, and other general literature. In this last class are not a few secular and frivolous titles, such as Plutarch's *Lives*, Edward Fairfax's *Godfrey of
Buloigne; or the Recoverie of Jerusalem*,[25] the works of
Ovid, *The right pleasant and variable tragical History of*

[24] Printed in G. E. Littlefield, *Early Boston Booksellers*, pp. 175-78, and in
Appendix B to John Dunton's *Letters from New England* (Prince Society,
1867). Until the present century this was the only known list of an
early Boston bookseller's stock, and it has called forth some curiously dis-
cordant comments. J. Truslow Adams (*The Founding of New England*,
Boston, 1921, p. 371n.) regards it as 'appallingly theological and dreary' (on
the same page he states that the New Englanders read no poetry but Uriah
[*sic*] Oakes and Michael Wigglesworth). Cyril A. Herrick goes to the
other extreme, declaring that Perry's stock 'would pass muster as satisfactory in many communities even today.'—"The Early New-Englanders:
What Did They Read?" reprinted from *The Library* (London, 1918). And
F. B. Dexter (*A Selection from the Miscellaneous Historical Papers of Fifty
Years*, 1918, p. 278) found only three quarters of Perry's stock to be
theological.

[25] An English translation of Tasso's *Gerusalemme Liberata*, which first
appeared in 1600.

Fortunatus whereby a young man may learn how to behave himself in all worldly affairs and casual chances (1676),[26] together with nine packs of playing cards.

Even more interesting are certain invoices of books sent from London to the Boston bookseller John Usher between 1679 and 1685.[27] These include a certain number of law books, such as Glisson's *Common Law Epitomized* (1661), Dalton's *Country Justice*, Coke's *Reports*, and *De Jure Maritimo, a Treatise of Affairs Maritime* (1677); practical works suitable for colonists, such as Cooke's *Mellificium Chirurgiae, or The Marrow of Chirurgerie* (1676), *Markham's Masterpiece, containing all Knowledge belonging to Farrier or Horse-Leach* (1675), Thomas Miller's *Compleat Modellist*, a famous treatise on shipbuilding (1676 or 1684), *The Boatswaine's Art, or the compleate Boats-waine;* Norwood's *Seaman's Companion* on navigation (1678); Vernon's *Compleat Compting-house, or The young Lad instructed in all the Misteries of a Merchant* (1678); Hannah Woley's *Queen-like Closet, or rich Cabinet, stored with all manner of rare Receipts for preserving, Candying, and Cookery. Very pleasant and beneficial to all Ingenious per-*

---

[26] And several other editions before 1700; see Arundell Esdaile, *A List of English Tales and Prose Romances* (London, 1912), pp. 54-56. Another item in Perry's inventory, *Alcibiades and Carolina*, must have been a romance, but I am unable to identify it. *Fortunatus* is second on a list of 42 'Histories' (*i.e.*, romances) available in English, which are recommended by Francis Kirkman in the preface to his *Famous and Delectable History of Don Bellianis of Greece*, ed. 1673 (Ms. dissertation of Alpheus W. Smith, Harvard College Library). Perry's stock includes most of the fiction we have mentioned in the text as best of Usher's stock.

[27] Printed by Worthington C. Ford, in *The Boston Book Market, 1679-1700* (Boston: The Club of Odd Volumes, 1917), and summarized in Wright, *op. cit.*, pp. 120-25.

sons of the Female Sex (1670); Bacon's *Resuscitatio* (an anthology of his works, 1671); More's *Utopia*, Hakluyt's and Sir John Mandeville's *Voyages;* Milton's *History of Britain* (1677), the *Miscellanea* of Sir William Temple (1679), biographies of the Earl of Shaftesbury (1683), Oliver Cromwell (1679), and Gilbert Burnet's *Life of the Earl of Rochester* (1680), and a number of jest books such as the perennial Scoggin, and the *Oxford Jests.*

There are at least eleven fictional works in Usher's two lists: the *History of Fortunatus* (our successful young man); the *History of Dr. Faustus* [28]—four and a half dozen of that; "Reynolds on Murther"; [29] *Pharamond, or the History of France. A Fam'd Romance, in Twelve Parts* (1677) (a translation from the French of *La Calprenède*); *The most Famous, Delectable, and pleasant History of Parismus —Prince of Bohemia* (1677), *The English Rogue, comprehending the most eminent Cheats of both Sexes* (1671), *The Famous History of Valentine and Orson* (1680), *The most pleasant History of Tom A Lincoln, The Life and Death of Guy, Earl of Warwick* (1681); *Clelia,* a translation of the ten-volume romance by Mademoiselle de Scudéry, and *Venus in the Cloyster, or The Nun in her Smock; in curious Dialogues, addressed to the Lady Abbess of Love's*

[28] *The Historie of the damnable life and deserved death of Doctor John Faustus* was first printed in London in 1592, and there were at least 8 more editions of it before 1679 and 4 more before 1700. Arundell Esdaile, *op. cit.,* pp. 46-47.

[29] John Reynolds, *The triumphs of Gods Revenge, against the crying, and execrable Sinne of Murther,* London, 1621, and at least 11 editions before 1680, Esdaile, pp. 117-18. All the others in this list, save the last, can be identified in Esdaile; the dates I quote are those of the latest edition before that of Usher's list where the book is mentioned.

Paradise.[30] Ecclesiastical in a sense, but hardly theological!

Of poetry, we find in these invoices Milton's *Paradise Lost*, Robert Wild's *Iter Boreale*, Sir Philip Sidney's *Arcadia*, with fifteen copies of *Argalus and Parthenia*, Quarles's poetical romance on the same theme; a dozen of *The Jovial Garland a Collection of all the newest Songs and Sonnets used in Court and Country* (1677); a dozen of a similar collection, *The Crowne Garland*, and half a dozen each of *The Garland of Delight* and *The Royall Arbor of Loyall Poesie . . . Triumph, Elegie, Satyr, Love, and Drollerie* (1663). Finally, we have two copies of the Earl of Rochester's *Poems on Several Occasions* (1680), a new edition of which was denied entrance to the United States by our customs authorities, less lenient than those of the puritan regime! [31]

[30] A translation from the French of the Abbé du Prat, London, 1683. But there must have been earlier editions, as this is mentioned as a book in the town gallant's library, in *The Character of a Town Gallant*, London, 1675 (Alpheus W. Smith, *op. cit.*, p. 149).

[31] Rochester's Poems are in an invoice of March, 1684, before the puritan regime in Massachusetts was superseded by the Dominion of New England. Professor T. J. Wertenbaker's remarks in *The First Americans*, p. 240, apropos the offerings of Boston booksellers, about the 'rigid control over men's thoughts and opinions exercised by the New England Theocracy,' seems to need some modification, either as to the rigidity of the control or the views of the 'theocracy.' I do not deny that the main interest in Boston was religious; I am simply endeavoring to show that there was enough demand for lighter literature and belles-lettres for booksellers to take account of it.

VI. LIBRARIES, PRIVATE AND PUBLIC

THE WARES offered by Boston booksellers do not exhaust the opportunities of New Englanders for obtaining books. A number of private libraries were brought over by the first settlers, and many of these collections were constantly increased, as Thomas Goddard Wright has shown, by orders from English booksellers, gifts from English friends, and purchases made during visits to England.[1]

The most important early private library in New England was that of Elder William Brewster of Plymouth Colony. As inventoried after his death in 1644, it comprised about 400 different works, of which at least one quarter had been imported after their owner's departure from England in 1620. A few were Elder Brewster's own surreptitious imprints at Leyden; a few others were practical, such as her-

---

[1] *Literary Culture*, chapters ii, iii, and pp. 110-14. Some curious remarks were made on New England libraries in Charles F. Thwing, *History of Higher Education in America* (1906), pp. 63-64: 'John Winthrop, who died in 1678 [*sic*], had a library of 269 books; and John Eliot, who is said to have had the largest library in New England between 1713 and 1745, had only 243.' He meant the John Eliot (d. 1719) whose inventory is in W. H. Emerson, *Genealogy and Descendants of John Eliot* (1903), pp. 37-38. Dr. Thwing was misled by some odious and highly inaccurate comparisons between New England and Virginian libraries in the early volumes of the *William and Mary College Quarterly*, on which J. Truslow Adams also relied (*The Founding of New England*, p. 370) for his 'refreshing contrast' of Virginian with New England libraries. The authoritative analysis of Virginia private libraries is in P. A. Bruce, *Institutional History of Virginia in the Seventeenth Century* (1910), I, 402-41. The samples he mentions are very similar to the books we find in New England: theology, almanacs and practical books, medicine, history, Latin classics, and a few romances. The largest library that he found inventoried had somewhat over 200 titles (pp. 427-28).

bals, books of surveying and medicine, and works on the
culture of silkworms and the surveying of timber. The
greater part of the collection was theological; as it had to
be, since for many years the owner preached thrice weekly.
But he also owned those constant features of any English
gentleman's library of that time, Bacon's *Advancement of
Learning*, Knolles's translation of Jean Bodin *de Republica*,
Machiavelli's *Prince*, and Sir Walter Raleigh's *Prerogatives
of Parliaments in England*.[2]

Your typical Plymouth Colony library comprised a large
and a small Bible, Ainsworth's translation of the Psalms, and
the works of William ("Painful") Perkins, a favorite theologian. But Myles Standish owned Caesar's *Commentaries*,
and *The Swedish Intelligencer*, an account of the campaigns
of Gustavus Adolphus. Governor Bradford, who had the
largest library in Plymouth after Brewster's, left copies of
Jean Bodin, La Primaudaye's *French Academie*, Guicciar-
dini's *History of Florence*, Peter Martyr's *Decades of the
New World*, and 'divers Duch books.' And his own great
history *Of Plymouth Plantation* proves that the Governor
made good use of these secular works when he wrote himself.

Undoubtedly the finest private library in New England
in the seventeenth century was that of John Winthrop, Jr.,
Governor of Connecticut. Containing over a thousand volumes as early as 1640, this collection gradually increased
until Winthrop's death in 1676; thereafter it was piously
preserved and even added to by his son Wait and his grandson John. The remnant (over two hundred and fifty volumes) of this library, which the Governor's descendants

kept intact and gave to the New York Society Library in the last century, proves that the collection was a truly remarkable one, as one would expect of a man of the younger Winthrop's wide attainments and scientific interests.[3] Besides scientific works, the Winthrop library contains books on religion, history, travel, philosophy, law, and sundry grammars and dictionaries. Half the books are in Latin, 71 in English, 23 in German, 17 in French, 12 in Dutch, 7 in Italian, 4 in Greek, and 1 in Spanish. Among those of a general cultural character, I have noted Scaliger's edition of the Latin poetry of Ausonius (Heidelberg, 1588); the curious *Théâtre du Monde* of Boistuau de Launai (1607); a Latin translation of Baldassare Castiglione's *Libro d'Oro* (or "Book of the Courtier," 1593); Cluvier's *Introductio in Universam Geographiam*, the standard geography of the century; an Italian translation of Erasmus' *Christian Prince* (Venice, 1543); a collection on political and economic theory, including Scudéry's *Curia Politiae* (London, 1654), Potter's *Key to Wealth* (London, 1650), Machiavelli's *Prince*, Jean Bodin *de Republica* and the *Vindiciae contra Tyrannos;* the first English translation (1659) of Pascal's *Lettres Provinciales*, and two volumes of the *Hymnes de P. de Ronsard, gentil homme Vandomois* (Paris, 1630); *The Historie of George Castriot, surnamed Scanderbeg* (London, 1596), *The Historie of the Troubles of Hungarie by Martin Fumee, Lord of Genille* (London, 1600), Camden's *Annales Rerum Anglicarum regnante Elizabetha* (London, 1627), the *Works of Hesiod* (Antwerp, 1603), and Steph-

---

[3] They are listed with brief titles, not very accurately, in the *Catalogue of the Society Library* (1850), pp. 491ff. The scientific ones are described by Dr. C. A. Browne in *Isis*, XI (1928), 325-42.

anus' *Greek Anthology* (1567). A library such as this, in the hands of so generous an owner as Winthrop, must have had a considerable intellectual influence on the better educated people in his successive places of residence—Ipswich, New London, and Hartford. Some of the volumes show unmistakable evidence of being borrowed by Winthrop's friends.

Thomas Jenner, a Cambridge alumnus who came to New England in 1635 at the age of twenty-seven, and ministered successively at Weymouth, Saco (Maine), and Charlestown, returned to England in 1650 leaving behind him a library of two hundred titles, which he sold to the Reverend John Eliot for £30.[4] The only nonreligious books in this collection are Camden's *Remains*, Richard Bernard's *Guide to Grand Jury Men* (with respect to witchcraft), *Cheape and good Husbandry*, and a few dictionaries and college textbooks. At the same time John Eliot bought the library of his former colleague, Thomas Weld, which contained one hundred and ninety-five titles of very much the same character, relieved only by an edition of Aristophanes.[5]

There is no need of repeating here the lists of significant books in private New England libraries of the seventeenth century that are printed by Thomas Goddard Wright, but some selections from manuscript lists in the probate records that escaped him may be of interest. Michael Wigglesworth, the parson poet, left in 1705 a small library valued at £16, including the *Institutiones Medicinae* of Daniel Sennert

---

[4] *C.S.M.*, XXVIII, 108, 111, and the titles of the Ms. Catalogue are expanded on pp. 113-36.

[5] *Idem*, 135-36.

(1619),[6] the *Praxis Medica* of Lazare Rivière (1640), an indexed *Materia Medica,* and Harvey's epoch-making work on the circulation of the blood (1628). The balance of Wigglesworth's library consisted of theology and college texts.[7] Samuel Brackenbury, a young physician who died in the smallpox epidemic of 1678, left a small library which included several works on chemistry, such as the *Basilica Chymica* (1609) of Oswald Croll, and the *Furni Novi Philosophici* (1648) and *Opus Minerale* (1651) of Glauber. The medical books include the collected works of Etienne de la Rivière (1663), *Medicina Practica* (1644) by Johannes Jonston, the *Thesaurus* by Dr. Adria of Mazara, Burton's *Anatomy of Melancholy,* and four books by Dr. Thomas Willis, physician in ordinary to Charles II: *Diatribae Duae* (1659) on intestinal fermentation and the urinary system; *Cerebri Anatome* (1664), *Pathologia Cerebri* (1667, a pioneer work on the nervous system), and *Pharmaceutice Rationalis* (1674).[8] A more extensive but less modern medical collection is found in the inventory of George Alcock, son and grandson of New England physicians, who was but three years out of college when he died, in 1676.[9] Of about one hundred titles in Alcock's library, at least half are medical. They include Harvey's *de Motu Cordis et Sanguinis* (1628), seven books by Daniel Sennert, an English translation (probably 1649) of the works of Am-

[6] These dates in parentheses are those of the first edition (so far as I can ascertain) of the works named. No dates are given in the inventories.

[7] Ms. Middlesex Court Files (East Cambridge), 24,860.

[8] Ms. Suffolk Probate Files, Boston, XII, 207-8. Brackenbury's inventory lists an unnamed work of Descartes.

[9] *C.S.M.,* XXVIII, 350-57.

broise Paré, Jean Fernel's *Universa Medicina* (1574), Van Helmont's *Ortus Medicinae* (1644), Thomas Bartholin's *Historiae Anatomicae* (1654), besides Galen, Hippocrates, and other ancient medicos. In the other half of Alcock's library, only ten or twelve are religious books; the rest are college classics and works of general literature, such as Cervantes' *Don Quixote* and *The Travels of Persiles and Sigismunda*, the epistles, and flores by Justus Lipsius, Plutarch's *Lives*, a *Thesaurus Poeticus*, Sir Thomas Browne's *Religio Medici*, and some of Bacon's works. The dates of publication of some of these books indicate that the New England physicians were not content with medical libraries brought over in the early days of the colonies, but were sending abroad for the newest and best works.

In other inventories, we find books of a different character. Daniel Russell, of Charlestown, who died in 1679 when less than ten years out of college, left the poems of George Herbert, Samuel Butler, Anne Bradstreet, and Michael Wigglesworth; a few college classics; a book of Characters (possibly Earle's or Thomas Fuller's);[10] *French Paraphrases* and *Decades Patavini; Seneca's Works in English* (doubtless the LeStrange translation, which later had a great influence on young George Washington); 'Homer's Illyeads'; two folio Chaucers; the favorite Parismus romance; a French and an Italian grammar; a work by 'Sir Walter Raughleigh'; a Machiavelli; Mrs. Rowlandson's *Narrative of the Captivity;* Barclay's *Argenis;* about half a dozen medical books of the more popular sort (Culpeper, Lowes, Bailey's *Directions for Health*, Ambroise Paré in

[10] Professor Chester N. Greenough has discussed 'Character' literature in his paper "John Dunton's Letters from New England," *C.S.M.*, XIV, 232-57.

English); numerous college texts; and '80 Pamphlets.' [11]

The Reverend John Norton left in 1663 a library of seven hundred and twenty-nine volumes, valued at £300. Exactly the same value is given to the library that the Reverend Thomas Hooker left at Hartford in 1647; but the Reverend John Davenport's library was appraised at £233 17s. at his death in 1670. John Cotton's library was valued by himself at £150 'though having cost much more.' [12] Unfortunately no titles in these four libraries are recorded.

The Reverend Benjamin Bunker of Malden left in 1669 about 80 volumes on religion and theology (including Suarez's *Metaphysica*), 25 of classics, belles-lettres, and college texts, and two of medicine. [13] The Reverend Jonathan Mitchell left in 1668 about 181 religious works, 75 of classics and the like, and 11 of medicine. Some of the unusual books in his inventory are the Histories by Sir Walter Raleigh and Alexander Ross, the Essays of Montaigne, several volumes of mathematics, including Norwood's *Trigonometry*, George Herbert's *Temple*, the *Poetae Minores Graecae* (common enough in the next century, but rarely found so early), the *Meditationes* of Descartes, Matthias Prideaux's popular *Introduction for Reading all Sorts of Histories* and an English translation (London, 1653) of the *Peregrinação* of Mendez Pinto in the Far East. [14] When the Reverend John Brock died in 1688, about 360 volumes of his library were inventoried,

[11] Ms. Middlesex Probate Court Files, docket 2,775.

[12] Franklin B. Dexter, *A Selection from the Miscellaneous Historical Papers of Fifty Years* (New Haven, 1918), p. 228.

[13] Ms. Middlesex Court Files, docket 3,508.

[14] *Idem*, docket 15,284. Mitchell makes a long quotation from Mendez Pinto in a memorial to the General Court of about 1662. *C.S.M.*, XXXI, 314.

and these included 16 titles in mathematics and physics, 15 in medicine, 18 histories, and 65 classics, belles-lettres, and grammars; the rest were religious, and there were one hundred volumes not listed by title.[15] It should be noted that inventories of these clerical libraries confirm the tradition that early New England ministers generally practiced medicine as well as religion.

All libraries so far mentioned belonged to college graduates. Unless a decedent owned a considerable number of books, the probate courts did not ordinarily make a list of them; but in the Essex Probate Records we have a few brief lists which probably indicate what literature the average New England household possessed, besides almanacs. John Symonds who died at Salem in 1671 left '2 old Bibles, a Booke of Doct. Prestons Works and a booke of Mr. Rogers works and a psalm booke,' the whole valued at 18s.[16] The Widow Rebecca Bacon, who died at Salem in 1655, left a large collection of plate and household furniture and a library consisting of '3 Bibles, a Concordance, Calvins *Institutions*, Luther upon the Galathians, Mr. Shepard's *Morality of the Sabath*, Nicholas Gibbins *Disputations*, Joshua Symonds bookes, 2 of Dr. Sibs and 1 of Mr. Preston, Markham and 10 smal bookes, £2.'[17] Here, as in many other instances, the appraisers noted the titles of folios, and of those that they recognized, while the others, which would probably have been far more interesting to us, are simply entered as 'small books' or as plain 'books.'

Edward Holyoke, founder of that family, died in 1660;

---

[15] Ms. Middlesex County Probate Records, VII, 108-20.
[16] *Probate Records of Essex County*, II, 249ff, 99, and I, 9.
[17] *Idem*, I, 229-30.

he had houses in Lynn and Rumney Marsh (Chelsea), and books in each. By will he directed that Broughton's works, a 'large new Testament in folio with wast pap[er] betweene every leafe' (evidently the family Bible), 'Mr. Ainsworth on the 5. bookes of Moses and the psalms,' a dictionary, and Tremellius' edition of the Vulgate, should go to his son in Springfield; the whole library was appraised at £20, not including certain books 'lent out and not Gott in.' [18]

Thomas Wells of Ipswich leaves to his son, in 1666, 'all the bookes, that I bought for his use, and my three phisicke bookes and the booke called the orthodox evangelist, the great sermon booke, and Hyelings *Geogripha*.' [19] And when William Casely, mariner, died on board the ketch *Eliza and Mary*, seven days out from Salem, he had with him 'One Bible, 4s., Mr. Smiths booke of the great assiz, 1s., 1 booke the voice of the rod, 1s. 4d., 1 Ditto Mr. Baxter Call to the unconverted, 6d.' [20] A rather serious selection to take to sea!

A tabulation of the inventories of estates in the probate records of Essex and Middlesex counties, by Dr. Shipton, shows a surprisingly large proportion of the population owning books; unfortunately many of the inventories have disappeared. But many of these estates in both counties were left by farmers, fishermen, servants, and poor widows. Hence they give us a fair cross-section of the book-owning population.

In New England outside Massachusetts, the probate records are not nearly so full. According to the researches of

[18] *Idem*, I, 313-14.
[19] *Idem*, II, 67. Peter Heylyn's folio *Cosmographie* is doubtless intended. A copy of it, owned by several college students of the seventeenth century, is in the Harvard College Library.
[20] *Idem*, II, 280.

ESSEX PROBATE RECORDS

Dates	Number Estates	Number Containing Books	Per Cent	Number of These Including Only Bibles	Per Cent
1635-64	381	149	39	30	20
1665-74	314	117	37	19	16
1675-81	306	124	41	26	21
1635-81	1,001	390	39	75	19

MIDDLESEX PROBATE RECORDS

1654-61	80	44	55	6	16
1667-73	99	66	67	9	16
1676-82	165	97	59	5	4
1689-92	96	56	58	4	7
1696-99	76	48	63	0	
1654-99	516	311	60	24	8

Franklin B. Dexter for Connecticut and Rhode Island, the smaller the library, the larger the proportion of theology.[21] An exception may be made of the library of William Harris, that lifelong adversary of Roger Williams, whose library of about thirty volumes in 1680 was over one-third law (no wonder he was able to annoy Roger!) and included Gervase Markham's *Gentleman Jockey* and Norwood's *Trigonometry*.[22] On the other hand, a respectable miller of Providence left but 'an old Bible, some lost and some of it torne'; and a citizen of Middletown, Connecticut, left nine Bibles and no other books. Edward Tench

---

[21] *Miscellaneous Historical Papers* (1918), pp. 274-83, or *A.A.S.*, n.s., XVIII, 135-47.
[22] *Idem*, XVIII, 136.

brought to New Haven six Bibles, about forty volumes of theology, two or three medical books, Dalton's *Country Justice*, one cookbook, and two works of practical husbandry. And one finds many inventories in which no book is mentioned but the Bible. But we are dealing with a period in which books, even in England, were few and precious in relation to their number and cost today, and when they percolated through to but a small proportion of the population.

At the end of the seventeenth century the two largest private libraries in Boston were those of Increase and Cotton Mather. The elder listed about six hundred and seventy-five titles in his possession in 1664, but from the great fire of 1676 saved not a hundred books from above a thousand.[23] Cotton tells us that his own library already amounted to between two and three thousand volumes in 1700.[24] Increase at once started to build up his library again; and from a list of duplicates that he later sold,[25] and from books that he read, as recorded in his diary, we know that he had many histories, geographies, books of modern science, classics, and works of general literature.

In the year 1686 Samuel Lee, an Oxford graduate and dissenting clergyman, emigrated to New England and became minister of Bristol, Rhode Island. Returning to England in 1691 he was made prisoner by a French privateer, and died in France. His library of well over a thousand vol-

[23] Catalogue printed by Mr. J. H. Tuttle in *A.A.S.*, n.s., XX (1910), 280-90; selections in Wright, *op. cit.*, pp. 178-79.

[24] *Diary*, I, 368.

[25] Wright, pp. 130-32. An invoice of books sent to Increase Mather by Chiswell, the wholesale bookdealer of London, with whom the Boston booksellers dealt is in W. C. Ford, *Boston Book Market*, pp. 14-15, 114-16.

umes was put on sale at Boston by Duncan Campbell, 'Book-seller at the Dock-head over-against the Conduit.'[26] Although this library was collected in England, its subsequent dispersion in New England gives it a certain interest for us; and the executors must have regarded Boston as a proper book market, or they would have shipped the lot to London. The books are divided in classes according to sizes, subjects, and languages, and the classification, as in most booksellers' catalogues, is not very exact; Aristophanes, for instance, is included with the philosophers. Of divinity in Latin there are about two hundred and fifteen titles, and in English, ninety-six. Of 'Physical Books,' including medicine and natural science, one hundred and nineteen. Of philosophy (including two works of Descartes), seventy-one. Of geography and cosmography, seventeen. Of mathematics, astronomy, and astrology, a considerable number. Histories in Latin, including one of Normandy, one of France, one of Byzantium, one of Hungary, Dugdale's *Monasticon*, works of Meursius, Cluvier, Vossius, and Plutarch, Selden's *Mare Clausum*, and Polydore Virgil, one hundred and twenty. Histories in English, including Sir Walter Raleigh's, Fynes Moryson's *Travels*, the *History of Scanderbeg*, an English naval history, Arthur Wilson's *History of the Reign of James I*, 'Sanydys History of China,'[27] a biography of Mary Queen of Scots, Howell's *History of London*, and natural histories such as Bacon's, and Evelyn's

[26] *The Library of the Late Reverend and Learned Mr. Samuel Lee* (Boston, 1693). This has been reproduced by photostat in the *Americana* series of the M.H.S., as it is the earliest American book catalogue. Cf. 2 *Proc. M.H.S.*, X, 540-44.

[27] Probably George Sandys' *Relation of a Journey . . . Containing a Description of the Turkish Empire* (1615).

Sylva, forty-five. Grammar-school and college textbooks, forty-five; law books, including the *Corpus Juris Civilis* and Grotius *de Jure Belli ac Pacis*, eight. Miscellaneous works included Selden's sumptuous *Marmora Arendulliana*; and there were over three hundred unclassified Latin books.

PUBLIC LIBRARIES

Of public libraries, in the modern sense—a library owned by a public body such as a church, town, or college—there were very few in New England in the seventeenth century. A town library was started in Boston by Robert Keayne, the merchant, who died in 1656. He bequeathed to the town his '3 great writing bookes' together with such of his 'Divinitie bookes and commentaries' as the ministers should think suitable for a public library; if the Town did not 'build a handsome room for the library' within three years, they were to go to Harvard College. The town met this challenge, and built a Town House (the predecessor of the present Old State House) where the library was kept. The Reverend John Wilson bequeathed to it ten volumes in 1674. In 1702, John Barnard was directed to make a catalogue of this Boston town library, and to reward himself by taking two duplicates; but the library was consumed in two Boston fires, in 1711 and 1747. It is unlikely that this town library amounted to anything more than a small collection of theology.[28] New Haven began a town library with a legacy of books which had belonged to Governor

[28] M. J. Canavan, "The Old Boston Public Library, 1656-1747," *C.S.M.*, XII, 116-31. Mr. Canavan also notes that King's Chapel, Boston, began a library in 1698 with a gift of 96 volumes from William III, and that the 214 volumes that remained of this library in 1823 were deposited in the Boston Athenaeum, where they still are.

Eaton and his brother. The collection contained about ninety titles: eleven stout folios by Calvin, and nineteen other folios, mostly theological, including Plutarch's *Lives*, Raleigh's *History*, and George Sandys' translation of Ovid which he made in Virginia. There were twenty-seven quartos, all but two theological, and all the smaller books were of divinity, save for a few college texts, More's *Utopia*, and a work on military discipline. Apparently this library received no additions during the thirty years of its existence. Modestly valued at £20 by the donor, it was sold by the town in 1689 for £12 18s. to the Reverend James Pierpont; and a number of the books eventually found a permanent resting place in the Yale University Library.[29]

The Harvard College Library was the largest single collection in New England at the end of the century. Begun in 1638 by John Harvard's bequest of about four hundred volumes, of which a catalogue is fortunately preserved,[30] it gradually increased by donation and bequest. In 1698, through the proceeds of selling over a hundred duplicates, the college was able to order for the library two important German annuals of science and general literature, the *Acta Eruditorum* and the *Miscellanea Curiosa, sive Ephemerides Medico-Physicarum Germanicarum*. By 1723 when the first catalogue of the College Library was printed, it composed about three thousand five hundred volumes, which I have analyzed as follows:

[29] Franklin B. Dexter, *op. cit.* (1918), pp. 223-34, with catalogue identified.

[30] The short titles are identified by Mr. Alfred C. Potter, in *C.S.M.*, XXI, 190-230. It was a good gentleman's library for the time, by no means exclusively theological; and the theology included many Catholic works, but very little of the polemical divinity of the day.

Theology, Bibles, Patristic Works, and Scholastic Philosophy 2,183
Ancient Philosophy, Logic, Ethics, Metaphysics . . . 137
History, Politics, Geography, Description, and Travel . 367
Physics, Natural History, General Science 131
Mathematics, Astronomy, Architecture, Navigation, Warfare 124
Hebrew and Other Oriental Languages 99
Greek Grammar and Literature 58
Latin Grammar and Literature 63
Dictionaries, Encyclopedias, Lexicons 105
Modern Literature (French, English, Italian, Renaissance Latin) 45
Law and Statutes 64
Medicine 58
Manual of Rhetoric, *flores*, etc. 35
Miscellaneous and Unidentified 47
_____
Total (of which 1,340 were in folio) . . . . 3,516 [31]

Although President Dunster had attempted to obtain money for law and medical books for the College Library, it was still weak in all subjects but theology; and for the very good reason that it was intended largely for what we should call graduate students in divinity. Undergraduates were expected to buy or borrow their textbooks, and were not encouraged to use the Library or permitted to borrow books from it without express permission. Nevertheless Samuel Lee, who knew books, called it 'a handsome library' in 1690.[32]

Ten years later the Yale College Library, through the donation of Bishop Berkeley and the collection made by

[31] S. E. Morison, *Harvard in the Seventeenth Century* (1936) I, 295.
[32] *C.S.M.*, XIV, 145.

Jeremiah Dummer, had a much more modern and service-able collection than its elder rival. Yet the Harvard Library contained a considerable number of valuable and curious works, most of which had probably been acquired in the previous century, and many of which cannot be found in any American university library today. For example, Sel-den's *Arundel Marbles*, several Roman missals and Uses of Sarum, a History of the Slavonic Churches by Jędrzey Węgierski (Regenvolsius), Kircher's pioneer work on hier-oglyphics, a manuscript *Trésor* of Brunetto Latini (the teacher of Dante), the charming Salmasius edition of Achilles Tatius' *Erotikon* (Leyden, 1640); two editions, including Halley's, of Apollonius Pergaeus' work on conic sections; the famous Spanish romance *Celestina: Tragico-media de Calisto y Meliboea*, two works on heraldry, an English translation of Nathaniel Ingelo's Italian romance *Bentivolio and Urania;* Giambattista della Porta's *Magia Naturalis* and several other works on magic and cabalistic philosophy; an Irish Old Testament, a German grammar, the earliest Tamil New Testament and Grammar; Purchas' *Chaldae seu Aethiopicae Linguae Institutiones*, and Mari-ano Vittorio's pioneer Ethiopic grammar (Rome, 1552); the works of Clément Marot, and Bella Pertica's com-mentaries on the Institutes and the Digest. Also a re-markable collection of political theory: Bodin *de Repub-lica* (Paris, 1586) and his *Six Bookes of Common Weal Englished by R. Knolles* (London, 1606), the *Republicas del Mundo* of Hieronymo Roman, Campanella's *Civitas Solis* (1623), Grotius *de Jure Belli ac Pacis* (1651), *de Im-perio* (1648) and other works, the *Vindiciae contra Tyran-nos*, George Lawson's *Examination of Mr. Hobbs his*

Leviathan (1657), Machiavelli *de Republica* (1599), Trajano Boccalini's *Pietra del Paragone politico* (1653), Marsiglio of Padua's *Defensor Pacis* (1692). This entire library, except for a few score of books that were out at the time (and they, of course, were the most modern ones), went up in smoke when Old Harvard Hall was burnt to the ground in 1764.

It would be an interesting and by no means insuperable task for one of our industrious bibliographers to make a catalogue of all the books that are known to have been in New England before 1700. My guess is that he would find about ten thousand separate titles, and that the number of copies of each work would range from several thousand of the Bible, and several hundred of the more popular works of puritan divinity, down to a single copy of the less common works. When one considers that Harvard College had less than six hundred students in the seventeenth century, and that no book is so little valued, easily lost, or readily destroyed as an obsolete college text, it seems amazing that Professor Arthur O. Norton, simply by browsing through six of our older libraries and pulling down likely volumes, has discovered over two hundred volumes with dated signatures of Harvard students of the seventeenth century. By what factor we should multiply this to reach the total number of books chewed up by these antediluvian college undergraduates, I haven't the faintest notion; nor can anyone tell what proportion the total books known to have existed in New England bears to the total volumes that New England actually possessed. All those here mentioned are mere samples from libraries and booksellers' lists that for one reason or another got recorded and saved; and the libraries, in turn, are mere samples of the whole number of libraries in New England during the century.

The mere fact that there is no mention of Shakespeare, Dryden, or Donne in lists found hitherto is no proof that their books were unknown in New England. Until 1933, for instance, nobody supposed that Spenser's works reached New England in the seventeenth century; but President Dunster's own 1611 folio of Spenser then turned up and was given to the Yale University Library. Evidence of the existence of at least one other reference is found in Elnathan Chauncy's student notebook. As interest in cultural history increases, and more sources are plowed up, new evidence comes to light that the New England puritans were not exclusively interested in theology, but had the literary taste common to educated Englishmen of their day.[33]

Such data as we now have indicate that there was little of importance in the English literature of the seventeenth century outside the drama that did not reach New England within a few years of publication; that many persons, especially college graduates, began private libraries at an early age, and increased them by purchases from England and from Boston booksellers. And the numerous quotations from ancient and modern works in writings by New Englanders prove that they read these books. The leading intellectual interest of New England throughout the century was in religion; but educated New Englanders

[33] There is one Shakespeare quotation—from *Venus and Adonis*—in Elnathan Chauncy's Commonplace Book (*C.S.M.*, XXVIII, 7). Judge Sewall found a folio of Ben Jonson in a tavern somewhere in Rhode Island in 1707, and copied out some extracts from it in his *Diary* (II, 167-68).

shared with their English contemporaries a healthy curiosity concerning modern literature, philosophy, and science, and a deep love for the literature of classical antiquity.

The local printing presses bore a very small part in producing this available literature. The real service of the local presses of Cambridge and Boston was to stimulate New Englanders to write books, and to afford a wider opportunity for printing them, than if the authors had remained in England. All in all, the New Englanders, by bringing over private libraries and purchasing and printing books, created a literary atmosphere that made their educational establishments far more effective, and counteracted the natural tendency of colonial conditions to insulate the people from European intellectual movements.

VII. THEOLOGY AND THE SERMON

So far I have confined my attention to the apparatus that the founders of New England provided, and the institutions they set up, in order to enjoy learning and literature. College, schools, libraries, and printing long outlasted the immediate purposes of their foundation; but the first test of them came in the second half of the seventeenth century, when the first American-born and American-educated generation began to grow up.

The founders of New England were primarily theologians on the intellectual side. Among the one hundred and thirty university alumni who came over by 1645, John Cotton of Boston, Thomas Hooker of Hartford, and John Davenport of New Haven were already marked men in the puritan party; and several others, such as Roger Williams of Providence, Nathaniel Ward of Ipswich, John Wilson and John Norton of Boston, Thomas Shepard of Cambridge, John Knowles of Watertown, William Hooke of Taunton, Samuel Eaton of New Haven, Peter Bulkeley of Concord, and Thomas Parker of Newbury, subsequently became well known in England through their American writings. These were mighty men in their day; it is to them and the universities where they were educated that New England owes her first intellectual impulse. Some of their works, composed in New England though mostly printed in Old England, are monuments of ingenuity, and good examples of effective presentation.

Thomas Hooker's *Survey of the Summe of Church Discipline* bears the same relation to the Congregational church as Richard Hooker's *Ecclesiastical Polity* to the Church of England. The pamphlet controversy on toleration between Roger Williams and John Cotton is significant in the history of free thought; and it was conducted in a generous manner, each acknowledging his opponent's gifts, and neither questioning the other's sincerity. Nathaniel Ward, the 'Simple Cobler of Agawam' was a social satirist and wit, as well as parson and pamphleteer; and several others were noted preachers and theologians, whose works the English booksellers were glad to publish. But from the point of view of American intellectual history, these men are not so interesting as those of the next generation, who were either born in the colonies, or who came over young and were educated there. The works of the second generation offer the first test of the founders' efforts 'to advance *Learning* and perpetuate it to Posterity.' So in speaking of the prose literature of seventeenth-century New England, I shall pass over the founders and begin with the writings of those who came over as children.

It would be pleasant to dwell on Bradford and William Wood and their generation, for, as J. Truslow Adams justly observes, there is a freshness and charm in their works that is wanting in later colonial writers; and he is doubtless right in ascribing a part of the change to 'living in the wilderness.' A wilderness may be very delightful for a man of wit and culture who knows he can return to civilization, but making a living on a frontier is a pretty grim business for an artist or scholar. Other explanations of the waning charm in New England prose are the puritan religion, and the intolerance of those who practiced it. At this point I split off from an agreement with Mr. Adams so rare that I would make the most of it. A mere reference to the France of Louis XIV or the England of Elizabeth is sufficient to prove that intolerance does not necessarily crush literary expression; and, conversely, the two English colonies that adopted a tolerant polity in the seventeenth century, Rhode Island and Maryland, were conspicuously barren in letters. Further, Mr. Adams declares that the concentration of New England intellectuals 'almost wholly upon the problems of election or damnation created a condition of ethical morbidity.' [1] But they did not concentrate on election and damnation, and as for morbidity, I cannot see it unless we are to call Keats, Shelley, and Walt Whitman morbid for writing poems on the theme of death. The puritans were indeed concerned with doing the will of God, and perhaps they overdid it; but the piety of great souls has produced some of the world's greatest literature. Moreover, if you will stay with me, I hope to show you some prose by Mrs. Rowlandson and others in which the quality of freshness is not wanting.

The changing character of New England literature is largely a counterpart of what was taking place in English literature. In that half-century English style was undergoing so profound a change that Addison, Swift, and Pope seem a world apart from Browne, Burton, and Milton;

[1] *The Founding of New England*, pp. 370-72. Mr. Adams, however, is not the only author to generalize for the whole of New England colonial literature from Wigglesworth's *Day of Doom*.

and they, in turn, seem separated by more than a generation from the great Elizabethans. Now, the older founders
of New England [2] grew up in the age of Shakespeare and
the King James Bible, when Englishmen had just discovered the beauty of their language, and were tossing it
about and playing with it, exuberant as a child who has just
learned a new game. New words were being coined by the
score; and in the hands of their first users they had all the
brightness and beauty of newly minted guineas. But by
the time the younger founders of New England [3] were beginning to write, many writers of English prose were becoming involved, intricate, and 'metaphysical,' as in the
sermons of Donne and Andrewes, Milton's prose, Browne's
Religio Medici, and Burton's *Anatomy of Melancholy.* At
its best this style had a balance, melody, and nuance that
has never been surpassed; at its worst it was characterized
by pedantic conceits and farfetched metaphors. By 1660 it
had become so overinflated that the Royal Society of scientists and virtuosi felt obliged to strew tacks in the road. For
the rising fraternity of scientists found this 'metaphysical'
style fatal to scientific accuracy. They exacted of their
members 'a close, naked, natural way of Speaking; positive
expressions, clear Senses; a native Easiness; bringing all

[2] Those born before 1595, such as Governor Bradford (1590), Governor
Winthrop (1588), Nathaniel Ward (1578), Francis Higginson (1586), John
Cotton (1584), Thomas Hooker (1586), Charles Chauncy (1592), John Wil-
son (1590), Henry Whitefield (1591), William Wood, and Thomas Morton.

[3] Such as Richard Mather (1596), John Davenport (1597), William Hooke
(1601), Roger Williams (1603), Thomas Shepard (1605), John Norton
(1606), John Winthrop, Jr. (1606), and the most famous teachers of early
New England: Woodmancy (1595), Wetherell (1600), Maude (1603), Dunster (1609), Corlet (1610), and Cheever (1616). For brief sketches of these
men, see Morison, *The Founding of Harvard College,* Appendix B.

Things as near the Mathematical Plainness as they can; and preferring the Language of Artizans, Countrymen, and Merchants, before that of Wits or Scholars.'[4]

A plain style naturally appealed to plain puritans; and among all the native New England writers, save Urian Oakes, and, in part, Cotton Mather, the plain style prevailed. But this does not mean that they cultivated plainness for its own sake, or sacrificed art in writing. In what he wrote and did, the New Englander used as much art as he was capable of. In architecture and silverware this is perfectly evident, as you may see for yourself by visiting the New England rooms in some of our modern museums of fine arts;[5] but it remains to be proved, in letters. Even the religious service of the primitive puritans seemed to some of the native-born rather too bald. Increase Mather, writing a preface for his son's *Accomplished Singer* (1721), says 'I would Encourage, especially our Younger People, to Learn the Skill, by which they may Sing Regularly; that so this Part of Divine Worship may be more beautifully carried on, and more generally delighted in.'[6]

PULPIT LITERATURE

With an intellectual class so largely clerical in occupation, and a public keenly interested in religion, a preponderant

[4] Thomas Sprat, *History of the Royal Society* (1702), sect. xx, pp. 111-13. Cf. Marjorie H. Nicholson, "The Early Stage of Cartesianism in England," *Studies in Philology*, XXVI (1929), 356-74, and H. S. V. Jones, "The Attack on Pulpit Eloquence in the Restoration," and "Science and Language in England of the Mid-Seventeeth Century," in *The Journal of English and Germanic Philology*, XXX (1931), 188-217, and XXXI (1932), 315-31.

[5] Especially the Metropolitan Museum of New York, the Boston Museum of Fine Arts, and the Nelson Museum in Kansas City.

[6] T. J. Holmes, *Increase Mather: A Bibliography of His Works* (1931), I. 27.

part of the intellectual energy of New England was expended on sermons. Puritans cultivated pulpit oratory as a fine art, even as did their Anglican contemporaries, John Donne and Lancelot Andrewes. The sermons of the first gloomy Dean of St. Paul's are well known to all students of English literature, and Bishop Andrewes is the subject of one of Mr. T. S. Eliot's best critical essays. Therein he notes the organic nature of Andrewes' style; his clarity and precision; his rhythm, cadence, and assonance; the skill with which he develops an idea, and the persistence with which he sucks the last bit of meaning out of a scriptural phrase or word. The nineteenth-century editor of Bishop Andrewes' sermons describes them as 'for the most part exegetical and practical. . . . They explain and they enforce a portion of Holy Writ, and they do it with such clearness and strength of reasoning, and with so powerful an appeal to the conscience, that they could hardly fail to have impressed the most careless and irreverent of those who heard them.' [7] And that would be a very good description both of the purpose and of the method of the New England sermons of the same century. Their purpose was exegetical and practical. They exposed—'opened up' was their favorite phrase—a passage of Scripture; and on it expended their best art and skill. They drew on a wealth of theological learning for support and enforced their points by homely or startling phrases, and appeals to the imagination and emotions of their audience. Here are three sample passages, all of the seventeenth century; one is from Lancelot Andrewes; a second was written in New England

[7] Preface to Lancelot Andrewes, *Ninety-Six Sermons* (Library of Anglo-Catholic Theology, Oxford, 1841-1853), I, viii-ix.

by Thomas Shepard, a puritan divine of the first generation; another, by Urian Oakes, a New England divine of
the second generation. See if you can tell which is which:

1.

If there have been abundance of sweet affections and sweet
refreshings, thereby rising up within the soul, without the death,
and killing, and removal of the contrary lusts and sins; it is certain
this soul was never truly filled nor satisfied with the Spirit of Gods
grace; for as it is with vessels, while they be filled with lime or
chaff, they cannot be filled with wheat or with water; so while the
heart is filled with some noisome distempers, it cannot be filled or
satisfied with the Lord. . . .

2.

Now then that God may not fail them, but go in and out before
them and bring them back with victory and triumph, and that we
all desire and pray for may so come to pass, Moses doth here out of
his own experience bestow an advice upon us. And Moses could
skill what belonged to war, as one that forty years together was
never out of camp. Which advice is, that among our military
points we would reckon the abatement of sin for one; that now
this time of our going forth we would go forth against sin too, and
keep us from it as we would keep us from our enemy. If we could
be but persuaded to reform our former custom of sin, it would
certainly do the journey good. That therefore with other courses,
some remembrance, some regard be had of this; that at this time sin
do not so overflow among us, be not so very fruitful as before time
it hath.

3.

That which makes Death so terrible is, that in the ordinary
course of it, it makes a perfect and perpetual separation between
the Sons and Daughters of men, and all the Fruits of the Love,
and Goodness, and Patience of the blessed God. Death passed
upon all men, for that all have sinned (Romans 5:12). And where
it Reigns and Triumphs, and is Victorious over any man, and
fastens its *Sting* in him (as I may allude to First Corinthians

15:55), it destroys him utterly by putting him into a condition of everlasting separation from God. Now this is the last Adversary that the believing Christian Soldier contends withal; though upon more advantageous terms than other men. . . .

A Believer cannot possibly make his way through all these Enemies, and tear down all this Opposition, without fighting. He skirmishes with these Enemies; yea, fights many a pitch'd battle against them. He must put on the whole Armour of God (Ephesians 6:11), and keep it on, and make use of the weapons of his Christian Warfare, and his Faith and other Graces will be soundly put to it. It costs him many a Bickering. He runs, and wrestles, and labours, and strives, and fights the good fight of Faith; as we might demonstrate by many Scripture instances. By *Fighting*, I mean a vigorous contending and conflicting with the enemies of his Soul, which is exprest variously by the Holy Ghost in Scripture. He must strive hard that will enter in at the strait gate (Luke 13:24); ordinary seeking will not do it. If the Believer put off his Armour, lay by his weapons, suffer the Sword of Truth to rest in the scabbard, and draw it not forth as there is occasion, . . . it will be impossible that he should break through those Legions of Devils, those Armies of Temptations, and make his way through those Adverse Powers that oppose themselves in his way to Happiness.

The first is from Thomas Shepard's *Parable of the Ten Virgins,* delivered in New England before 1649 and printed in London in 1660.[8] The second is from Bishop Lancelot Andrewes' Ash Wednesday sermon of 1599.[9] The third is from Urian Oakes's Artillery Sermon of 1672.[10]

Before quoting further passages from New England sermons, a word on New England theology. Although of the Calvinist family, the New England theology of the seven-

---

[8] Part ii, pp. 84-85.
[9] *Ninety-Six Sermons* (Oxford, 1841), I, 321-22.
[10] *The Unconquerable, all Conquering, more then Conquering Souldier* (Cambridge, 1674), p. 11.

teenth century was not Calvinism; Jonathan Edwards, the
first really original theologian and philosopher that this
province produced, was the first New England Calvinist.
The seventeenth-century New Englander preached what
historians of theology call the federal or Covenant system,
expounded by their favorite English writers, John Preston,
Richard Sibbes, and William Ames, whose works are
found in almost every recorded New England library. The
God of John Calvin was both absolute and arbitrary. After
Adam's fall the human race was destined to eternal damnation, but through the merits and intercession of Christ,
God consented to save a certain predetermined number
from hell. He selected these by methods known only to
himself, with complete arbitrariness so far as men might
discern. The key text of Calvinism is Romans, ix. 18,
'Therefore hath he mercy on whom he will have mercy,
and whom he will he hardeneth.' But the God of New
England, though absolute, was not arbitrary. So far as his
dealings with men were concerned, he had voluntarily
placed himself under a code: the Covenant of Grace. This,
as interpreted by our theologians, meant that God's re-
deeming grace was bestowed on any person who sincerely and completely believed in God, and surrendered
himself to God. Such a one, no matter how grievously he
had sinned, could join the Covenant, and lay hold on
Grace. And as Christ's death and passion gave full and sufficient satisfaction for all the sins of the world, there were
no personal sins, however great, that would not weigh as
a feather in the scale against our Saviour's merits. That is
what Samuel Sewall meant when he recorded in his diary,
'I pray'd this noon that God would give me a pardon of

my Sins under the Broad Seal of Heaven. . . . I hope I doe thirst after Christ.'[11]

Among the early exponents of this Covenant theology in New England were Thomas Shepard of Cambridge, and Peter Bulkeley of Concord. Bulkeley's *Gospel Covenant, or the Covenant of Grace Opened* (London, 1646), is the most important treatise. Although highly praised by Tyler for its intellectual robustness: 'one of those massive, exhaustive, ponderous treatises into which the Puritan theologians put their enormous Biblical learning, their acumen, their industry, the fervor, pathos, and consecration of their lives, the literary quality is not remarkable. A clearer exposition of Covenant theology is to be found in the sermons and treatises of Samuel Willard who, born in 1640 during Bulkeley's ministry at Concord, was graduated from Harvard in 1659; and after several years' service in the frontier town of Groton, became minister of the Old South Church in Boston. This excerpt from his *Barren Fig Tree's Doom* (a book of sixteen sermons and three hundred pages on the parable of the fig tree, printed at Boston in 1691) is interesting not only for substance, but for style—the plain style, eschewing all conceits, metaphors, and hard Latin words, that came into vogue at the Restoration.

Gods tenderness hath been already declared to you, in and of all that patience which he hath used with you, and the cost that he hath laid out upon you. God will for ever be acknowledged, and you shall be enforced to confess, that he did not deal with you as he might have done, that he did not execute all the rigour of his Justice upon you which you deserved: Hear how Christ expostu-

[11] *Diary*, I, 351 (October 25, 1691).

lates with Jerusalem in this regard, Matthew 23, 37 [O Jerusalem, Jerusalem, *thou* that killest the prophets, and stonest them which are sent unto thee, how often would I have gathered thy children together, even as a hen gathereth *her* chickens under her wings, and ye would not!]. . . . All the offers of grace made to you; and all the strivings of his holy spirit with you, and all the long time wherein he waited upon you, will witness for him, that you undid your selves, that you were the blameable cause of your own destruction: every time that he came and said to you, *Oh turn! why will you die? receive instruction and live,* which you slighted, will say that you undid your selves. . . .

Then, in order 'to encourage such as have long lived barren in God's vineyard,' Willard warns them that when people begin to 'rouse themselves, . . . and seek after God in earnest,' Satan tries to persuade them that it is too late, 'they have sinned beyond a pardon.' On the contrary,

there is merit enough in the satisfaction of Christ to answer for all your sins and provocations . . . there is a compleat payment made to it by the blood of Christ, and therefor read *Matthew.* xii. 31 [Wherefore I say unto you, All manner of sin and blasphemy shall be forgiven unto men]: yea and by the accepting and pardoning of such a one as you are, . . . will God also be glorified.[12]

The same doctrine had been stated by Willard even better in an earlier sermon:

Your many weaknesses and infirmities cannot undermine or subvert your safety; they cannot destroy or breake the peace that is made in Christ between God and you; they may, if fallen into through neglect of duty, and remissness in your spiritual watch,

[12] Willard, *Barren Fig Tree's Doom* (Boston, 1691), pp. 193, 276, 278. In these sermons I have expanded the Biblical references, in square brackets, since I understand that the ministers always read such quotations aloud, but gave the reference only in the printed version to save space.

procure you the displeasure of a father, discovering itself in his chastizing of you with affliction: but can never alienate his heart from you, though your grace be faint, and your corruptions strong . . . yet still all shall be well at the last: Jesus Christ your advocate is pleading for you, and presenting the merit of his righteousness in your account. . . .[13]

People do not write English like that by accident. Willard had very happily combined the 'choiceness of the phrase, and the round and clean composition of the sentence, and the sweet falling of the clauses' that Lord Bacon praised in the English of his day, with the conciseness and exactness inculcated by the scientists. He had achieved a style.

By almost all shades of religious opinion in seventeenth-century England, the sermon was regarded as the most important form of prose literature, and it was one which had preserved a striking continuity of form and design from the orations of ancient Greece, through the Christian centuries. And the puritans emphasized it more than did any other branch of the church. In an austere, unliturgical service, it provided a touch of the ritual that all men crave even when they deny it stoutly; for the sermon followed accepted rules of rhetoric and design; it was supposed to be a work of art, and often was.[14]

An admirable training for sermon writing and delivery was provided by the rhetorical discipline in the college, where each of the four classes spent an entire day on rhetoric every week, every student gave a Latin oration once a

[13] *A Briefe Discourse of Justification* (Boston, 1686), pp. 163-64.
[14] W. Fraser Mitchell, *English Pulpit Oratory from Andrewes to Tillotson* (London, 1932), pp. 112-14.

month, and 'publike Exercises of oratory' in the 'mother-
tongue' are mentioned in the college laws of 1642-1646.
Rhetoric was defined in one of the commencement theses
as 'the art of speaking and writing with elegance' (*ornate*).
Correct speaking in Latin was supposed to have been
learned by the freshman in grammar school; fine speaking
he learned in college. He studied it mainly from classical
models in Latin and Greek, especially Cicero, Demosthenes, and Isocrates, from a variety of Latin textbooks
and from phrasebooks. Just before Samuel Willard entered
college, one of the Harvard tutors was Michael Wigglesworth, author of *The Day of Doom*. As an exercise for his
master's degree, Michael delivered two orations 'In Praise
of Eloquence,' the manuscript of which has been preserved. A few extracts from one of them will give the drift:

Eloquence gives new luster and bewty, new strength new vigor,
new life unto trueth; presenting it with such variety as refresheth,
actuating it with such hidden powerful energy, that a few languid
sparks are blown up to a shining flame. And which is yet more:
Eloquence does not onely revive the things known but secretly
convay life into the hearers understanding rousing it out of its former slumber, quickning it beyond its naturall vigor, elevating it
above its ordinary conception. . . .[15]
Like a mighty river augmented with excessive rains or winter
snows swelling above its wonted channel bear's down banks and
bridges, overflows feilds and hedges, sweeps away all before it, that
might obstruct its passage: so Eloquence overturn's, overturn's all
things that stand in its way, and carrys them down with the ir-
resistible stream of its all controuling power. . . .

[15] This passage is also interesting as stating a theological doctrine particularly cultivated by the Covenant theologians: that the first spark of God's
grace upon which the sinner may, if he will, build salvation, is commonly
conveyed by sermons (comment by Perry Miller).

And to those modest students who say eloquence is all very well, but we can never attain it, he replies:

Go too therefore my fellow-students (for to you I address my speech) . . . give me leav to say: Let no man hereafter tel me I despair of excelling in the oratoricall faculty, therefore 'tis bootless to endeavor. Who more unlike to make an orator than Demosthenes except it were one who had no tongue in his head? yet Demosthenes became orator optimus. Tell me not I have made trial once and again, but find my labor fruitless. thou art not the first that hast made an onset, and bin repelled; neither canst thou presage what renewed endeavors may produce. Would you then obtain this skill? take Demosthenes his course. gird up your loines, put to your shoulders, and to it again, and again, and agen, let nothing discourage you. Know that to be a dunce, to be a stammerer, unable to bring forth 3 or 4 sentences hanging well together, this is an easy matter; but to become an able speaker, hic labor, hoc opus est. Would you have your orations pleas, such as need not be laughts at? why follow him in that also. Let them be such as smell of the lamp, as was sayd of his. not slovenly I mean, but elaborate, such as savor of some paines taken with them. A good oration is not made at the first thought, nor scarce at the first writing over. Nor is true Eloquence wont to hurry it out thick and threefould, as if each word: were running for a wadger: nor yet to mutter or whisper it out of a book after a dreaming manner, with such a voyce as the orator can scantly heare himself speak; but to utter it with lively affection, to pronounce it distinctly with audible voyce. But I shall burden your patience no further at the present. . . .

All this fervor was intended to make ministers more effective; for in seventeenth-century New England none other had opportunity for oratory. Lawyers were a despised class without professional status, and the only political speech of the century that has been preserved is John Winthrop's on Liberty. Yet the art of oratory was taught in the antique and humane tradition, with no special reference to divinity. Only after he had taken his first degree, and begun specific preparation for the ministry, did the Harvard student deliver practice sermons.

Of almost equal importance with rhetoric for the training of the puritan preacher was logic, the third subject of the medieval trivium. Grammar taught one to write and speak correctly; rhetoric to do it elegantly; and logic to do it reasonably. In college commencement theses it is described as the art that regulates the reasoning faculty, and teaches the student to think straight; as 'the Mercury of the Arts, at the service of all.' Whether a sermon was expository, imprecatory, or polemic, the art of logic was required; and in the works of Peter Ramus, the great French reformer and teacher of the previous century, New England students had an excellent logical *organon* of which Milton's *Ars Logicae* was merely a digest. In 1686 a manual of Cartesian logic by tutor William Brattle was placed in the hands of his students.

The accepted method of preparing and delivering a sermon, among the puritans, was to write the whole thing out, but deliver it from memory, without notes.[16] John Warham, an Oxford graduate who became the first minister of Windsor, Connecticut, was much criticized for using brief notes in the pulpit; but this method, recommended by Richard Baxter and practiced by the Mathers, gained vogue toward the end of the century. The sermon was timed by an hourglass for minimum, not maximum length. A preacher who ended within the hour was con-

---

[16] Mitchell, *op. cit.*, p. 25. This method was advised by William Perkins, in his *Art of Prophecying* (1592), which was the favorite puritan manual of the art of preaching, at least to 1660. Mitchell, pp. 19, 99.

sidered deficient in duty; Edward Johnson describes listening with rapt attention to a sermon by Thomas Shepard which must have been over two hours long, since 'the glasse was turned up twice.' [17] Throughout the century the New England people never seemed to have enough sermons. Every church had two on the Lord's Day, attendance at which was compulsory, and one weekly 'lecture,' —a sermon unaccompanied by prayer or other devotion or teaching—which no one need attend who did not so desire. Yet in the 1630's there was so much running about from one town to another to hear these weekday lectures that the General Court of Massachusetts tried to fix them all on the same day. The parsons protested, reminding the legislators that people had come to New England expressly to hear sermons; the General Court then passed a resolve to the effect that weekday lectures should end early enough for people to get home before dark!

Members of the congregation often provided themselves with inkhorn and paper to take notes on the sermon; and many thick notebooks closely written with sermon abstracts by laymen survive.[18] From the English grammar schools the puritans imported the cruel practice of requiring schoolboys and college students to take notes on sermons, and repeat them afterwards.[19] A system of shorthand had been especially devised for getting down as much of the sermon as possible. In pious families every sermon was hashed over, and the children catechized on the main

---

[17] *Wonder-Working Providence* (1910 ed.), p. 135.

[18] E.g., Robert Keayne's notes on John Cotton's sermons, at the M.H.S.; and the famous notebook in shorthand on Thomas Hooker's sermons, at the Connecticut Historical Society.

[19] Mitchell, *op. cit.*, pp. 31-33, gives an account of the practice in England.

points; in the college, President Chauncy 'had the Morning Sermon repeated at noon, and the Afternoon Sermon repeated at night, and both the sermons repeated once more in the evening, before the next Lord's Day: at which times he still took occasion to reinforce the more notable truths, occurring in the sermons, with pertinent applications of his own.'[20] There is preserved a closely written notebook of the discourses that one student suffered under twice every Lord's Day in 1670-1671. After a sermon by the President in February the student notes: 'A very could day. I could write no more in the after noone then I did in the fore noone. So let it suffice.'

Good literature is always helped by good criticism; and the puritan preacher was in a very different position from the modern clergyman whose congregation expects only not to be too much bored. He had a highly critical as well as appreciative audience, critical not only of his matter but of his method. Almost everyone was mentally alert for Biblical texts with which to trip up the parson. All who had been to grammar school knew somewhat of rhetorical method, as a basis for a technical criticism; almost everyone else had heard other ministers, and was only too ready to compare one with another. Hence the New England parsons were kept 'right up on their toes.' They were responsible not only to Christ, but to their flock; the Lord and Saviour must be served, and the hungry and very critical sheep fed, with high-class diet. And there was always the hope that a sermon would bring about, in some members of the congregation, the emotional crisis known as conversion. Of that there were many il-

[20] *Magnalia* (1702), book iii, 137.

lustrious examples; Cotton, Hooker, Shepard, and Wilson had been turned from seeking success to the service of Christ by the famous pulpit orators of old Cambridge.

Only a small fraction of the sermons preached in New England have been preserved, and more than half of them still remain in manuscript, often in the form of a listener's notes. We cannot assume that the best sermons reached the printed page. Churches engaged their parsons fresh from college, and, barring quarrels or accidents, kept them during life; hence some of the most effective and eloquent preachers were in remote frontier parishes far from a printing press. Such a man as Solomon Stoddard of Northampton might be invited to give an election sermon, and so establish a reputation that opened the Boston or Cambridge press to his other works; but a minister of Boston or the neighborhood had by far the greater opportunity for publication, since his congregation was likely to contain a printer or bookseller looking for copy. Thus Samuel Willard, the most prolific in printed sermons after the Mathers, published but one sermon during the twelve years of his ministry at Groton but burst into print as soon as he obtained a Boston pulpit.

The New England clergy did not produce much controversial theology, the chief intellectual sport of their predecessors in England. The church synod of 1637 defined the limits of permissible speculation, and in 1646 the General Court of Massachusetts Bay passed a law condemning to banishment anyone who broached certain 'damnable heresies.' The only New England writer who ventured to brave that prohibition was a layman, William Pynchon of Springfield. His book on the Atonement, although printed in London, was given the honors of a public burning when a copy of it arrived in Boston; the author, although one of the principal founders of the Colony, was deprived of his magistracy. He returned to England rather than make a full retraction of his heresies.[21] Hardly an encouragement to further speculation! New England publications on theology were mainly expository, or defenses of stands already taken: works such as John Norton's reply to Pynchon; a symposium on baptism and communion entitled *First Principles of New-England* (Cambridge, 1675); and a joint *Letter Released by the Ministers of New England to Mr. John Dury* (Boston, 1675), a stern reply to an overture from that indefatigable advocate of Protestant union.

New England theological literature seems arid to anyone who values the Catholic tradition, since it ignored the mystical aspects of faith; and it seems inhuman to a liberal Christian, because it takes no account of the humanity of Jesus. But we must remember that in the seventeenth century only two approaches to Jesus were permissible to any Christian: the mystical and the theological. Mysticism, so productive of beautiful poetry and devotional literature, was regarded by puritans with deep suspicion. The *Imitatio Christi* was as far as they cared to go in that direction, and that was farther than popular hostility to 'popery' permitted. Nineteenth-century writings on the 'man Jesus' would have seemed as blasphemous to puritans of the sev-

---

[21] *Proc. M.H.S.*, LXIV, 102-5. For a discussion of Pynchon's doctrine, and John Norton's reply to it, see F. H. Foster, *A Genetic History of the New England Theology* (University of Chicago Press, 1907), pp. 16-21. The condemned book, *The Meritorious Price of our Redemption* (London, 1650), is devoid of literary merit.

enteenth century as they do to Catholics of today. Puritans regarded Jesus as very Son of very God, sent to guide men's conduct in this life, and to carry out the divine plan of salvation. The human aspect of Jesus simply did not interest them, or indeed many intelligent Christians, until the romantic era.[22] It was the Word that counted; the 'personality' of Jesus was a matter of no moment whatsoever.

The only aspect of theology to which New England made a distinct contribution was the political. Richard Mather's *Platform of Church Discipline* (Cambridge, 1649), and Thomas Hooker's posthumously printed *Survey of the Summe of Church Discipline*, and John Cotton's *Way of the Congregational Churches Cleared*, both of which came out in London in 1648, served as constitutional law for the Independent churches in England, as well as for the Congregational churches in New England.[23] But there was one plank in the New England platform that within thirty years proved very embarrassing. A Church, as Mather, Hooker, and Cotton defined it, was the communion of 'saints' (the elect), in a given parish. You could be admitted only by satisfying the church that you were of the elect; and only the children of church members could be baptized. In other words, the New England theologians imagined that they could create a visible church coterminous with the invisible church; they expected that God would give them the technique to recog-

[22] A. D. Nock, *Conversion, the Old and the New in Religion from Alexander the Great to Augustine of Hippo* (1933), p. 210.

[23] See Perry Miller's article on Thomas Hooker in *N.E.Q.*, IV, 663-712, which proves the essential agreement of Hooker and Cotton on polity, correcting the superficial account of both men in V. L. Parrington, *The Colonial Mind* (Vol. I, *Main Currents in American Thought*), pp. 27-62. They did differ on certain theological points, but not in the way that Parrington states.

nize the recipients of divine grace. But God did not prove
to be so accommodating. As time elapsed, and many instances occurred of highly sanctimonious church members
committing 'damnable villanies and bestialities,' [24] the puritans' belief in their ability to distinguish the sheep from the
goats became somewhat shaken. And the failure of large
numbers of adults to prove their sanctity and gain admission to the church left their children unbaptized, without
the fold.

Faced by the dilemma of being consistent to the point
where church membership would dwindle away to the
vanishing point, or breaking down the system in order to
keep the churches going, the New England ministers held
a synod in 1662, which threshed the whole matter out.
The result was a system known as the Half-Way Covenant, by which the children of adults who were not com-
municants could be baptized if their parents made a mere
profession of faith. As the adoption of this Half-Way
Covenant was optional with every church, it produced a
considerable crop of controversial literature by President
Chauncy, John Allin, John Davenport, Increase Mather,
and others; a closely reasoned group of pamphlets in which
the one side showed the more logic, and the other the more
statesmanship. This compromise satisfied nobody, and was
swept away in the next century after revivalism had been
evoked to keep church membership up to an appreciable
majority of the church congregations. [25]

[24] See instances in Cotton Mather's *Magnalia* (1702), book vi, 38ff.
[25] Perry Miller reviews the literature of the Half-Way Covenant, and dis-
cusses the issues, in *N.E.Q.*, VI, 676-715.

After 1662, as before, the larger number of printed sermons were expository, developing and explaining some Biblical text within permissible limits. Many of them were expositions and applications of Christian ethics, such as Samuel Willard's sermon on *The Danger of Taking God's Name in Vain* (1691), in which he points out about two dozen different ways of breaking the third commandment. Seventeenth-century puritan parsons were not tolerant. They regarded heresy as a poison and were continually exhorting magistrates to silence or punish the Quakers and Baptists; they took a gloomy view of human nature, and were always inclined to attribute the pursuit of pleasure by young people to innate depravity. Willard, for instance, in *The Peril of the Times Displayed* (Boston, 1700) noted (pp. 112-114) a number of 'bad *Symptoms* that are upon the *Rising Generation*.'

It hath been a frequent observation, that if one Generation begins to decline, the next that followeth grows worse, and so on, till God poureth out his Spirit again upon them; and for the most part some desolating Judgments intervene . . . alas, how doth vanity, and a fondness after new things abound among them? how do young persons grow weary of the strict profession of their fathers, and become strong disputants for those things which their Progenitors forsook a pleasant Land for the avoidance of . . . that their posterity might be removed from the temptations of? Besides, it is almost a general complaint of Family Governours, that their Children and Servants are weary of the yoke, and are not willing to be under their Command . . . that they are in combination with one another, and do joyn hand in hand in . . . debauching of themselves with their night revels, and meetings in bad houses, to drink and game . . . and these also the Children of Godly Parents, and such as have been carefully and religiously Educated.

In the 'Election' and 'Artillery' sermons the clergy made a particular point of dealing with social and political subjects. On 'general election,' the spring day set for counting the votes for governor and assistants, it was customary in each colonial capital for a clergyman to deliver the election sermon before the assembled magistrates, and as many people as could crowd into the largest meetinghouse in town. On this important occasion the preacher was apt to choose a topic of public concern; and most of the election sermons at Boston, together with some of those delivered at Hartford, were printed. A typical election-day preacher dwelt on the virtues of our ancestors, the decay of public and private virtue, the remissness of magistrates in punishing wickedness and vice, the crying abuses and particular sins that needed cure; and he was apt to wind up by prophesying calamity if the community did not repent and do works meet for repentance. Samuel Willard, in the Boston election sermon of 1682, declares that his predecessors did not relish this self-imposed role of Jeremiah:

They delivered not these messages, without many heavy pangs and throes, upon their own spirits. This roll was bitter to them, and with a great deal of reluctancy and unwillingness did they declare themselves. I my self have heard some of them expressing what Combats, what Wrestlings they have had in their own minds, how loth to speak, how fearful about their message, how well they could have been content to enjoy the good-will of the People, and how greatly unwilling they were to be an occasion of adding to the guilt of those that had already run too deep an account with God: . . .

He does not entertain much hope that his political audience will take his warnings to heart for

Such is the unhappy entertainment that plain-dealing and open-hearted reproofs do meet with in the World, that when they are most needed, they can be least born: The fouler the stomack, the more nauseous is the Physick: when the malady is come to a dangerous Crisis, and every symptom bodes a sad and sudden change, men are better pleased with a cheating quack, that disembleth the disease, and engageth all shall be well, then with an honest and faithful Physitian, who tells them the distemper is malignant, the issue dubious, and, without the application of some speedy and extraordinary means, desperate.

Many people, he says, are of the opinion

that the foundations of this People are unmovable; that our civil constitutions, and Church Covenants have so engaged the presence of God with us, that we ly out of the reach of forraign mischeif. Thus the *Athenians* once chained down the Image of *Minerva*, their Tutelary Goddess, to her station, and so thought they had secured themselves from all dangers of being subjugated by any enemy, or oppressed with any evil.

But if the rulers of the Bay Colony

can tolerate the dishonour of Christ, let me boldly say, I believe he will soon and signally testifie his dislike of it.[26]

And within two years, the Bay Colony lost her precious charter. Don't say we clergy didn't warn you!

The annual Artillery sermons were delivered before the still flourishing Ancient and Honorable Artillery Company of Boston, or the shorter-lived Cambridge Artillery, at an annual muster and drumhead election of officers. Preparedness for war and the duty of a Christian soldier were the usual subjects of such discourses as were printed.

[26] Samuel Willard, "The Only sure way to prevent threatened Calamity," in *The Childs Portion* (1684), pp. 163-64, 181, 192-93, 195.

But on more occasions than one, the assembled defenders of Massachusetts Bay heard the same ardent hope for peace between the nations for which we are still yearning. Urian Oakes, for instance, declared in 1672:

I am no Friend to warre, but an unfeigned lover of Peace. I long for an End of the warres and Bloudsheds, the Destructions and Desolations that the poor world is filled withal. O when will this Iron Age expire, and that glorious Morn appear, that Lightsome Day dawn, wherein the Nations shall beat their swords into plough-shares, and their spears into pruning-hooks, neither shall Nation lift up sword against Nation, nor the sons of men learn warre anymore? The God of Peace will certainly put an end unto these miserable doings ere long. In the mean time it is the wisdom and duty of the people of God to improve all advantages that are providentially put into their hands, to secure their peace and precious enjoyments, and to put themselves into posture and condition of disputing it with those that may invade or assault them.[27]

Alas, that goal seems almost as far distant now as in 1672.

[27] *The Unconquerable, all Conquering, more then Conquering Souldier* (Cambridge, 1674), pp. 37-38.

VIII. HISTORICAL AND POLITICAL LITERATURE

HISTORICAL literature is the only other native prose in seventeenth-century New England of which we have enough examples for generalizing. In this class I would include histories, biographies, chronicles, and original narratives of secular experience. The New England habit of writing history began early, with Governor Bradford of Plymouth and it has grown upon us in the course of time, as you have had reason to observe. Clio is seldom allowed by her foolish votaries to appear in her proper character; she is clothed in strange disguises, from the whig blue-and-buff to the hammer and sickle. In seventeenth-century New England she wore the preacher's gown. The main object of our primitive historians was to prove that God, in spite of occasional severe chastenings, had a very special interest in New England as a holy experiment in Christian living. Indeed, the subtitle of one of these early chronicle-histories, Edward Johnson's *Wonder-Working Providence of Sion's Saviour in New England* frankly reveals the author's motive.

In accordance with my plan, I shall pass over the writings of the founders who had been educated in England, and barely mention our first crop of histories: Johnson's story with the long title; Governor Bradford *Of Plymouth Plantation*, incomparably the best of New England colonial histories;[1] Governor Winthrop's *Journal*, which

[1] For this great book and its author, see the Introduction to my edition, *Of Plymouth Plantation* (New York: Knopf, 1952).

he intended to revise for publication as a History of New England; Thomas Morton's highly diverting *New English Canaan*, William Wood's *New England's Prospect*, written with gay humor and Elizabethan verve, albeit the author was a puritan of the first generation.[2] I shall confine myself to history as a form of intellectual activity among those born or at least educated in New England.

The first native New Englander to burst into print with a history was Nathaniel Morton of Plymouth. His *New-Englands Memoriall: or, A Brief Relation of the most Memorable and Remarkable Passages of the Providence of God, manifested to the Planters of New-England in America; with special Reference to the first Colony thereof, Called New-Plimouth*, was printed on the college press at Cambridge in 1669.[3] It was an official publication, paid for by the Colony of New Plymouth with 'twenty pound in country pay' (*i.e.*, corn); plus 'a barrell of marchantable beefe to Mr Greene, the printer,' when he complained of 'a hard bargaine about the printing of the booke.'[4] (Would that we could now get histories printed on such easy terms!) The author of this work emigrated from England at the age of ten. He was brought up by his uncle, Governor Bradford, and for forty years served as secretary of the Plymouth Colony. In a foreword 'to the Reader' by John Higginson and Thomas Thacher, he is informed that 'it is very expedient

[2] This may seem an unwise generalization, in view of the little we know about William Wood; but he lived at Salem both before and after his book came out, and the work was dedicated to Sir William Armine, one of the puritan gentry of Boston, Lincolnshire, whose wife was one of the chief supporters of John Eliot's work among the Indians.

[3] Albert Matthews in *C.S.M.*, XIV, 269-70. A facsimile of the first edition was printed for the Club of Odd Volumes, Boston, in 1903.

[4] *Plymouth Colony Records*, V, 25.

that (while sundry of the Eldest Planters are yet living) *Records* and *Memorials of Remarkable Providences* be preserved and published . . . that New England, in all times to come, may remember the day of her smallest things.'[5] Morton admits in his dedication to Governor Prence of Plymouth, 'the greatest part of my intelligence hath been borrowed from my much honoured Uncle, Mr. William Bradford' and from 'certain *Diurnals* of the honoured Mr. *Edward Winslow*.' And, as good as his word, Morton's *Memoriall* turns out to be little more than an abridgment of the Bradford History (which was destined to remain in manuscript almost two centuries longer), and of Winslow's *Journal*, part of which had already been printed to advertise the colony.[6] Morton does give the *Mayflower* her name, which Bradford nowhere mentions; and he asserts that the Dutch bribed Captain Jones to keep the Pilgrims away from the Hudson, which modern historians regard as highly improbable. But from the point where Bradford's history leaves off, Morton becomes a mere chronicler, and he has practically nothing to say on any other colony than his own. Nevertheless, Morton deserves at least a footnote in American historical literature; for it was he who started the Pilgrim tradition. By printing even an abridged version of Bradford's noble and touching

[5] This foreword is not found in all editions of *New-England's Memoriall* (Boston, 1721; Newport, 1772; Plymouth, 1826; Boston, 1826; Boston, 1855). The last, or 6th edition, which includes John Davis' notes to the 5th, is the best.

[6] In "Mourt's Relation," so called from the signature 'G. Mourt,' to the preface 'To the Reader.' The real title of this pamphlet is *A Relation or Journall of the beginnings and proceedings of the English Plantation settled at Plimoth in New England* (London, 1622), and its real character, selections from the journals of Bradford and Edward Winslow. There are several modern editions.

story, he disclosed the services and sufferings of the little band who came over on the *Mayflower*. Long before the public had been given the text of Bradford, his homespun nephew had incorporated the Pilgrim Fathers in American folklore; and the Pilgrims are still America's favorites, in spite of all that historians have said on the priority of Jamestown and the superiority of Boston.

Similar in character to Morton's *Memoriall* was the story of New England by William Hubbard. Born in England about the year 1621, he came over with his father at the age of fourteen and graduated from Harvard College with its first class, in 1642. He lived in Ipswich for several years as a planter. At the age of thirty-five he entered the ministry, and in 1658 was ordained pastor of the church in Ipswich, an office in which he served for forty-five years.[7] Master Hubbard appears to have been a commonplace parson, but a genial and easygoing neighbor, who borrowed money that he could not (or at least did not) repay, joined his parishioners in resisting Governor Andros' taxes, and at an advanced age married his housekeeper, a sprightly young widow. The manner of his end may be envied by all historians. At the age of eighty-two he retired from the pulpit. On a pleasant September afternoon he attended the Thursday lecture of his successor, followed by a good dinner at the house of Colonel Appleton, the squire of Ipswich. Returning home, the aged historian had a cold supper, retired, and died quietly in the night.

[7] The best account of Hubbard's life is in Samuel G. Drake's introduction to his edition of Hubbard's *Narrative of the Late Troubles* (Roxbury, 1865). See also Sibley, *Harvard Graduates*, I, 54-62, and the *Dictionary of American Biography*.

We do not know why or when Hubbard began his *History of New England*, but it was finished about the year 1680. Apparently the Boston bookseller-publishers would have none of it, since Hubbard offered the work to the General Court as an official history. The first committee appointed to deal with the manuscript refused to wrestle with the author's unusually bad copy, and in 1682 the General Court resolved that whereas it was a duty 'to take due notice of all occurrences and passages of God's providence' toward Massachusetts Bay, and whereas Mr. Hubbard had compiled 'a history of this nature,' the Colony Treasurer should pay him £50 provided he would make a fair copy. This he attempted to do, and in 1683 the court ordered the Treasurer to pay Mr. Hubbard 'half of the said summe,' a discount that will surprise nobody who has wrestled with Hubbard's manuscript. It had to await publication until 1815.[8]

Hubbard's *History* was sucked dry of factual material by Cotton Mather, Thomas Prince, and Governor Thomas Hutchinson, long before it got into print; and the work had no literary merit to give it a renewed lease of life. The style is pedestrian where it is not obscure; Hubbard had an unfortunate trick of prolonging sentences, clause after clause, until they reached the length of a paragraph. He was a lazy writer, preferring to incorporate lengthy passages from Morton's *Memoriall* and Winthrop's *Journal* rather than look things up in the records; and he was un-

---

[8] In 2 *Coll. M.H.S.*, V-VI; also printed separately in one volume. The transcribing for the press was very badly done; the second edition (Boston, 1848), edited with notes by William T. Harris, is better. The original ms. is in the M.H.S.

fortunately too modest to enlarge on matters of his personal experience. Ten pages of description of his daily life at Ipswich, or of reminiscence of early Harvard might have given Hubbard a certain immortality; as it is, the most valuable contribution he made was to interview Roger Conant of Beverly and so preserve for us a different version of the founding of Massachusetts Bay from Winthrop's. The general tone of the Hubbard history is much more secular than that of Morton. Special providences are not so abundant, even at the founding, nor did he make the mistake of Thomas Prince, who felt obliged to begin his history with the creation of the world, making New England the acme of human aspiration since Adam's fall. Hubbard began with Columbus, and so managed to get down to 1680. Nineteen of the seventy-seven chapters are devoted to events between 1651 and 1680. Hubbard did not confine himself, like Morton, to a single colony; and his book concludes with an interesting description of New York City and Colony, lifted almost word for word from Daniel Denton's *Brief Description of New York* (1670).[9] His description of Long Island shows an appreciation of the beauties of nature that is rare among colonial writers, especially in the seventeenth century, when nature was an enemy to be subdued rather than a friend to be enjoyed.

[9] Denton too was a New Englander, son of Richard Denton, a graduate of the University of Cambridge who was minister successively at Wethersfield, Connecticut, Stamford in the New Haven Colony, and Hempstead, L. I. Cf. Hubbard's *History* with the 1902 edition of Denton's *Description*, pp. 40–42. Hubbard never wrote anything himself when he could borrow what he wanted from some other book; but we should not dismiss him as a plagiarizer, since in his preface he disclaims any higher title than that of 'compiler.'

In May you shall see the woods and fields so curiously be-
decked with roses, and an innumerable multitude of other delightful flowers, not only pleasing to the eye, but smell, that you may
behold nature contending with art, and striving to equal, if not
excel many gardens in England. Nay, did we know the virtue of
those plants and herbs growing there (which time may more discover), many are of opinion, and the natives do affirm, that there
is no disease common to the country, but may be cured without
materials from other nations.[10]

This description, explains Hubbard at the conclusion of
his History, is 'thought necessary to be published for the
encouragement of many that may have a mind to remove
themselves thither, as for a satisfaction to others that would
make a trade thither.' Perhaps this tactless suggestion that
all good New Englanders go to New York before they
die, either to live or to trade, was the reason why the General Court of Massachusetts refused to give such a manuscript the honors of publication!

Before his *History of New England* was presented to
the General Court, Hubbard had won his spurs as historian
of the Indian wars. The English, like other Europeans,
have always had a great curiosity about American Indians,
and an appetite for stories of Indian fighting. With the outbreak of King Philip's War in the summer of 1675, English booksellers saw their opportunity; and before the end
of that year one Dorman Newman 'at the Kings-Arms in
the Poultry, and at the Ship and Anchor at the Bridg-foot
on Southwark side' brought out an exciting narrative of the
first few months of the struggle entitled *The Present State
of New-England . . . Faithfully Composed by a Mer-*

[10] Hubbard (1848 ed.), p. 671.

chant of Boston and Communicated to his Friend in London.[11] Whoever the author may have been,[12] his success was immediate; *The Present State* was followed up by a *Continuation of the State*, a *New and Further Narrative*, purporting to be by the same author; and at least six other pamphlets, some of them little more than news bulletins of four to eight pages.[13] One of the earliest to come out was written by Edward Wharton, a New England Friend, who ascribed the outbreak of the war not to the Indians' cussedness, but to God's taking a just vengeance on Massachusetts puritans for their persecution of Quakers.[14]

If anything were required to make the Boston authors take pen in hand, it was just such an accusation as that. The puritan clergy agreed that King Philip's War was a divine judgment, but they were divided in opinion as to whether God was manifesting his displeasure for moral lapses among the younger generation, or for the magistrates' being too easy on Quakers and other heretics.

Increase Mather, minister of the Second Church in Boston, was about twenty years out of college when the war broke out. He had already published eight or ten sermons and tracts, of no great distinction. Mather was already jot-

[11] Reprinted in C. H. Lincoln's *Narratives of the Indian Wars* (1913), in Original Narratives of Early American History.

[12] Lincoln and others have supposed, on the authority of the initials 'N. S.' appended to the *Continuation of the Present State* and the *New and Further Narrative* (also printed in the above-mentioned volume) that the author was Nathaniel Saltonstall (d. 1707); but he was not a merchant of Boston.

[13] These are listed in Justin Winsor, *Narrative and Critical History*, III, 360n, and five of them are reprinted by S. G. Drake, in *Old Indian Chronicle*, eds. 1836 and 1867. The best collection of the originals is in the John Carter Brown Library.

[14] *New Englands Present Sufferings under their Cruel Neighbouring Indians* (London, 1675).

ting down occurrences 'without any thought of publication' (says he), when the 'astounding mistakes' of the
anonymous *Present State* decided him to publish a 'true
History of this affair.' [15] The Quaker tract, coming under
his eyes, made him speed up; but it was difficult (as historians always find) to write as fast as events happened.
Nevertheless, on August 24, 1676, twelve days after the
death of King Philip had ended the war in southern New
England, the manuscript of Increase Mather's *Brief History of the Warr with the Indians in New-England* was
in the hands of John Foster, the Boston printer. The same
year it was reprinted in London. Mather at once began to
write a prelude to the history, giving the story of Indian
troubles from the early settlements to 1675. William Hubbard beat him to it, with a full-dress history of Indian warfare that made Mather's prelude superfluous; but Mather
did not think that anyone could do it as well as himself,
and the popular thirst for narratives of Indian fighting was
not yet slaked, so in 1677 Mather published in Boston *A
Relation of the Troubles which have hapned in New-
England by reason of the Indians there. From the Year
1614 to the Year 1675.*

William Hubbard's contribution, *A Narrative of the
Troubles with the Indians,* was printed at Boston the same
year, and a few months later in London, with the confus-
ing title *The Present State of New-England.* [16] Cotton
Mather, who was a boy in college at the time of King
Philip's War, wrote a brief account of it entitled *Arma*

[15] T. J. Holmes, *Increase Mather: A Bibliography of His Works,* I, 71;
K. B. Murdock, *Increase Mather, the Foremost American Puritan* (1925),
p. 110.
[16] The two title pages are reproduced in S. G. Drake's edition of 1865.

Virosque Cano, about the year 1695, which was printed in his famous *Magnalia Christi Americana* (London, 1702).

It is interesting to compare these three histories of Indian warfare: Increase Mather's, Hubbard's, and Cotton Mather's. The last is not only the best from a literary point of view, but the only one with any literary merit whatsoever. Increase Mather wrote, as he always did, a plain straightforward narrative without imagination, distinction, or dramatic sense. Hubbard's was the fullest and most accurate story of the war, and has proved to be the most enduring; it was six times reprinted before the definitive edition by Drake in 1865. Hubbard had a rich resource in nouns and adjectives of opprobrium: King Philip is a 'savage miscreant,' a 'treacherous and perfidious Caitiff,' 'Ungrateful, perfidiously False and Cruel,' a 'bloody wretch' of 'inveterate Malice and wickedness,' who began his rebellion in cold blood, with 'nothing of any Provocation from the English,' an accusation from which the Quaker accounts of the war have attempted to clear the Indians.[17] But apart from the invective it is a very pedestrian piece of writing.

Cotton Mather, despite his occasionally dropping into lamentable verse, and his pedantic intrusion of parallels to Roman history, was the only one of the three authors with any historical imagination, or sense of style. A typical passage of Cotton Mather at his best may be seen in his de-

[17] The second Quaker narrative is Eaton's, reprinted in C. H. Lincoln, *Narratives of the Indian Wars*, pp. 7-17. By some authorities, the manuscript of this work is supposed to have been the Quaker narrative 'fraught with worse things than meer mistakes' that hastened Increase Mather's composition of his *Brief History;* but it seems much more probable that Mather was referring to Edward Wharton's *New Englands Present Sufferings* (London, 1675).

scription of the Great Swamp Fight on December 19, 1675, the toughest battle in New England previous to Bunker Hill:

The Connecticut-forces being also arrived on Dec. 18, they presently marched away by break of day, the next morning, through cold and snow, and very amazing difficulties, enough to have *damn'd* any ordinary fortitude, for eighteen miles together. The Indians had a fort raised upon an island of about five or six acres, in the midst of an horrid swamp, which fort, besides its palisadoes, had a kind of wall or hedge about a rod thick encompassing of it. The entrance of this fort was upon a long tree over the water, where but one man could pass at a time, and this was waylaid after such a manner, that if our men had attempted that passage, they must have perished. Only by the help of *Peter* [a friendly Indian] they discovered a *vulnerable heel*, as I may call it, yet left in the fort at one corner, where there was a gap supplied only with long trees about four or five foot from the ground, over which men might force their way; though against this they had built a block-house, from whence a bloody storm of bullets, (and enough to make every man like the poor man in the twelve signs of the Almanack) was to be expected by them that should make their approaches there. Our men came up to the swamp about one a clock, and immediately and courageously pressing through the swamp, from whence the Indians begun to fire upon 'em, they advanced unto that part of the fort which was most accessible: . . . Nothing in the world could be more magnanimous than the spirit which now carried on both leaders and soldiers in the enterprise now before them: They leaped over the trees of death, into the spot of ground where death in all its terrors was to be encountered; the fall of the valiant leaders, no less than six of them, namely, Davenport, Gardiner, Johnson, Gallop, Seely and Marshal (tho' it rendered the place worthy of the name which the Romans put upon the abhorr'd place where their beloved commander Drusus died, namely, *Scelerata Castra*) did but add fire to the rage of the soldiers; they beat the enemy from one shelter to another, till they had utterly driven them out of all their sconces; and at last they set fire to the fort, from which the surviving Indians fled into a vast cedar-swamp at some distance off. . . . . No less than seven hundred fighting Indians were destroyed, as it was afterwards confessed, in this desperate action; besides three hundred which afterwards died of their wounds, and old men, women and children, *sans* number; but of the English about *eighty five* were slain, and an *hundred and fifty* wounded. And now, *sic magnis componere parva!* Reader,

> *And now their mightiest quell'd, the battel swerv'd,*
> *With many an inrode gor'd; deformed rout*
> *Enter'd, and foul disorder; all the ground*
> *With shiver'd armour strown, and on a heap,*
> *Salvage and Sagamore lay overturn'd,*
> *And fiery, foaming blacks; what stood, recoil'd*
> *Orewearied, and with panick fear surpris'd.*[18]

Nevertheless, we cannot award Cotton Mather the literary laurels of King Philip's War. The classic that came out of that desperate struggle is an unpretentious personal narrative by Mrs. Rowlandson, wife of the minister at the frontier settlement of Lancaster. First issued from the local Cambridge press in 1682, Mrs. Rowlandson's narrative was eagerly snapped up, reprinted the same year both here and in London, and reissued again and again in chapbook form, hawked about the countryside for a few pence the copy; even in the present century it has had at least three editions.[19] A few extracts from it will show the qualities that made it so deservedly popular. Instead of the literary flourishes, the long prefaces and complimentary poems with

[18] Mather, *Magnalia* (1702), book vii. 49-50.

[19] *The Soveraignty and Goodness of God . . . being a Narrative of the Captivity and Restauration of Mrs. Mary Rowlandson. . . . Written by Her Own Hand for Her private Use, and now made Publick at the earnest Desire of some Friends* (Cambridge, 1682). It is reprinted in C. H. Lincoln, *Narratives of the Indian Wars* (1913), and separately by the Houghton Mifflin Company, in 1930.

which the three clerical historians begin, Mrs. Rowlandson opens with a bang:

On the tenth of February, 1675, came the Indians in great numbers upon Lancaster. Their first coming was about sun-rising. Hearing the noise of some guns, we looked out: several houses were burning, and the smoke ascending to heaven. There were five persons taken in one house; the father, the mother, and a sucking child they knocked on the head; the other two they took and carried away alive. There were two others, who being out of their garrison upon some occasion, were set upon; one was knocked on the head, the other escaped. Another there was, who, running along, was shot and wounded, and fell down; he begged of them his life, promising them money, (as they told me,) but they would not hearken to him, but knocked him in head, and stripped him naked, and split open his bowels. Another, seeing many of the Indians about his barn, ventured and went out, but was quickly shot down. There were three others belonging to the same garrison who were killed; the Indians getting up upon the roof of the barn, had advantage to shoot down upon them over their fortification. Thus these murderous wretches went on burning and destroying [all] before them.

At length they came and beset our own house, and quickly it was the dolefulest day that ever mine eyes saw. The house stood upon the edge of a hill; some of the Indians got behind the hill, others into the barn, and others behind any thing that would shelter them; from all which places they shot against the house, so that the bullets seemed to fly like hail; and quickly they wounded one man among us, then another, and then a third. About two hours (according to my observation in that amazing time) they had been about the house before they prevailed to fire it (which they did with flax and hemp which they brought out of the barn, there being no defence about the house, only two flankers at two opposite corners, and one of them not finished). They fired it once, and one ventured out and quenched it, but they quickly fired it again, and that took. Now is the dreadful hour come, that I have often heard of (in time of war, as was the case with others) but now mine eyes see it. Some in our house were fighting for their lives, others wallowing in their blood, the house on fire over our heads, and the bloody heathen ready to knock us on the head if we stirred out. Now might we hear mothers and children crying out for themselves, and one another, *Lord, what shall we do?* Then I took my children (and one of my sisters her's) to go forth and leave the house: but as soon as we came to the door, and appeared, the Indians shot so thick, that the bullets rattled against the house, as if one had taken an handful of stones and threw them, so that we were fain to give back. We had six stout dogs belonging to our garrison, but none of them would stir, though [at] another time, if an Indian had come to the door, they were ready to fly upon him and tear him down. The Lord hereby would make us the more to acknowledge his hand, and to see that our help is always in him. But out we must go, the fire increasing, and coming along behind us, roaring, and the Indians gaping before us with their guns, spears, and hatchets, to devour us. No sooner were we out of the house, but my brother-in-law (being before wounded, in defending the house, in or near the throat) fell down dead, whereat the Indians scornfully shouted, and hallooed, and were presently upon him, stripping off his clothes. The bullets flying thick, one went through my side, and the same (as [it] would seem) through the bowels and hand of my dear child in my arms. One of my elder sister's children, named William, had then his leg broken, which the Indians perceiving, they knocked him on the head. Thus were we butchered by those merciless heathens, standing amazed, with the blood running down to our heels.[20]

There is unconscious humor in her remarks on tobacco, when King Philip, during her captivity, offered her a smoke:

Then I went to see King Philip. He bade me come in and sit down, and asked me whether I would smoke it, (a usual compliment now-a-days amongst saints and sinners) but this no way suited me. For though I had formerly used tobacco, yet I had left it ever since I was first taken. It seems to be a bait the devil lays to

[20] Mrs. Mary Rowlandson, *The Narrative of the Captivity and Restoration* (Boston, 1930), pp. 3-6.

make men lose their precious time. I remember with shame, how formerly, when I had taken two or three pipes I was ready for another, such a bewitching thing it is. But I thank God he has now given me power over it. Surely there are many who may be better employed than to lie sucking a stinking tobacco-pipe. . . .

During my abode in this place Philip spake to me to make a shirt for his boy, which I did, for which he gave me a shilling. I offered the money to my master but he bade me keep it, and with it I bought a piece of horse flesh. Afterwards he asked me to make a cap for his boy, for which he invited me to dinner. I went, and he gave me a pancake, about as big as two fingers. It was made of parched wheat, beaten, and fried in bear's grease, but I thought I had never tasted pleasanter meat in my life.[21]

Moreover, this comparatively uneducated woman was responsible for starting a new branch of prose literature: personal narratives of captivity among the Indians (of which John Williams's *Redeemed Captive* is the best known example) that flourished through the eighteenth and early nineteenth centuries.

Two narratives by actual fighters in King Philip's War have been preserved, but neither is in the same class with that of the valiant Mrs. Rowlandson. Captain Thomas Wheeler's *True Narrative of the Lord's Providences in various Dispensations towards Captain Edward Hutchinson of Boston and my self* is the more typical of the time and place. It was published as an appendix to a thanksgiving sermon after the war was over, but did not satisfy the public taste, for there was no reprint until the nineteenth century.[22] Captain Wheeler describes how his com-

[21] *Idem*, pp. 29-30.
[22] The tract in which Wheeler's narrative is incorporated is entitled *A Thankfull Remembrance of Gods Mercy to several Persons at Quabaug or Brookfield, Partly in a Collection of Providences about them, and partly in a Sermon preached by Mr. Edward Bulkley, Pastor of the Church of Christ at*

pany was ambushed by the Indians near Brookfield, and made good its retreat to a garrison house in that then isolated settlement. There

The barbarous heathen pressed upon us in the house with great violence, sending in their shot amongst us like hail through the walls, and shouting as if they would have swallowed us up alive; but our good God wrought wonderfully for us, so that there was but one man wounded within the house, viz.—the said Henry Young, who, looking out of the garret window that evening, was mortally wounded by a shot, of which wound he died within two dayes after. There was the same day another man slain, but not in the house; a son of Serjeant Prichard's adventuring out of the house wherein we were, to his Father's house not far from it, to fetch more goods out of it, was caught by those cruel enemies as they were coming towards us, who cut off his head, kicking it about like a foot-ball, and then putting it upon a pole, they set it up before the door of his Father's house in our sight.

The night following the said blow, they did roar against us like so many wild bulls, sending in their shot amongst us till towards the moon rising, which was about three of the clock; at which time they attempted to fire our house by hay and other combustible matter which they brought to one corner of the house, and set it on fire. Whereupon some of our company were necessitated to expose themselves to very great danger to put it out. Simon Davis, one of the three appointed by my self as Captain, to supply my place by reason of my wounds, as aforesaid, he being of a lively spirit, encouraged the souldiers within the house to fire upon the Indians; and also those that adventured out to put out the fire, (which began to rage and kindle upon the house side,) with these and the like words, that *God is with us, and fights for us, and will deliver us out of the hands of these heathen;* which expressions of his the Indians hearing, they shouted and scoffed, saying: *now see*

Concord (Cambridge, 1676); copy in the New York Public Library. Wheelers' narrative is reprinted in *Collections New Hampshire Historical Society,* II (1827), 5-23. Joseph I. Foot, *An Historical Discourse Delivered at West Brookfield* (West Brookfield, 1843), and *Old South Leaflets,* no. 155, from which my quotation is taken.

how your God delivers you, or will deliver you, sending in many shots whilst our men were putting out the fire. But the Lord of hosts wrought very graciously for us, in preserving our bodies both within and without the house from their shot, and our house from being consumed by fire, we had but two men wounded in that attempt of theirs, but we apprehended that we killed divers of our enemies.

The Indians' 'several stratagems to fire us' are told in great detail; and Captain Wheeler admits that the garrison would have been overcome 'had not the only wise God (blessed for ever) been pleased to send us . . . the worshipful Major Willard with Captain Parker of Groaton, and forty-six men more with five Indians to relieve us in the low estate into which we were brought.' The honoured Major and his company surpassed 'those beastly men, our enemies skilful to destroy' and the Indians decamped, after burning every other building in the village. And so Captain Wheeler's company, with such people of Brookfield as had not been slaughtered, were able to make good their escape. 'Oh that we could praise the Lord for his great goodness towards us!' concludes the pious Captain:

Praised be his name, that though he took away some of us, yet was pleased to spare so many of us, and adde unto our dayes; he help us whose souls he hath delivered from death, and eyes from tears, and feet from falling, to walk before him in the land of the living, till our great change come, and to sanctifie his name in all his ways about us, that both our afflictions, and our mercies may quicken us to live more to his glory all our dayes.

One other combatant, Captain Benjamin Church, left a personal narrative of the war. It was dictated to his son

Thomas, and published at Boston in 1716, with a title that marked the passing of the puritan century. Mrs. Rowland-son's publisher made a concession to the Wonder-working Providence school of thought by beginning the title to her Narrative with *The Soveraignty and Goodness of God;* Wheeler's conviction that the Lord was his ally, he made plain to all; but Church's account is called *Entertaining Passages relating to Philip's War.* Entertaining the narrative certainly is, rapid in movement and robust in flavor; my impression is that the literary son took down the language of his fighting father accurately. Even so, the doughty Colonel, who had fought two more wars against the Indians since 1676, felt obliged to pay his tribute to the God of Hosts in the preface:

> Through the Grace of God, I was Spirited for that work and Direction in it was renewed to me day by day . . . I was ever very sensible of my own littleness and unfitness, to be imployed in such Great Services; but calling to mind that God is strong, I endeavoured to put all my confidence in Him, and by His Almighty power was carried through every difficult action: and my desire is that His name may have the Praise.[23]

Mrs. Rowlandson, Captain Wheeler, and Colonel Church were unlearned people, who wrote plain, straightforward tales of their personal experiences, without conscious art. Very different in character are the historical works of Cotton Mather, the universal genius of New England at the close of the seventeenth century.

---

[23] Preface to 1716 edition, as reproduced in *The History of King Philip's War by Benjamin Church* (H. M. Dexter, ed.), Boston, 1865. This was the fifth edition of *Entertaining Passages.*

Cotton had the misfortune to be an infant prodigy, who never succeeded in sublimating the egoism and exhibitionism that are apt to make precocious children offensive. The son of Increase Mather, born in 1663, he entered college in his twelfth year, an unwholesomely pious and priggish boy. When the sophomores attempted to kick some sense into Cotton, he was taken home to be tutored by his father, returning only to take the examinations and receive his degree at the age of fifteen. On that occasion he was complimented by President Oakes on his two names, representing the highest piety, wisdom, and erudition in New England. And Cotton Mather's life was an attempt to fulfill the expectations of his elders, and disappoint the low opinion of those young hoodlums who had knocked him about in college.[24] Shortly after his eighteenth birthday, Cotton became assistant to his father in the North Church; and for the rest of his life he remained a minister of Boston, eagerly devouring every book that came his way, telling people their duty on every public question and private problem, and tossing off several printed works annually; the total number reached the incredible figure of four hundred and fifty. His learning was only equaled by his conceit, and by the unpopularity which has pursued him ever since. Hardly a writer before the present century has said a good word for Cotton Mather; and he has become the scapegoat for most of the offenses which his community committed against nineteenth-century notions of toleration and liberalism.

Cotton Mather published history, biography, essays, ser-

[24] Lucien Price, in *N.E.Q.*, II, 327-31.

mons, fables, books of practical piety, theology, and verse.[25] He was sensitive to the stylistic currents of his day, and wrote in several of them, even in the manner of the "Spectator" essays; but on the whole he preferred the prolix English of certain Jacobean writers. For, as he explained in his one essay on style, the reader should have something for his money: 'the real Excellency of a Book will never ly on *saying of little*.' His great work, the *Magnalia Christi Americana*—or Ecclesiastical History of New England—

> *In that quaint* Magnalia Christi, *with all strange and marvellous things,*
> *Heaped up huge and undigested, like the chaos Ovid sings.*[26]

was the most ambitious attempt to prove that God had showered special providences on New England. It was all written before 1700, though not printed until 1702. Almost anything you can say about the *Magnalia* will be true, in part; for it has a bit of everything, in matter, style, and method. The author could be disarmingly candid, as in the passages where he describes without mincing words the vices of certain pious-seeming church members; yet he could suppress the truth, as in the flabby biography of a minister who had been expelled from his parish after attempting to administer the Lord's Supper while in an advanced state of intoxication. He was both credulous and critical, kindly and harsh. The larger part of the *Magnalia*

---

[25] K. B. Murdock, ed., introduction to *Selections from Cotton Mather* (Harcourt, Brace and Company, 1926), p. xxxi.
[26] Whittier, "The Garrison of Cape Ann."

is written in a prolix, surcharged, parenthetical and con-
ceited style, modeled on that of Burton's *Anatomy of Melancholy*. Yet Cotton Mather could write clear, nervous,
concise English when he would, as we have seen in his account of the Swamp Fight. "The Memorable Action at
Wells" in *Decennium Luctuosum* is positively thrilling.[27]
His biography of John Eliot, first printed in 1691 and included in the *Magnalia*, is still the best life of the Indians'
Apostle; and *Pietas in Patriam, or the Life of William
Phips*, is as good reading now as when it first appeared.
Mather glossed over the vulgarities and immoralities of this
self-made hero, as was only decent to the memory of a
parishioner; but in terse, vigorous English he describes
enough fighting, treasure-hunting, mutinies, shipwrecks,
and other adventures to satisfy the most red-blooded
reader.[28] The lives of Eliot and Phips, and some of the
others in the *Magnalia*, are a worthy beginning for New
England biographical literature.[29]

It may also be claimed for Cotton Mather that he was
the first native-born political pamphleteer of his province.
So long as their charter governments endured, the New
Englanders had little occasion to write political pamphlets.
Roger Williams had indeed shown his skill at that form of
literature, and set a standard of magnanimity toward op-

[27] Boston, 1699; reprinted as chapter vii in book vii of the *Magnalia*, and in
C. H. Lincoln, *Narratives of the Indian Wars* (1913); the Wells action is on
pp. 232-40.
[28] Reprinted in the *Magnalia*, and Murdock's *Selections from Cotton
Mather*.
[29] The earliest New England biography, however, is Increase Mather's
Life and Death of Richard Mather (Cambridge, 1670), a work wholly devoid
of art. For editions, see T. J. Holmes, *Increase Mather: Bibliography*, I,
323-27.

ponents that unfortunately did not last, while Samuel Gorton attained heights of vituperation where nobody could follow him. Robert Child and Edward Winslow exchanged literary insults in London, with *New-Englands Jonas Cast Up* and *New-Englands Salamander*, and a number of repatriated New Englanders, such as Hugh Peter, Thomas Weld, and Nathaniel Ward, entered the lists under the Commonwealth. But these were men who had been born and educated in the old country. Although the New England colonies had annual elections, they did not countenance political speeches and campaign literature. But in 1685 they were placed under the arbitrary government of Sir Edmund Andros. His control of the press prevented the people from printing what they thought of him; but on receiving news of the probable success of William of Orange early in 1689, the New Englanders deposed Sir Edmund Andros, resumed their charter governments, and proceeded to justify themselves in a series of political tracts.

On April 18, 1689, the very day of the revolt in Boston, *The Declaration, of the Gentlemen, Merchants, and Inhabitants of Boston, and the Country adjacent*, was read from the balcony of the Town House to the crowd below. This document had been drafted by Cotton Mather, then twenty-six years old; it was shortly after printed in both Boston and London.[30] Mather must have written the *Declaration* in a great hurry, yet it is most artfully composed. King James's Dominion government is tied up to the famous Popish Plot, and Sir Edmund's policy is de-

---

[30] C. M. Andrews, *Narratives of the Insurrections* (Original Narratives), p. 168.

scribed in just such terms as to appeal to those Englishmen who had driven King James out, and called King William in. Nothing, of course, is said about Sir Edmund's introduction of Anglican worship, his long overdue breaking of the puritan monopoly in religion. One of the paragraphs may be quoted as a sample of Mather's political style:

> The Government was no sooner in these Hands, but Care was taken to load Preferments principally upon such Men as were Strangers to and Haters of the People: and every ones Observation hath noted, what Qualifications recommended a Man to publick Offices and Employments. . . . But of all our Oppressors we were chiefly squeez'd by a Crew of abject Persons fetched from New York, to be Tools of the Adversary, standing at our right Hand; by these were extraordinary and intollerable Fees extorted from every one upon all Occasions, without any Rules but those of their own insatiable Avarice and Beggary; and even the probate of a Will must now cost as many Pounds perhaps as it did Shillings heretofore; nor could a small Volume contain the other Illegalities done by these Horse-leeches in the two or three Years that they have been sucking of us; and what Laws they made it was as impossible for us to know, as dangerous for us to break. . . .

As in 1775, the Boston rebels made a point of placing their version of events in the hands of the English public before the royal officials had any opportunity to state the other side. Deacon Nathaniel Byfield of Bristol, Rhode Island, wrote *An Account of the Late Revolution in New-England* only eleven days after the event, which Increase Mather had printed in London in June, 1689, as a preface to son Cotton's *Declaration*.[31] This gave the Bostonians a

---

[31] *Idem*, pp. 168-69; reprinted, pp. 170-75. There was also an Edinburgh edition.

six months' start, at least; for it was not until 1690 that there appeared in London an elaborate defense of the Andros regime, and reply to Mather, by John Palmer, one of the 'abject Persons fetched from New York' to whom Cotton Mather had adverted.[32] The same year was printed *New-England's Faction Discovered*, probably by Joseph Dudley or Edward Randolph.[33] But the New Englanders kept the presses hot pouring forth replies. Samuel Sewall the diarist is joint author of *The Revolution in New England Justified*,[34] an extremely wordy pamphlet that answered Palmer point by point; and a group of former councilors of the Dominion, led by William Stoughton, printed *A Narrative of the Proceedings of Sir Edmond Androsse and his Complices* that told their personal experiences of his 'despotism.'[35]

At the time of the Glorious Revolution of 1688 Increase Mather was in England seeking relief for his colony from James II, and hoping to obtain restoration of the colony and college charters. During his residence in London, he issued four tracts attacking the Dominion government and defending the Revolution. But the most interesting New England printed pamphlet on the 1689 uprising was on the other side. *The People's Right to Election*, printed on the Bradford press at Philadelphia in 1689,[36] was the work

---

[32] *An Impartial Account of the State of New England*. Reprinted in *Andros Tracts* (Boston, Prince Society, 1868), I, 21-41.

[33] London, 1690, reprinted in Andrews, *Narratives of the Insurrections*, pp. 253-67.

[34] Boston, 1691. Reprinted in *Andros Tracts*, I, 63-132.

[35] Boston, 1691. Reprinted *ibid.*, pp. 133-47, and in Andrews, *Narratives*, pp. 239-49.

[36] Reprinted in *Andros Tracts*, II, 85-102, and *Collections of the Connecticut Historical Society*, I, 57-81.

of a native scholar and conservative, Gershom Bulkeley. Son of the first minister of Concord, and son-in-law of President Chauncy, Bulkeley had lived in Connecticut since his graduation from the college in 1655, as minister of Wethersfield, physician, army surgeon in King Philip's War, and official under Andros. A careful study of the life and works of this curiously versatile man is long overdue. J. Hammond Trumbull declared that 'overweening self-importance, obstinate adherence to his own opinions or prejudices, a litigious spirit and the peculiarities of his political creed, detracted from his usefulness, and kept him almost continually at strife with his parish, his neighbours or the government of the colony.'[37] That may well be; but Bulkeley was a close friend and associate of John Winthrop, Jr., sharing the Governor's interest in natural and occult sciences, and he was easily the first scholar in Connecticut after the Governor's death. *The People's Right to Election* shows that he also had a sound knowledge of constitutional law; for he pointed out that after the Connecticut charter had been legally vacated, it was nothing less than rebellion to elect an assembly as though the charter were in force. Bulkeley argues convincingly the legality of the Andros government, in which he himself was a magistrate, and humorously advises the people against hasty action. Orders are expected from William and Mary for settling and regulating the government, so why anticipate matters? 'And the Town-Clerke of *Ephesus* could say, that these things being so, *you ought to be quiet & do nothing rashly*.' In calm and dignified language he reminds the people that they are subjects of the King, and have no

[37] *Andros Tracts*, II, 84.

right to assume powers of self-government without his permission.

Fortunately for Connecticut, their Majesties had many more pressing objects of their attention. Month after month slipped by, and no word came from Whitehall. Bulkeley and the like-minded grew more and more restive at paying taxes to a *de facto* government acting under a nullified charter. It does not appear that the Connecticut government did anything to molest them personally; but in September, 1692, this little 'tory' group addressed their complaints to Governor Fletcher of New York, for transmission to the King. Their Address and Petition was accompanied by "Some Objections against the Pretended Government in Connecticut " by Gershom Bulkeley.[38] In the meantime, James Fitch of Connecticut had circulated two manuscript replies to Bulkeley's printed tract. In order, as he supposed, to answer these, and to bolster up his argument against the resumed charter government, Bulkeley amplified "Some Objections" into a lengthy manuscript entitled "Will and Doom, or the Miserie of Connecticut by and under an Usurped and Arbitrary Power." The preface is dated December 12, 1692.[39]

This Connecticut controversy has never received the attention it merits because, for want of a printing press in that colony, the several tracts were circulated in manuscript and promptly forgotten. Of Fitch's two pamphlets, no copy is now known to exist. And when Bulkeley's works

[38] Printed in *Documents relative to Colonial History of New York*, III, 849-54.

[39] Printed with introduction by C. J. Hoadley, from the copy in the Public Record Office, in *Collections of the Connecticut Historical Society*, II (1895), 69-269.

were recovered from manuscript depositories and printed, they ran so counter to what had become a Connecticut superstition on the presumed democracy of that colony, that few people paid any attention to them. "Will and Doom" is unquestionably the ablest colonial writing that came out of the 'Glorious Revolution'; and one of the ablest of colonial political tracts prior to the American Revolution.

In the preface, Bulkeley adverts to the defamation of his little party

as if they were enemies to government and friends to none but popish, French, and arbitrary government, yea papists, wicked incendiaries, disturbers of the peace, (because they endeavoured and desired that the government and peace might have been preserved,) Jacobites, Edmundites, such as serve the devil and the pope, reprobates, &c. And, having thus dressed us in bearskins, they sport themselves in baiting of us. All this while, as they have no shadow of any warrant from their majesties for the exercise of this government to which they now pretend . . .

Having thus compelled us, they must excuse us if we lay open the naked truth, and represent things in their own colors. There is a time to speak, as well as a time to be silent, and truth speaks as the thing is. . . .

After a few pages of argument from the Bible, Bulkeley declares the political principles which he believes to be of God, and which should determine the polity of Connecticut. I regret that we have insufficient space to quote the whole, but these passages show clearly enough Bulkeley's drift, and the reason why this frontier Filmer has never become a hero of American history:

That authority of government is a right of ruling over others. That civil government is the ordinance of God.

That all lawful civil authority is (not of man but) of God, and is founded in right; and it is of God not only by permission but by justification and donation; it is ordained by him and given by him; the kingdom, the power, the throne and the judgment are his.

Monarchy is the best form or kind of civil government.

The king of England is (as was said of Solomon) the chief or supreme governor in all his dominions, over all persons and in all causes.

The king is the minister of God for our good, and the fountain of all lawful civil authority within all his dominions. . . .

Laws are essential to government. God himself (with reverence be it spoken) cannot punish his own creature without a law broken.

The laws of nature and right reason are the standard of all human laws. *Ipsae etenim leges cupiunt ut jure regantur*, and whatsoever is unreasonable is, therefore, unlawful. An unreasonable law is a law against law.

Unlawful, usurped, or tyrannical authority is truly no authority, and is call'd authority but by a catachresis, because it is not of God, neither ordained by him, tho' it may be permitted by him. There is no power but of God: therefore the power which is not of God is no power: an idol is nothing in the world.

We owe no obedience to any man contrary to that obedience we owe to God; and, by proportion, we owe no obedience to any inferior governors contrary to that obedience we owe to the king.

Legal obedience to lawful authority, whether active or passive, tho' it be unto death, is no slavery, but due subjection, which we are to yield for conscience sake and for the Lord's sake.

Rebellion against the king is a mediate rebellion against God, and it is like the sin of witchcraft. . . .

Liberty and property are natural rights, grounded upon the essential liberty of man's will, given him by his Creator, and upon the individuality of his person, and so belongs to every man by the law of nature: there can be no stealing against the 8th command, (which is a part of the law of nature,) if there be no such thing as property in nature. . . .

We think that the Colony of Connecticut is *de jure* (we wish we could say *de facto*) as much subject to the government of the crown of England as London or Oxford. The realm of England is the mother that bare us: we are a swarm out of that hive: we are natural subjects of that crown, born within the king's dominions: our allegiance is original or natural, and perpetual: their majesties are our political father and mother, but we are a great way off, and the more remote we are from them the nearer we are to violence and injustice, and the more remediless; and, therefore, have so much the more need of a speedy and thorough good settlement.

The main body of "Will and Doom" is equally interesting. Bulkeley first reviews Connecticut history. The Fundamental Orders naturally are abominable in his sight; and the government erected by those arrogating to themselves the title of freemen, 'in imitation (as it seems) of the corporation government erected in the Massachusetts,' carried on pretty much as it pleased under the Royal Charter of 1662. 'This corporation is stept into the throne and become king, or tantamount.' Citing one Connecticut law after another for the passage of which there was no color of authority in the Charter, he concludes, 'in fine, we have no law but Will and Doom, no security of anything: if we have any case depending, we have nothing to expect but the discretion of the court.' In other words, Connecticut had established a government of men and not of laws. 'Our judges had need be men of greater wisdom and integrity than we can find among them, else this latitude of law must needs make our yoke very heavy and intolerable.'

Many pages of argument are required to prove that charter government ceased in 1687 (in spite of the Charter Oak!) and that the magistrates commissioned by Sir Edmund Andros (including the author) were the lawful government of Connecticut. And he makes the interesting point that the 'tyranny' of Andros for the first time established in Connecticut the liberties of an English subject.

For the Charter of 1662 (and the same might be said of the Fundamental Orders of 1639, and the Massachusetts Bay Charter of 1629) gave no liberties to the 'People,' only to the 'freemen,' *i.e.*, members of the Corporation created thereby, and those to whom they subsequently extended the franchise. 'The other people of Connecticut, who yet were many times the greater number of the people,' had nothing to do with it. Instead of Andros 'invading the liberties' of the Connecticut people, 'The truth is, we had been so deprived of all law and liberty, and made so blind, that we had never yet known the liberties of free and natural subjects if it had not been for Sir Edmund Andros his government.' And, asserts the author with considerable humor, many of the assemblymen were only too glad of the change of regime:

> Do they think that nobody took notice how Sir E. A. was caressed by them? How brisk and jocund they were at that time? What liberal healths some of them (for all indeed are not addicted to such frolicks) drank then, and afterwards in remembrance of it? Were not all his excellencies proceedings fair and candid? Did he use any fraud or put any force upon them?

Bulkeley becomes rather tedious when he tries to prove that the mere holding of an election in May, 1689, after Andros had been imprisoned in Boston, was a horrid rebellion; but his bitter humor returns when contrasting the 'Will and Doom' taxation of the restored charter government with the mild if paternal sway of Andros.

> If ever there was or can be a Turkish, French, arbitrary and tyrannical government in Connecticut, it is so now. They cry out against Sir Ed. Andross, but their little finger is thicker than his

loins. We will not say that nothing was arbitrary or amiss in Sir E. A.'s time; but now all is arbitrary, and we have nothing but Will and Doom. . . .

Sir Edmund Andros rates them a penny, and they find fault: they have no more right than he, if so much, and yet they rate us groat after groat, and if he will not pay they call us rebels, and the prison is good enough for us. We had no 4d. nor 8d. in Sir Edmund's time.

Well, but, say they, it is for support of the government, and government must be supported. Why, but Sir Edmund's rates were for the support of the government also, and if your corporation be not able to support its government, let it fall. But, say they, Sir Edmund imposed his rates by advice of his council, chosen by the king, in which we had no vote, without any assembly of our election, and this was not right. Why, so the corporation imposes taxes on us by the advice of their common council chosen by their freemen, wherein we have no votes, without any assembly of our election, and this is as wrong as the other.

Bulkeley is certainly not afraid to go the whole way. He pays no homage to representative government. He would rather Sir Edmund Andros rate him a penny, than the 'corporation of Connecticut' rate him eight pence. One able ruler is far better than 'omnipotent democraticks.' General assemblies are no use but to run up taxes and to 'ruin the country; and this they will certainly do, if they be let alone.' There follows some amusing though unfair satire on the ambitious military expeditions of Connecticut during King William's War. And the reverend author concludes:

Sovereignty in a king is a sceptre of gold, but in the hands of a subject it is a rod of iron: and so we find it. No man in the world so sovereign as usurping subjects: they are as absolute and arbitrary as the great Turk, so far as they dare to go. It is now above three years and an half that we have been drudging under this tyrannical anarchy, for the want of their majesties lawful government, and we are almost destroyed by it. We are quite weary and sick of Will and Doom, and can bear it no longer, but must either betake ourselves to their majesties for their protection and government, or we must submit ourselves and posterity to become the hereditary servants of servants and scorn of fools, or we must take up arms, or, lastly, quit the dominion. We choose the first course. . . .

But alas for Bulkeley and his little party of loyalists; they were more royalist than the King. Queen Mary in 1694 announced 'our gracious intention to continue our royal protection' to the people under their existing government; which undoubtedly represented what the great majority desired. Rhode Island was similarly indulged; but Massachusetts, in spite of her vigorous pamphlet campaign, and the persistent lobbying of Increase Mather, was too important a trading center to be given such complete autonomy. The diplomacy of Increase Mather procured for the new Province of Massachusetts Bay a charter in such form that a generous measure of self-government was assured; and this result, though displeasing to most of the people, was ably defended by him in *A Brief Account concerning Several of the Agents of New-England: with some remarks on the New Charter*.[40] The accuracy of this narrative, says Professor Andrews, 'is beyond impeachment, as every statement of fact . . . can be supported by references to the journals of the houses, the acts of the Privy Council, and the journal and papers of the Lords of Trade. As a defense of his own course the narrative is convincing,

[40] London, 1691. Reprinted in *Andros Tracts,* II, 271-96, and Andrews, *Narratives of the Insurrections,* pp. 276-97.

and as an argument in behalf of the new charter it is a state paper of high rank.' [41]

Thus, before the puritan century came to an end, political literature had begun; and in these tracts of the Revolution of 1689, we can already discern the qualities of the literature of 1765-1775. A generation that had produced little but sermons, theological tracts, and histories of Indian wars, was nevertheless prepared for political disputation; and, during the next seventy years, New England writers showed the same skill in baiting royal governors and showing up tory sophistry, as formerly they had employed in fighting the Indians and beating the devil.

[41] *Ibid.*, pp. 274-75.

IX. VERSE

New england was founded at a period when almost everyone who could read at all, read poetry, and many attempted to write it; when all grammar-school boys were taught to write Latin verse, and almost everyone sang the songs that are found in the countless 'garlands' of the day. Colonial conditions are never favorable to poetry; you will not find much place in anthologies of English verse for the poets of Canada, Australia, South Africa, the West Indies, and the thirteen American Colonies. Great poetry is not commonly produced by tillers of the soil, nor yet in a garret under conditions of semistarvation; by and large, the great poets of modern times have flourished in a society that was capable of giving them adequate support, by court pensions or offices, ecclesiastical livings, professorial chairs, or a wide market for their productions. Poetry almost requires a cultivated leisure class, not only for supporting the poet, but for giving him the necessary stimulus and criticism to keep him up to the mark. Although it is difficult to compare poetry of one language with that of another, it is probable that the best American colonial verse was written in Spanish, in Mexico and Peru, where there was a wealthy and cultured leisure class, and a viceregal court that rewarded occasional verse by profitable offices in the state and church. French Canada, however, seems to have been barren of any form of literary expression, except travelers' tales and Jesuit Relations; and in the English colonies, puritan New England was the only section that put forth any appreciable quantity of verse in the seventeenth century.

Approaching literature from the social rather than the critical point of view, I cannot dismiss early New England verse-makers as negligible merely because they are not to be mentioned in the same breath with Milton, Donne, and Dryden. Anne Bradstreet may not have been a really great poetess although, if we compare her work with that of her English contemporary Katherine Phillips, the 'Matchless Orinda' who was so much admired in mid-century London, she does not come off badly. So I shall approach poetry as an expression of the thought, feeling, and emotions of the times, or as a literary record of contemporary life.

Poetry, like other manifestations of intellectual life in seventeenth-century New England, was dominated by religion. College students relished the pastoral and amorous and witty poetry of their day, copied it into their notebooks, and doubtless learned some of it by heart; some of them tried without success to imitate it in the only medium at their disposal, the annual almanacs. Benjamin Tompson attempted an epic of King Philip's War, and some of Anne Bradstreet's best poems are lyrical; and I suppose we may allow them also to be amorous, even though addressed to her husband. But for the most part, early New England verse was religious both in motive and expression. Here, again, the puritan was limited by the nature of his religion. He abolished all the traditional church holidays, and he was very much opposed to symbols, such as the cross and the sacred heart; hence he cut himself off from a whole range of devotional and festival poetry open to the

Catholic. Milton, indeed, wrote the "Ode on the Morning of Christ's Nativity"—but Milton was first a poet, only secondarily a puritan. Consequently the New Englanders, in their religious poetry, were confined to four principal forms: rhymed translations from the Bible to be sung as hymns in divine worship; didactic poetry intended to drive home some portion of the puritan creed, religious lyrics expressing the poet's own emotions, and controversial poetry aimed at some other sect than the writer's own.

As the two Bay Psalm Books, *The Whole Booke of Psalmes* (1640), and the much better version, *The Psalms Hymns and Spiritual Songs of the Old and New Testament* (1651), were by puritans born and educated in England, I shall say nothing further about them here,[1] but will proceed directly to the didactic poetry of Michael Wigglesworth. The celebrated, not to say notorious, author of *The Day of Doom*, who is generally regarded as a typical poet of the puritan colonies, was typical only in his background, his sincerity, and his deeply religious feeling. The son of plain Goodman Wigglesworth, he was brought out to New Haven in his seventh year, in 1638, prepared for college under Ezekiel Cheever, and graduated at the head of his class in 1651. For three years thereafter he served as college tutor, and apparently was one of the most beloved and successful who held that office. His glowing oration in praise of oratory we have already quoted.

---

[1] For the same reason, I have omitted to mention William Morrell's *New-England, or a Brief Ennaration* (1625), the drinking song in Thomas Morton's *New English Canaan*, the doggerel verse in Edward Johnson's *Wonder-Working Providence* (1654) and William Wood's *New Englands Prospect* (1635), or the narrative poetry of John Wilson, which is reprinted in K. B. Murdock, *Handkerchiefs from Paul* (1927).

Wigglesworth was a loving and affectionate tutor to his Harvard pupils: yet he wrote that dreadful epic *The Day of Doom*, which pictures Jehovah as a God of wrath, and Christ as an implacable and merciless judge consigning to eternal hell-fire the souls of men who had refused his proffer of saving grace. It is Michelangelo's Last Judgment, in jogging ballad metre.

I dislike making selections from *The Day of Doom*,[2] since it works up to a climax in a highly artistic manner; but you will not expect us to print the whole. At the day of doom, after silencing with the most blighting casuistry the reprobates' petition for grace, Christ pronounces their sentence in these words:

> *Ye sinful wights and cursed sprights,*
> *that work Iniquity,*
> *Depart together from me for ever*
> *to endless Misery;*
> *Your portion take in yonder Lake,*
> *where Fire and Brimstone flameth;*
> *Suffer the smart which your desert,*
> *as its due wages claimeth.*

Then comes the climax:

> *As chaff that's dry, as dust doth fly*
> *before the Northern wind,*
> *Right so are they chaséd away,*
> *and can no Refuge find.*

[2] Of the first edition, 1662, no copy exists; the best modern reprint is edited by K. B. Murdock (New York: The Spiral Press, 1929). See J. W. Dean on Wigglesworth in the *New England Historical and Genealogical Register*, XVII (1863), 129-46, and separate reprint.

These, and other verses quoted in this chapter, have been edited to the extent of modernizing the spelling and punctuation; but most of the capitals are left, as they were intended for emphasis.

They hasten to the Pit of Woe,
*   guarded by Angels stout,*
Who to fulfil Christ's holy Will,
*   attend this wicked Rout;*

With Iron bands they bind their hands
*   and cursèd feet together,*
And cast them all, both great and small,
*   into that Lake forever,*
Where day and night, without respite,
*   they wail, and cry and howl*
For tort'ring pain which they sustain
*   in Body and in Soul.*

Josiah Quincy, a late sufferer under fire-and-brimstone sermons, records that the Andover meetinghouse was so frigid in winter that 'the vivid description of those sultry regions to which the vast majority of the human race were hastening lost something of the terror they were meant to excite.' [3] Certainly the First Church of Malden, over which Master Michael Wigglesworth officiated, wanted no central heating plant in the coldest of old-fashioned winters.

There are two hundred and twenty-four stanzas of *The Day of Doom*. It was the most popular poem that New England has ever known. The eighteen hundred copies of the first edition of 1662 were snapped up within a year, which means that in New England about one in every five-and-twenty persons bought a copy; and few there must have been who did not read it, or have it read to them. Such a circulation is beyond the wildest dreams of the most high-pressure publisher of modern fiction. There were at least three more American and two London editions in the

[3] Josiah Quincy, *Figures of the Past, from the Leaves of Old Journals* (Boston, 1883), p. 7.

seventeenth century; and at least six in the next century, beside divers others of which no copy has survived, printed on broadsheets and hawked about the country like ballads. A little over a century ago there were old people in New England who could repeat the whole of it by heart. Book of the Month, forsooth! *The Day of Doom* was the Book of the Era; happily Cotton Mather's prophecy that it would prove the Book of the Ages was not fulfilled.

This poem has a social significance far transcending its quality as poetry. For in simple words that everyone would understand, and in a metre that was easily memorized, it carried home to every man, woman, and child the essential message of New England's intellectual class: that man was free to choose eternal bliss or eternal damnation; that his salvation rested on his will to believe, on his own efforts to meet that saving grace which Our Lord proffered to him:

> *Not for his* Can *is any man*
> *adjudgéd unto Hell,*
> *But for his* Will *to do what's ill,*
> *and nilling to do well.*

Very seldom in history has an intellectual class succeeded so well in breaking through to the common consciousness. Another century passed before any appreciable number of the New England people were open to any sweeter conception of God than that of *The Day of Doom*.

Yet the author of this macabre ballad was no beefy sadist, but 'a little, feeble shadow of a man,' so tender of conscience that he feared lest an inordinate zeal for his pupils' progress and welfare would draw off his own affections from Christ; so sensitive that it caused him keen anguish to decide whether or not on the Sabbath he should inform a neighbor that his barn door was banging. And his recently published diary [4] indicates that he frequently succumbed to the sins of the flesh. It was his intense desire to save men from the dreadful fate impending over them that drove him to perpetrate this ethical monstrosity. What cared he for the nightmare terror his words would bring to generations of little children, if he could but awaken them to the awful consequences of sin? So to describe his vision he drew on all the logic he had learned at college, and all the artistry that was in him. Artistry was never employed more conscientiously in a moral cause; but many a better cause enjoyed less artistry:

> *And by and by the flaming Sky*
> *shall drop like molten Lead*
> *About their ears, t'increase their fears,*
> *and aggravate their dread.*

> * * *

> *For day and night, in their despight,*
> *their torment's smoak ascendeth.*
> *Their pain and grief have no relief,*
> *their anguish never endeth.*
> *There must they ly and never dy,*
> *though dying every day:*
> *There must they dying ever ly,*
> *and not consume away.*

The Day of Doom was not Wigglesworth's only poem. In 1699 appeared *Meat out of the Eater; or, Meditations concerning the necessity and usefulness of Afflictions unto*

God's Children, which had many printings in the colonial period.[5] But the most artistic of his poems was not printed in his own day. It was called "God's Controversy with New England, written in the time of the great drought, Anno 1662"[6] and shows a much more flexible art than *The Day of Doom*, for the metre is varied with the theme. The ballad stanza is employed to describe the pristine vigor and simplicity of New England, which God had transformed into a safe and peaceful refuge from the troubles of Europe. But the people have not lived up to God's expectation of them. The Almighty addresses them in tones of stern reproof:

> *What should I do with such a stiff-neckt race?*
> *How shall I ease me of such foes as they?*
> *What shall befall despisers of my Grace?*
> *I'll surely bear their candle-stick away,*
> *And lamps put out. Their glorious noon-day light*
> *I'll quickly turn into a dark Egyptian night.*

The ballad form returns to depict the terrible consequences of God's wrath to come, of which a drought the previous summer was simply the first installment. But the poem closes on a high note of love and faith, addressed to the poet's own countrymen:

> *Ah dear New England! dearest land to me;*
> *Which unto God hast hitherto been dear,*
> *And mayst be still more dear than formerlie,*
> *If to his voice thou wilt incline thine ear.*

[5] Bibliography in Oscar Wegelin, *Early American Poetry* (1930), I, 90-91.
[6] Printed in *Proc. M.H.S.*, XII, 82-93; analyzed by F. O. Matthiessen, in *N.E.Q.*, I, 500-3.

Consider well and wisely what the rod
Wherewith thou art from yeer to yeer chastized,
Instructeth thee. Repent, and turn to God,
Who will not have his nurture be despized.

*   *   *

Cheer on, sweet souls, my heart is with you all,
And shall be with you, maugre Sathan's might,
And whereso'ere this body be a thrall,
Still in New-England shall be my delight.[7]

From Michael Wigglesworth we gladly turn to Anne
Bradstreet, one of the two poets of early New England
whose work has endured; and the greatest American poetess
before Emily Dickinson. Although Anne came over at the
age of eighteen, already two years a wife, we may fairly
claim her as a daughter of New England; for all her poetry
was written here, and it showed a steady improvement as
she became older and more remote from the springs of inspiration abroad. It is a brave chapter in early American history, the story of this young gentlewoman brought up in
the luxury and refinement of the Earl of Lincoln's household, delicate in health and tortured by a recurrent illness
that physicians could not cure, faithfully performing in a
frontier village the duties of a magistrate's wife and devoted mother to eight children, yet weaving her thoughts
of God, her love for her kind, and the wild beauty of the
untamed New England countryside into verse that still
endures.

Like much colonial and provincial poetry, Anne Bradstreet's earliest verse was imitative, inspired by the scrip-

[7] *Proc. M.H.S.*, XII, 90, 93.

tural epics of Guillaume du Bartas, which Joshua Sylvester had translated before she was born. The strained language and euphuistic conceits of Sylvester's Du Bartas were a bad influence on Anne; but they gained her an early hearing, which original poetry might not have done. Her brother-in-law John Woodbridge took to London a manuscript of her imitative poems which had passed the rounds of an admiring circle of friends, and had them printed in 1650 as *The Tenth Muse lately sprung up in America, By a Gentlewoman in those parts.* This was the book that was the subject of Anne's playful verses, 'At thy return my blushing was not small,' which I have already quoted. The misprints were many and shocking. 'French Lewis' the king, for instance, became 'French Jewes' in print; but even if properly proofread, *The Tenth Muse* would hardly have secured Anne permanent fame, although it is mentioned as "not yet wholly extinct" by Edward Phillips, in his *Theatrum Poetarum* of 1675. Seeing her works in print cured Anne of the Du Bartas disease. Henceforth she obeyed Sidney's injunction, 'Look in thy heart, and write.' The second edition of her poetry, *Several Poems compiled with great variety of Wit and Learning, full of Delight,* edited by one of her sons and printed at Boston six years after her death, in 1678, included much that she had written in the last twenty years of her life; but many of her best poems, which her son did not publish, as too intimate, remained in manuscript until the nineteenth century.

Religion was the dominant motive of Anne Bradstreet's verse; but unlike Wigglesworth she wished not to instruct and warn, only to express her personal emotions. "The

Flesh and the Spirit," a favorite of modern anthologists,[8] is one of the best expressions in English literature of the conflict described by St. Paul in the eighth chapter of his Epistle to the Romans; a conflict that was evidently part of the personal experience of the poetess. The prose meditation that she left to her children shows that she had often been beset by doubts 'whether there was a God.' And her faith seems to have been rekindled, not so much by the orthodox means of prayer and reading the Scripture, as by the 'wondrous works' of nature that she observed in her quiet contemplation by the Merrimac River as it flowed unvexed to the sea.[9]

Child of the seventeenth century though she was, Anne would have been far happier had she been brought up under 'Nature's God' of the Century of Enlightenment. Of this may some of the thirty-three stanzas of her "Contemplations," the most finished and musical of her religious poems, bear witness:

> *Some time now past in the Autumnal Tide,*
> *When Phoebus wanted but one hour to bed,*
> *The trees all richly clad, yet void of pride,*
> *Were gilded o'er by his rich golden head.*
> *Their leaves and fruits seem'd painted, but was true*
> *Of green, of red, of yellow, mixéd hew,*
> *Rapt were my senses at this delectable view.*

> *I wist not what to wish, yet sure thought I,*
> *If so much excellence abide below;*
> *How excellent is He that dwells on high?*

---

[8] Reprinted in Louis Untermeyer, *American Poetry from the Beginning to Whitman* (1931), pp. 73-77, and Conrad Aiken, *American Poetry 1671-1928* (Modern Library, 1929), pp. 1-4.

[9] *The Works of Anne Bradstreet in Prose and Verse* (J. H. Ellis, ed.), pp. 9-10.

Whose power and beauty by His works we know.
Sure He is goodness, wisdome, glory, light,
That hath this under world so richly dight:
More Heaven than Earth was here no winter and no night.

* * *

I heard the merry grasshopper then sing,
The black-clad cricket, bear a second part,
They kept one tune, and played on the same string,
Seeming to glory in their little Art.
Shall Creatures abject, thus their voices raise?
And in their kind resound their Maker's praise:
Whilst I as mute, can warble forth no higher layes?

* * *

Under the cooling shadow of a stately elm
Close sat I by a goodly rivers side,
Where gliding streams the rocks did overwhelm;
A lonely place, with pleasures dignified.
I once that lov'd the shady woods so well,
Now thought the rivers did the trees excell,
And if the sun would ever shine, there would I dwell.

Another group of her poems expresses simple domestic affections: "Upon her son Samuel's going to England"; "Upon her daughter's recovery from a Fever"; "In her solitary hours in her Husband's absence"; "Verses upon the burning of our house."

When by the ruines oft I passed,
My sorrowing eyes aside did cast,
And here and there the places spy,
Where oft I sat, and long did lie.

Here stood that trunk, and there that chest;
There lay that store I counted best:
My pleasant things in ashes lie,
And them behold no more shall I.

> *Under thy roof no guest shall sit,*
> *Nor at thy Table eat a bit.*

And, best of all, the verses "To my dear and loving Husband," so human, simple, yet inevitable in language, so devoid of contemporary conceits or religious dogma. Save for one obsolete accent (perséver instead of persevere) they might have been written at any time during the last three centuries.

> *If ever two were one, then surely we.*
> *If ever man were lov'd by wife, then thee;*
> *If ever wife was happy in a man,*
> *Compare with me ye women if you can.*
> *I prize thy love more than whole mines of gold,*
> *Or all the riches that the East doth hold.*
> *My love is such that rivers cannot quench,*
> *Nor aught but love from thee, give recompence.*
> *Thy love is such I can no way repay,*
> *The heavens reward thee manifold, I pray!*
> > *Then while we live, in love lets so perséver,*
> > *That when we live no more, we may live ever.*

The only New England writer of love lyrics yet discovered, comes from the Old Colony, where the sons of the Pilgrim Fathers were not notably addicted to verse. Everybody knows about the Courtship of Myles Standish, but few have heard of the courtship of John Saffin. John came over from England in 1644 at the age of twelve as a ward of Governor Edward Winslow, in whose house he grew up. At the age of twenty-one or two, he fell in love with Martha Willet. 'In Splendid Beauty She did much Excell,' as he wrote in one of his poems. She was a daughter of Thomas Willet the fur trader, who by this time had become an Assistant of the Colony. Mr. Willet gave consent to the match on condition that John make some money first; and to help do that, arranged that he should go to Virginia as a merchant.

Upon departing, John went to the Willet house to say goodby to his fiancée, but found her asleep and kissed her without awaking her. And, en route to Virginia, he wrote a poem to Martha, of which these are a few of the lines:

> *Sweetly, my Dearest, I left thee asleep,*
> *Which silent parting made my heart to weep;*
> *"O wake her not, so sweetly let her lie!"*

*   *   *

> *Thus in sad silence, I alone and mute,*
> *My lips bade thee farewell with a salute,*
> *And so went from thee. Turning back again,*
> *I thought one kiss too little; then stole twain,*
> *And then another. But, no more of this,*
> *Count with yourself how many of 'em you miss!*

John and Martha remained true to each other during his four years' absence in Virginia. Then, having made a modest fortune, he sailed home in one of those small two-masted vessels called a pinnace to claim his bride. And on the voyage, he paraphrased for her benefit Quarles' *Argalus and Parthenia*, in these words:

> *Sail, gentle pinnace, Zepherus doth not fail*
> *With prosperous gales; sail, gentle pinnace, sail!*
> *Proud Neptune stoops and freely condescends*
> *For's former roughness now to make amends;*
> *Thetis with her green mantle sweetly glides*
> *With smiling dimples singing by our sides.*
> *Sail, gentle pinnace! Zepherus does not fail*
> *With prosperous gales; sail, gentle pinnace, sail!*

John and Martha were married shortly after his return, and he continued to write poetry to her during the twenty years of their happy married life.[10]

From the example of the long concealment of John Saffin's and Edward Taylor's poems, we may infer that much lyrical poetry was written in the English colonies that never reached the printed page. Anne Bradstreet's was preserved only because of the devotion of her family, and the fame of *The Tenth Muse.*

Closely allied to religious poetry was the elegiac. This was the most abundant form of verse in the puritan century, since it was a natural outlet for grief at the death of an eminent or a beloved person. The puritan creed forbade funeral services, for which no authority could be found in Scripture; the most that could be done was an extempore prayer by the minister at the house of the deceased, among his family and friends, who then accompanied the corpse from house to grave in silence, and buried it without a funeral note. The minister might preach a funeral sermon the following Sabbath, but this did not become usual until the eighteenth century. Hence it was inevitable that those who had, or believed that they had the poetic gift, should burst out in a threnody of woe. Sewall's diary shows that manuscript elegies were attached to the coffin, and copies passed around to the mourners. These verses were often printed and distributed to friends, or, in the case of eminent persons, sold at the bookshops and by the country hawkers. Doubtless the printed elegies that survive are only

[10] *John Saffin His Book* (*1665-1708*) with an Introduction by Caroline Hazard (New York: Harbor Press, 1928).

a small minority of those that were written; and some are still found in manuscript form in our older libraries.[11]

These broadside, or pamphlet elegies, as they occasionally grew to be, followed a set form brought over from England. The writer made up one or more anagrams on the name of the deceased, and composed a poem, usually in the classic elegiac metre, on the theme suggested by the anagram. Take, for instance, the elegy *Upon the Death of the Virtuous and Religious Mrs. Lydia Minot . . . the Mother of Five Children, who Died in Child-Bed of the Sixth, and together was Interred January 27, 1667.* This broadside is adorned by a rude woodcut of a skull and crossbones, pick and shovel, grim reaper, hourglass with the sand run out, and other conventional emblems of death. The name *Lydia Minot*, with some straining at the vowels, yields three anagrams:

> *I die to al myne*
> *I die, not my Al*
> *Day is my Lot*

And on each of the three the unknown poet appends a painful poem.

Occasional verse seldom rises above the indifferent, and the New England broadside elegies are no exception. But Urian Oakes, in an ambitious elegy that disregarded the standard form, attained dignity, pathos, and even beauty in this kind. It was an elegy on his lifelong friend Thomas Shepard, Jr., minister of Charlestown; and was printed at

[11] A corpus of family elegies, written by the Tompsons, has been printed by K. B. Murdock, in *Handkerchiefs from Paul* (1927).

Cambridge in 1677.[12] These are a few of the fifty-two stanzas:

> Art, Nature, Grace, in him were all combin'd
> To shew the world a matchless Paragon:
> In whom of radiant virtues no less shin'd,
> Than a whole Constellation: but he's gone!
> > He's gone alas! Down in the dust must lie
> > As much of this rare Person as could die.

> His look commanded reverence and awe,
> Though mild and amiable, not austere:
> Well humour'd was he (as I ever saw)
> And rul'd by Love and Wisdom, more than Fear.
> > The Muses, and the Graces too, conspir'd
> > To set forth this rare piece, to be admir'd

> * * *

> My dearest, inmost, bosom-friend is gone!
> Gone is my sweet companion, Soul's delight!
> Now in an huddling crowd I'm all alone,
> And almost could bid all the world goodnight;
> > Blest be my rock! God lives; O! let Him be,
> > As He is all to all, in all to me.

Controversial poetry seems to have been used only by the New England Quakers, to vent their indignation against the persecutions to which they were subject by the dominant puritans. The spirit of their poems is better than their art; their significance lies in the fact that even the Quakers, plainest and starkest of all the Protestant sects, thought art well employed to express their feelings in verse, when a plain prose might equally well have conveyed their message. In the Massachusetts Historical Soci-

---

[12] Reprinted in *Early American Poetry IV. Elegies and Epitaphs* (Boston: Club of Odd Volumes, 1896).

ety is a broadside entitled *Innocency's Complaint against Tyrannical Court Faction in Newengland*, signed 'George Joy, Mariner, 1677,' which the bibliographers assign to the Cambridge press.[13] Sailor George, of whom nothing else is known, does not mince his words:

> *The* Massachusetts *is alike for Crime*
> *Unto* Judea, *in Christ Jesus' Time*
> *Here Laws are extant, that doth terrify*
> *Well meaning men, and Liberty deny*
> *In serving God, except in their own way.*

Better known, because the author was the maternal grandfather of Benjamin Franklin, is Peter Folger's *Looking Glass for the Times*, written in 1676 but not printed until the following century.[14] Peter was one of the leading citizens of Nantucket; and his "Looking Glass" reflects an honest lover of religious liberty, if not a poet:

> New-England *they are like the* Jews,
> *as like, as like can be;*
> *They made large promises to God,*
> *at home and at the sea:*
> *They did proclaim free Liberty,*
> *they cut the Calf in twain,*
> *They passed between the part thereof:*
> *O this was all in vain!*

> *   *   *

> *I am for Peace, and not for War,*
> *and that's the reason why*

[13] Wegelin, *op. cit.*, p. 47. The type certainly looks like Samuel Green's, but how did this diatribe against the government pass the censorship?

[14] Reprinted from an 18th-century edition in *Rhode Island Historical Tracts*, no. 16 (Providence, 1883). Wegelin, *op. cit.*, p. 32, lists an edition of 1677 at the American Antiquarian Society.

I write more plain than some men do,
that use to daub and lie.
But I shall cease and set my name
to what I here insert,
Because to be a libeller,
I hate it with my heart.
From Sherborn Town, *where now I dwell,*
my Name I do put here,
Without offence your real friend,
it is Peter Folger

The most ambitious narrative poem of the century was inspired by King Philip's War. Benjamin Tompson, the author, was born at Braintree in 1642, the son of the minister; graduated from the college in 1662, taught school successively in Boston, Charlestown, Braintree, and Roxbury, and in all four places eked out his income by practicing medicine. He was frequently called upon for elegies, and several of them were printed. Like other godly persons he was persuaded that the Indian war was a divine chastisement on New England for the luxury and extravagance that had crept in through trade with the West Indies and Southern Europe; and *New England's Crisis*,[15] among other things, is a homely document on the contrast between New England life in the first and the third generations. It is patterned after Francis Quarles' "Historie of Sampson." The Prologue opens:

The times wherein old Pompion *was a Saint,*
When men fared hardly yet without complaint
On vilest cates; the dainty Indian maize
Was eat with clam-shells out of wooden trays

* * *

[15] Boston, 1676; reprinted in H. J. Hall, *Benjamin Tompson . . . His Poems* (1924), pp. 49-71.

> *These times were good, Merchants cared not a rush*
> *For other fare than* Jonakin *and* Mush.
> *'Twas ere the neighbouring* Virgin-land *had broke*
> *The hogsheads of her worse than hellish smoke,*
> *'Twas ere the Islands sent their presents in,*
> *Which but to use was counted next to sin.*
> *'Twas ere a Barge had made so rich a freight*
> *As chocolate, dust-gold and bits of eight.*
> *Ere wines from* France *and* Moscovado *too*
> *Without the which the drink will scarcely do,*
> *From Western Isles, ere fruits and delicacies,*
> *Did rot maids' teeth and spoil their handsome faces.*

The poem itself opens with an imaginary speech of King Philip to his subjects, in which effective use is made of Indian words and Indian English:

> *This no wunnegin, so big matchit law,*
> *Which our old fathers fathers never saw.*
> *Me meddle Squaw me hang'd, our fathers kept*
> *What Squaws they would wither they wakt or slept.*
> *Now if you'll fight I'll get you English coats,*
> *And wine to drink out of their Captain's throats.*

In what the author modestly styles

> *lamenting words*
> *I dare not stile them poetry but truth,*
> *The dwingling products of my crazy youth,*

he relates the early attacks on villages:

> *The mother* Rachel*-like shrieks out 'My child!'*
> *She wrings her hands and raves as she were wild.*
> *The bruitish wolves suppress her anxious moan*
> *By cruelties more deadly of her own.*

The last episode of the poem humorously describes the

work of women patriots raising a mud fortification on Boston neck when the capital was threatened:

> *A tribe of female hands, but manly hearts*
> *Forsake at home their pasty-crust and tarts*
> *To knead the dirt, the samplers down they hurl,*
> *Their undulating silks they closely furl.*
> *The pick-axe one as Commandress holds,*
> *While t'other at her awk'ness gently scolds.*

In proportion to her numbers, early Harvard was more fertile in poets than at any subsequent period of her history; and considering the few opportunities of college students to break into print, a surprising amount of their verse has survived. We owe most of it to the college printers and their almanacs. From 1646, if not earlier, a young graduate was chosen to make the calculations and prepare the copy for this annual. An almanac is a fussy thing to set up and print, and the retail price of threepence barely covered the cost of production. So our authors were rewarded with a little space which they could fill with poetry (provided it was appropriate) or, if their tastes ran that way, a popular scientific essay. Thus the Cambridge almanac became the annual poetry magazine of New England.

Samuel Danforth, who graduated in 1643 at the age of fourteen, is the earliest college almanac poet whose work has been preserved. Danforth had been an unwholesomely pious freshman, whose shocked comments when 'reciting to his Tutor out of the Heathen Poets' are recorded with approval by Cotton Mather. But college so broadened young Danforth's intellectual horizon, that he not only learned to enjoy but to imitate said Heathen Poets in his *Almanack For The Year of Our Lord 1647*. The spaces there are occupied by a somewhat obscure allegory on contemporary events, of which the stanza for September may serve as example. The 'four heads' are the United Colonies of New England, the 'hive' is Harvard College, and the last two lines are apparently intended to suggest that the college be aided by a tax on the fishing industry:

> *Four heads should meet and counsel have,*
> *The chickens from the kite to save,*
> *The idle drones away to drive,*
> *The little Bees to keep i'th hive.*
> *How honey may be brought to these*
> *By making fish to dance on trees.*

Next year, the homespun muse has already become more polished. The Almanac for 1648 opens thus, in March:

> *Awake ye western Nymphs, arise and sing:*
> *And with fresh tunes salute your welcome spring,*
> *Behold a choice, a rare and pleasant plant,*
> *Which nothing but it's parallel doth want.*
> *'Twas but a tender slip a while ago,*
> *About twice ten years or a little moe,*
> *But now 'tis grown unto such comely state*
> *That one would think't an Olive tree or Date.*

And each month celebrates one of the fruits of the New England tree: Justice, Liberty, Peace, Plenty, and the like. Samuel Danforth returns to current events in the Almanac for 1649, and shows no little skill in fitting the barbarous names of Pequot chieftains into English verse.[16]

Samuel Bradstreet, son of the poetess and teaching fellow in the college, attempted to spice up the Almanac for

---

[16] All the poems from this and the 1647 and 1648 almanacs are printed in K. B. Murdock's *Handkerchiefs from Paul*, pp. 104-11, with notes.

1657 with a poem on Apollo wooing Tellus, the earth Goddess. One imagines that his mother was not very proud of the attempt, almost the worst, if not the very worst, attempt of our almanac poets.

More happily we return to Tellus and Hellas in the Almanac for 1671, by Daniel Russell (A.B. 1669), who poured the classical tradition into the New England scene, and from that alembic distilled a dozen eclogues in the true Virgilian tradition.

MARCH

The Starry Monarch now in's full career,
Comes marching up to our North Hemisphere,
And by his burning beams, our Frigid Zone,
Doth metamorphize to a temperate one;
Re-animating with Celestial Fire,
Those lifeless natures, Hiem's caus'd t'expire:
And causing Tellus t'doff her winter vest.
For joy of th'spring, her new-come, welcome guest.

APRIL

The airy choristers, they now begin
To warble forth their native musick in
The new-leaf'd boughs; and in each pleasant field,
By Nature's art their curious nests do build.
Now big with hopes, the toiling country swain
Buries in th'Earth his multiplying grain,
On which the Heavens do fertile showers distill,
Which th'Earth with fruits, the swain with joy doth fill.

MAY

Dame Tellus *cloathed in a grass-green coat,*
By Flora's *curious needle-work well wrought,*
'Gins to appear; for now the meads abound
With fragrant roses, and with lilies crown'd.
The Proverb's verifi'd, that April *showers*
On Maia's *fields do rain down glittering flowers;*

And now the croaking crew, late all a-mort,
By their night-chantings, their new life report.

JUNE

The smiling fields, attired in their suits
Of taste-delighting, and eye-pleasing Fruits;
Their strawb'ry mantles now begin to wear,
And many orchards, cherry-cheekt appear.
Now Sol *in's crabbed throne doth take his place,*
Where he performs his longest daily race:
Soon after which, the day's length 'gins to fade,
And Phoebus, *Cancer-like, turns retrograde.*

JULY

Now Ceres' offspring's numerous everywhere,
And mighty Armies of tall blades appear
In many fields, all rank'd and fil'd they stand
Ready for battle: with whom hand to hand
Fierce husbandmen with crooked cutlash meet,
And being victors lay them at their feet.
This don't suffice; together th'blades are bound,
Transported home, and soundly thresh'd on th' ground.

AUGUST

Now Sol *and* Mercury *near th'* Virgin *meet,*
Where in conjunction they each other greet,
The best of Aspects; which doth signify,
Advancement to the Sons of Mercury.
And now the verdant meads begin to feel
The sharp encounter of the mowers' steel:
The noble vines with grapes, the grapes begin
To swell with Bacchus, *which is barell'd in.*

SEPTEMBER

The Indian *stalks, now richly fraught with store*
Of golden-colour'd ears, seem to implore
By humble bowing of their lofty head,
From this their load to be delivered.

Pomona's *daughters now at age, and dight*
With pleasing beauty, lovers to invite
In multitudes: it's well if they escape
From each of these, without a cruel rape.

OCTOBER

Now the Æolian Lords and Commons meet
In Parliament, where it is voted fit,
Yea and resolv'd upon, what-e're it cost,
They'll king it over all, and rule the roost,
Which to effect, it is agreed by all,
That blust'ring Boreas *shall be General*
Of their great Forces; and then to't they go,
And Tellus' *Kingdome first they'll overthrow.*

NOVEMBER

Where thundring Boreas, *with his troops doth shake*
The trembling woods, and makes the trees to quake:
The leaves for very fear the trees have left,
Which of their July *garb, now're quite bereft:*
The fruits, those pleasant fruits, the painted flowers,
The flow'ry meads, gay fields, and shady bowers,
Are now destroy'd; and th'Earth's depriv'd of all
Her summer glory by this wasting Fall.

DECEMBER

Exit Autumnus: *Winter now draws near,*
Armed with Frost i'th van, with snow i'th' Rear;
Whose freezing forces cause men to retire,
For help to th'fortress of a well-made Fire.
Phoebus *himself, as if with panic fear*
Hereat affrighted, now in's full careere
Doth post away, and speeds him from our flight
In greatest haste, bidding the World good-night.

JANUARY

The Northern Captains' siege still fiercely lasts,
And still the roaring canons of his blasts
Are fired off; which brings both Land and Sea
His chained captives quickly for to be:

And lest they should rebel, if load they lack,
Mountains of Snow are heap'd on Tellus' *back;*
The lofty swelling waves, stout Neptune's *pride*
Are made a packhorse on which men may ride.

FEBRUARY

And now the World's *bright torch, whose radiant light*
Dispels the gloomy mists of black-fac'd Night:
The twelve Herculean *labours of his sphere,*
Completed hath, and periodiz'd the Year,
But not his motion: Nature's law commands
That fiery Phoebus' Chariot *never stands,*
Without a miracle; and that it be,
Still termed corpus semper mobile.

It did not take much education or gift of poesy to write this sort of thing; but at least the effort was made. One of the best old English customs, for young men to make verses, was being carried on without a break, hand in hand with the classical tradition. Flora, Ceres, Bacchus, and Pomona were making the acquaintance of the wild roses, cornfields, grapes, and apple orchards of New England.

As recently as 1937 another New England seventeenth-century poet was unearthed by the indefatigable Thomas H. Johnson of Lawrenceville. This is the Reverend Edward Taylor (c. 1644-1729), minister and physician in the Massachusetts frontier town of Westfield.[17] The discovery created a sensation among students of American literature, and every anthology of American poetry that has since appeared has included some of Taylor's poems.

[17] Mr. Johnson announced the discovery and printed a few samples of Taylor's verse in *N.E.Q.*, X (1937), 290-322, and published *The Poetical Works of Edward Taylor* in 1939 (see review by S. Foster Damon in *N.E.Q.*, XII, 777-80). Additional poems are printed by Mr. Johnson in *N.E.Q.*, XVI (1943), 280-96.

Edward Taylor belonged to what one might call the second Puritan migration, that of the Restoration, which gave us, among others, Charles Morton and Dr. Samuel Lee.[18] Coming to Boston with his father when over twenty years old, he entered Harvard College, where he was class-mate and chum to Samuel Sewall the diarist. Immediately after graduating in 1671, he became minister of the First Church of Westfield, and there lived, completely un-known to the great world, during the remaining fifty-eight years of his life.

For reasons unknown and unexplained, Taylor chose to hide his poetical light under a bushel; and his manuscript book, containing some four hundred pages of verse, was left to his heirs with the injunction that they were never to be published. (But if he really meant that, why did he not destroy them?) Only two stanzas, so far as is known, actually were printed in his lifetime. These, on the death of one of his children, were sent by way of consolation to his classmate Sewall who had been similarly afflicted; and Sewall had them incorporated in a printed sermon which Cotton Mather preached on the death of the Sewall boy.[19] Here are the two stanzas, as re-edited by the author for his manuscript collection:

> But pausing on't, this Sweet perfum'd my thought,
>   Christ would in Glory have a flow'r choice, prime;
> And having choice, chose this my branch forth brought.
>   'Lord! take! I thank Thee thou tak'st aught of mine;
>   It is my pledge of glory; part of me
>   Is now in it, Lord, glorified with Thee.'

[18] See below, Chapter X.
[19] *N.E.Q.*, XIV (1941), 199-41.

> *Grief o'er doth flow; and nature fault would find*
> *Were not Thy will my spell, charm, joy and gem.*
> *That as I said, I say: 'Take, Lord, they're Thine.'*
> *I piecemeal pass to glory bright in them.*
> *I joy, may I sweet flowers for glory breed,*
> *Whether Thou get'st them green, or lets them seed.*

In his very numerous poems, Taylor drew similes from the humble occupations and common things of his community—the spinning and weaving, plowing and reaping, the wild flowers, the hens and chickens, the cows and sheep, even the dogs and cats. In "God's Determinations," a colloquy between Christ, the Christian soul, and Satan, the devil appears as a cur dog, and the soul begs Christ for succor in these words:

> *I know he is Thy cur, therefore I be*
> *Perplexed lest I from Thy pasture stray,*
> *He bows and barks so veh'mently at me.*
> *Come, rate [20] this cur, Lord; break his teeth, I pray!*
> *Remember me, I humbly pray Thee first,*
> *Then halter up this cur that is so curst.*

Jesus then replies in language such as Taylor and his wife must have used to calm their children when frightened by a savage dog:

> *Peace, peace, my honey! do not cry,*
> *My little darling, wipe thine eye,*
> *O! cheer, cheer up, come see!*
> *Is anything too dear, my dove;*
> *Is anything too good, my love,*
> *To get or give for thee?*

[20] "To chide vehemently" (Dr. Samuel Johnson).

If in the Several[21] *thou art,*
This yelper fierce will at thee bark—
That thou art Mine, this show.
As Spot barks back the sheep again,
Before they to the pound are ta'en,
So he—and hence 'way goes.

But if this cur that bows so sore,
Is broken-tooth'd, and muzzled sure,
Fear not, my pretty heart!
His barking is to make thee cling
Close underneath thy Saviour's wing;
Why did my sweeting start?

And if he run an inch too fur,
I'll check his chain, and rate the cur;
My chick, keep close to me.
The poles shall sooner kiss and greet,
And parallels shall sooner meet,
Than thou shall harméd be.[22]

A large part of Taylor's compositions consists of a series of "Preparatory Meditations" before administering, or partaking of, the Lord's Supper. These owe their style as well as their conception to George Herbert; they are a continuous outpouring of the author's love for God. There are no fewer than 221 of these Meditations of from three to twenty-one stanzas each; and they were written over a period of forty-four years. From these it is difficult to choose. To appreciate Taylor, one should read the whole; the total effect is overwhelming. But as my readers will expect a sample, here are two stanzas. In one, from "The Experience" which follows Meditation No. 1, dated 1682,

[21] An enclosed pasture.
[22] *Poetical Works of Edward Taylor,* pp. 60-61.

Taylor is trying to describe his ecstasy at the 'flame' of the Lord's real presence in the sacrament; it has even made him presumptuous:

> *Oh! that that Flame which thou didst on me cast*
> > *Might me enflame, and lighten ev'rywhere.*
> *Then Heaven to me would be less at last,*
> > *So much of Heaven I should have while here.*
> > *Oh! sweet though short! I'll not forget the same.*
> *My nearness, Lord, to thee did me enflame.*
>
> *I'll claim my Right—Give place, ye Angels bright!*
> > *Ye further from the Godhead stand than I;*
> *My nature is your Lord, and doth unite*
> > *Better than yours unto the Deity.*
> > *God's Throne is first, and mine is next; to you*
> > *Only the place of waiting-men is due.*

And there follows a "Reflextion" after the Lord's Supper, on the theme of the Rose of Sharon:

> *Shall Heaven and Earth's bright glory all up lie,*
> > *Like sunbeams bundled in the sun in Thee?*
> *Dost Thou sit, Rose, at table head, where I*
> > *Do sit, and carv'st no morsel sweet for me?*
> > *So much before, so little now! Spread, Lord,*
> > *Thy rosy leaves, and me their glee afford.*
>
> *Shall not thy Rose my garden fresh perfume?*
> > *Shall not Thy beauty my dull heart assail?*
> *Shall not Thy golden gleams run through this gloom?*
> > *Shall my black velvet mask Thy fair face veil?*
> > *Pass o'er my faults, shine forth, bright sun, arise,*
> > *Enthrone thy rosy self within mine eyes!* [23]

Such intensity of devotion, such richness in color and imagery, one looks for in the Anglo-Catholic poets rather

---

[23] *Idem.,* pp. 124-26.

than among puritans. Naturally, the question has been asked, the suggestion made, that Taylor feared to make his verses public lest his sacramental ecstasy seem lush and even 'idolatrous' to his contemporaries. But the answer to that query and insinuation is a definite 'no!' For the New England puritan, the Eucharist had a very special appeal as evidence and reminder of Christ's supreme sacrifice for him; the sacrament could not have been more significant if he had believed, with the Catholic, that the bread was Christ's very flesh, and the wine His very blood. There was nothing unusual, for a New England puritan clergyman, in Taylor's sweet inner life or in his fervid adoration of his Saviour. The uncommon thing about him is his expression of it.

This poetry, which he allowed nobody outside his own family to see, reached an artistic excellence that no one else in New England attained until the nineteenth century.

X. SCIENTIFIC STRIVINGS

IT APPEARS to be a common notion that the New England puritans were hostile or indifferent to science, while nourishing and coddling various pseudoscientific superstitions, such as astrology, demonology, and witchcraft. The German social historian Troeltsch declared that puritanism was hostile to natural science, wishing all things to be explained supernaturally—the same old charge that has been made time and again against Catholicism.[1] Dr. Dorothy Stimson, on the contrary, finds that the principal English scientists of the 'century of genius,' those who founded the Royal Society, observed nature, and made experiments, were men of puritan background.[2]

In the colonies we find the relation between puritanism and science to be much the same as between puritanism and literature. Religion proved a stimulus rather than a restraint, because the clerical leaders of the community were well-educated men, curious about what was going on, eager to keep in touch with the movements of their day, receptive to new scientific theories. The scientific production of colonial New England was negligible, even compared with that of Mexico; yet more than in other English colonies. As a rough test, let us see how many colonists were elected fellows by the Royal Society of London, the

[1] Quoted in H. J. C. Grierson, *Cross Currents in English Literature of the Seventeenth Century* (London, 1929), p. 192n.

[2] Dorothy Stimson, "Puritanism and the New Philosophy in Seventeenth Century England," *Bulletin of Institute of History of Medicine*, III (1935), 321-34. Cf. Theodore Hornberger, "Puritanism and Science," *N.E.Q.*, X (1937), 503-15; and James B. Conant, "The Advancement of Learning during the Puritan Commonwealth," *Proc. M.H.S.*, LXVI (1942), 3-31.

great scientific academy of the English-speaking world: one from South Carolina, three from Virginia, three from Pennsylvania (including Benjamin Franklin), and eleven from New England. And one of the New Englanders, Governor John Winthrop of Connecticut, was proposed for membership before the Royal Society obtained its charter, and chosen fellow at the first regular election, May 20, 1663.

The scientific strivings of New England are, moreover, a test of their receptivity to new ideas. For the puritan colonies were founded, and their college of liberal arts established, before the New Philosophy (as the new science was generally called) had obtained a foothold in the English universities. The university men among our founders were brought up in the Aristotelian explanation of reality, which, with a few Platonic and other accretions, had satisfied the learned world through the Middle Ages. In all the other slopes of intellectual activity that I have mentioned in these lectures, New England started at the top of the hill, and was given a stout shove by her first founders. Science alone was at the foot of the hill, bogged down in the old, soft snow of scholasticism; New Englanders of the younger generation had to pull it up Mount Bacon, where the English lads were already having a good time, and make a fresh start.

The university-trained founders of New England had been to Oxford and Cambridge at a time when mathematical and other sciences, in those universities, were at their lowest ebb. English boys, in 1640, went through seven years of grammar school and four years of college without studying any more mathematics than the plain ciphering they had learned at dame school. At Oxford and Cambridge geometry was looked upon as a practical subject, fit only for mechanics; and algebra was not studied. Consequently the necessary mathematical basis for scientific research was wanting. A student like John Pell or William Oughtred who showed mathematical tastes obtained no substantial encouragement, such as a college fellowship; and the best scientific work in England went on outside and independent of the universities. This absence of mathematical training in Oxford and Cambridge, not any imaginary hostility of puritanism to mathematics,[3] is the obvious reason why Harvard College started off with a very inadequate mathematical program. President Dunster, to be sure, got him an English Euclid, and a Peter Ramus' *Royal Road to Geometry*, and made it possible for some at least of his pupils to learn surveying; but Thomas Brattle who graduated in 1676 under President Oakes, wrote that he had to study mathematics by himself. In a letter written long after to Flamsteed, the Astronomer Royal, Brattle describes amusingly how he was stumped by the fifth proposition of Euclid, and in searching other books for a solution, found that this was the famous *pons asinorum*. He finally managed to cross it; once across, the rest came easy.[4]

In physics, which then comprehended all the physical, chemical, and biological sciences, the founders of New England and the first generation of college students were

[3] As stated by Professor David Eugene Smith, in his *A History of Mathematics in America before 1900* (Chicago, 1934).

[4] Brattle to Flamsteed, December 15, 1703, Archives of Royal Observatory.

in an equally bad way. Cambridge University students as late as 1650 studied physics in digests of or commentaries on Aristotle's physical books. They were taught, as Dante had learned in the thirteenth century, and as John Milton apparently still believed, that the universe was composed of four elements: earth, air, fire, and water, among which the qualities

> . . . *hot, cold, moist, and dry, four champions fierce*
> *Strive here for mast'ry, and to battle bring*
> *Their embryon atoms* [5] . . .

The first scientific textbooks used at Harvard were the works of Keckermann, an industrious German compiler who died before the physical concepts of Aristotle had been much disturbed by new discoveries; J. J. Scaliger *de Subtilitate*, a truculent attack on Cardan which in the opinion of university wits had completely silenced the critics of scholastic physics; and the *Physiologia* of Johannes Magirus, a professor at Marburg who died in 1596. This manual, a mere digest of Aristotle with commentaries, enjoyed an undeserved popularity on the Continent and in England well into the seventeenth century. By 1663 Harvard students were making fun of scholastic physics in some of their theses. The Class of 1671 got rid of the obsolete Magirus textbook by locking up their tutor who insisted on lecturing from it, until he resigned in a huff, taking Magirus with him.[6]

Astronomy affords the best test of the New England attitude toward science, for the astronomical theories and

---

[5] *Paradise Lost*, ii. 898-900. Cf. Dante, *Paradiso*, vii. 124-125.
[6] Diary of Edward Taylor, *Proc. M.H.S.*, XVIII, 15.

discoveries of Copernicus, Galileo, and Kepler were not only the most spectacular, but the most disturbing of the age. Copernicus's hypothesis that the earth spun around on its own axis and revolved about the sun; Galileo's demonstration that God was not the immediate source of astral energy; Kepler's proof that the planets followed, not the circular path which was supposed to reflect divine perfection, but elliptical orbits; moved man first to astonishment, then to anger. It mattered not whether he was Catholic or Protestant, since the reformers had accepted the same philosophical explanation of reality as the schoolmen. Doubtless the majority of Protestants approved when in 1633 the Inquisition forced Galileo to recant his heliocentric theory, as 'contrary to Holy Scripture.' Oxford, though she had a chair of astronomy as early as 1619, lacked an exponent of the new astronomy for thirty years more. When Maestlin, the German astronomer who encouraged Galileo and taught Kepler, wrote a college textbook of astronomy, he dared not, because of his official position in the University of Heidelberg, adopt the Copernican hypothesis, but declared that the earth was immobile. Astronomy was the dangerous subject in the universities around 1620, as politics and economics in our own day; the thing for which professors got fired because they did not 'co-operate.' Catholic universities were forbidden to teach Copernican astronomy until the end of the eighteenth century; of course many if not most of them disregarded the prohibition.

Hence, we need not be surprised that the first generation of college students in New England were taught the astronomy of the ancients, the Ptolemaic system. They learned little of the universe that Dante did not know. Our fixed and stable earth is the centre of all existence. About her atmosphere revolve nine transparent and concentric orbs, the 'crystal spheres,' which 'move in melodious time.'[7] In each of the first seven heavens a single planet is embedded; the eighth heaven of the fixed stars, the firmament, is 'thick inlaid with patines of bright gold';[8] the ninth or *primum mobile,* diaphanous in substance and invisible to human eyes, but giving forth the deepest tone in the music of the spheres, revolves at incredible speed inside the tenth heaven, the immutable empyrean. There dwells God the prime mover, with all the glorious company of heaven and the souls of the blessed dead.

Not long were our colonial students allowed to retain their cosmographic innocence; and as soon as they learned about the New Astronomy, they were eager to tell the world about it. *Astronomia Instaurata* by Vincent Wing, the first Englishman who made a satisfactory popular exposition of the Copernican system, was apparently 'adopted' at Harvard shortly after its first appearance in 1656; for an essay based on it is printed in the annual New England almanac for 1659. These almanacs, as we have seen, were compiled by Harvard tutors or graduate students, and often employed by them as a medium for college poetry. Zechariah Brigden, who had worked his way through college by 'ringinge the bell and waytinge in the hall,' received the almanac assignment for 1659, and started a new fashion by using his empty space for a popular essay on

[7] Milton, *On the Morning of Christ's Nativity,* xiii.
[8] *The Merchant of Venice,* v. 1.

astronomy.[9] Quoting Wing, Kepler, Galileo, Gassendi, and other authorities, Zechariah gives a brief digest of the Copernican system, which he calls 'the true and genuine Systeme of the world' and answers the principal objections made from Scripture texts which, he says, should not be taken literally. God was writing for the common people, often in parables, and not attempting to indicate the nature of his Universe in a few texts.

The reception of this almanac is significant. Both President Chauncy and John Winthrop, Jr. sent copies of it to the Reverend John Davenport, the famous minister of New Haven. Mr. Davenport observed that Galileo, Gassendi, and Kepler meant nothing to him; that the young author appeared to be setting himself up as the eighth sage; that we lived in a fixed place, not a revolving planet; and that the objections from Scripture were not answered. 'However it be,' he writes to John Winthrop, Jr., 'let him enjoy his opinion; and I shall rest in what I have learned, til more cogent arguments be produced.'

Now, I wish to rub this in! Much has been written about the bigotry of the New England clergy, and Davenport was one of the least liberal of that group; yet he does not demand that Brigden be fired from Harvard, or kept out of the pulpit. He simply agrees to disagree with the young radical. The new astronomy, which had to fight the church and the clergy in almost every other country, was accepted by and even propagated by the clergy in New England. The clerical government of the college sponsored these annual almanacs which frequently contained a popu-

[9] Reprinted in *N.E.Q.*, VII, 9-12.

lar essay on the new astronomy; and clergymen like the Mathers were the chief patrons and promoters of the new science.

The pseudo science of astrology seems never to have had any standing at Harvard. A long series of commencement theses, beginning in 1653, prove that it was the favorite butt of undergraduate disputants at these academic festivities.

Fortunately for the new astronomy, the seventeenth century was rich in comets, the observation of which added greatly to our knowledge of the universe, and enabled Newton to correlate Kepler's discoveries with his own, and work out the laws of gravitation. Theologians had long considered comets within their province, as heavenly portents of disaster; and it was not without a struggle that they relinquished these 'blazing stars' to the scientists. The first comet to stimulate literary activity in New England was that which appeared at the turn of the years 1664-1665. Samuel Danforth, the almanac poet, was now minister of Roxbury, but retained his interest in astronomy. In 1665 he had printed at Cambridge a tract of one hundred and twenty-two pages called *An Astronomic Description of the late Comet or Blazing Star, with a brief Theological Application thereof*. And for the Almanac of 1665 Alexander Nowell, who had graduated the previous June, wrote an essay called "The Suns Prerogative Vindicated," quoting observations by European astronomers (such as Seth Ward, the Savilian Professor at Oxford) through 'optick tubes' (telescopes), and concluding with remarks on comets. Both the young man and the elder minister admit that comets proceed from natural causes, are subject to mathematical laws, and are composed of the same stuff as

stars—a somewhat advanced position in 1665. Nevertheless, they insist that comets are divine portents of impending disasters. For surely God must be a better mathematician than we! [10]

Before the next important comet came along, Harvard
College had acquired a telescope from John Winthrop, Jr.,
then Governor of Connecticut. The younger Winthrop
was easily first in scientific interest among New Englanders in the seventeenth century. Educated largely through
his own reading and travels (since he had spent but two
years at Trinity College, Dublin), he came to New England at the age of twenty-five, bringing with him a large
library full of scientific books. The surviving remnant of
it, in the New York Society Library, contains fifty-two
relating to chemistry and alchemy, thirty-three on medicine, twenty-seven on mathematics and physics, twelve on
witchcraft, astrology, and occult lore.[11] Winthrop, like
many intellectuals of his day, was interested in almost
every branch of science. He was a practicing physician,
and dispensed medicines of his own compounding to the
poor. He prospected for minerals, assayed ores that he
found in New England, dabbled in alchemy, organized the
first ironworks and salt-pans in New England, and showed
a keen interest in optics and astronomy. But his principal
interest, as his books indicate, was in chemistry. That had
not yet attained the dignity of a separate discipline. Chem-

[10] Nowell's essay was thought so good by John Josselyn, the English tra-
veler, that he printed it in his *Two Voyages to New England* (London,
1674). It is reprinted in Sibley, *Harvard Graduates*, II, 149-51. Considerable
correspondence between Increase Mather and English divines on comets
will be found in 4 *Coll. M.H.S.*, VIII.

[11] The library is described by Dr. C. A. Browne, in *Isis*, XI (1928), 328-41;
cf. Chapter VI, above.

istry was regarded as a branch of physics, somewhat under ill repute with the *cognoscenti* because the object of most of the early chemists was to discover the philosopher's stone and transmute base metals into gold. Winthrop's collection of works on chemistry and alchemy includes several books that belonged to John Dee, the celebrated mathematician, astrologer, and reputed magician of Queen Elizabeth's reign.

There were not many people in New England who could share Winthrop's chemical tastes and enthusiasm. One of them, George Stirk or Starkey, a lad from Bermuda, graduated from the college in 1646 and shortly after went to England, where he became a famous practitioner of medicine and an experimental alchemist. Robert Child (M.D. Padua), another of Winthrop's scientific friends, was expelled from Masachusetts in 1647 for daring to ask toleration for Presbyterians. But Jonathan Brewster and Gershom Bulkeley remained. The former, son of Elder Brewster of the Pilgrim church, maintained a trading post at the site of Norwich, Connecticut, when Winthrop was living at New London, and like him had a private laboratory for chemical experiments. Bulkeley did the same at his parsonage on the Connecticut River. These three were constantly interchanging books. Among Winthrop's English scientific friends and correspondents were Robert Boyle, the Earl of Clarendon, Sir Kenelm Digby, Prince Rupert, Sir Christopher Wren, and Samuel Hartlib; among his European correspondents were Glauber, Kepler, and Van Helmont. He became, as we have seen, one of the earliest fellows of the Royal Society. Sir Kenelm Digby and others begged him to live in London, and not to hide his light in a remote corner of the world; but he remained faithful to New England, and died while Governor of Connecticut in the midst of King Philip's War.

One of Winthrop's many scientific interests was astronomy. His library contained the second edition of Tycho Brahe's *Astronomia Instaurata*, Kepler *de Stella Nova*, and two other works by him. Upon Winthrop's return from England in 1663, he brought a three-and-a-half-foot telescope, the first that is known to have been imported into the English colonies. The Governor set it up at Hartford; and through it on a bright August night in 1664 observed a star which he supposed to be a fifth satellite of Jupiter. Of course he must have been mistaken, for the fifth satellite was not observed until 1892, at the Lick Observatory; and Winthrop, to do him credit, was unwilling to communicate his 'discovery' to the Royal Society until it was confirmed by others.[12]

Henry Oldenburg, secretary of the Royal Society, kept writing to the Governor urging him to 'season and possesse the youth of New England' with 'this reall Experimental way of acquiring knowledge, by conversing with, and searching into the works of God themselves,' rather than the 'notional and disputacious School philosophy.'[13] The more progressive spirits of the Royal Society were committed to the experimental method of broadening scientific knowledge, as urged by Lord Bacon; but our college students as yet had no facilities for checking by their

[12] His letter about it to Sir Robert Moray is printed in F. E. Brasch, *The Royal Society . . . in the American Colonies*, p. 7, and *Proc. M.H.S.*, XVI, 220-21.

[13] *Idem*, p. 230; cf. 239, 240, 244.

own observations what they learned of the new discoveries in books. Governor Winthrop, weighted with age and the cares of office, found little time or inclination to 'look upon the constellations of the heavens, or the planetts.' [14] In 1672 he presented the college with his telescope and sundry attachments, which were enthusiastically acknowledged by the three tutors, one of whom, Alexander Nowell, had already written on comets. [15] Shortly after, the Governor wrote to his son in Boston to inquire if the college students had observed anything worth while. The reply is lost, and we know nothing of what use was made of the college telescope for eight years.

In the year 1680 there appeared in the eastern sky a great comet, sometimes called Newton's. It excited astronomers all the way from Poland to Mexico, terrified the ignorant, provoked sundry controversies between scientists and theologians, [16] and impelled Isaac Newton along the line of reasoning that led to his greatest discovery. Thomas Brattle, the young Harvard graduate who later complained of the slight assistance he had in mathematical studies, observed the comet of 1680 through the college telescope, printed his observations in the local almanac for 1681, and communicated them to Flamsteed, the Royal Astronomer at Greenwich, who in turn sent them to his friend Newton. In the *Principia*, after quoting several 'rude' observations of this comet, Newton says that 'those made by Montenari, Hooke, Ango, and the observer in New England,

[14] 2 *Proc. M.H.S.*, IV, 266.

[15] *N.E.Q.*, VII, 17-18.

[16] One of these is well described by Irving A. Leonard, in his paper on Don Carlos de Sigüenza, the Mexican astronomer (*University of California Publications in History*, XVIII, pp. 58-61).

taking the position of the comet with reference to the fixed stars, are better.' This, Brattle wrote to Flamsteed many years later, 'was no small comfort to me, that I was none of the last of all the Lags.'

Considering his limited equipment, Brattle's observations are remarkable. Independently he recognized the fact that a comet which disappeared at perihelion into the glare of the sun's rays and reappeared on the other side of the sun was one and the same comet. His observations were valuable to Newton because, being based on fixed stars rather than on azimuths and altitudes, they helped him to determine the orbital elements of a comet moving in an ellipse. Hence our little college telescope, used by a careful and intelligent observer, contributed its mite toward helping Newton to test Kepler's three laws, to work out the law of gravitation, and to write the great *Principia*.

The college telescope did not long remain idle. In 1682, Halley's Comet made one of its periodical visits to the earth, and was viewed through our 'optick tube' by both Mathers. Increase Mather incorporated his observations, with much reading that he had done in Hevelius' *Cometographia* (Danzig, 1668), in a work called *Kometographia, or a Discourse Concerning Comets* (Boston, 1683). Cotton Mather had something to say on the subject in his second published work: *The Boston Ephemeris, An Almanack for MDCLXXXIII* (Boston 1683). His younger brother, Nathaniel Mather, before graduating from the college in 1685, published in *The Boston Ephemeris* for that year a list of astronomical discoveries which shows that he was keeping up with the work of Hooke, Cassini, and Flamsteed, as reported in the *Philosophical Transactions* of the

Royal Society. Thomas Brattle himself contributed to the *Philosophical Transactions* some observations he and Henry Newman made by a brass quadrant with telescopic sights of an eclipse at Cambridge in 1694. By the turn of the century the college had acquired a new telescope, a foot longer than Winthrop's; and with this Brattle made observations until his death in 1713—after which William Brattle was elected Fellow of the Royal Society on the strength of what his brother Thomas had done.

Increase Mather preached two sermons entitled *Heaven's Alarm to the World* and "The Latter Sign" on the occasion of the Comet of 1680.[17] *Kometographia* was a more elaborate treatise. Two only of the ten chapters related to the nature of comets; the other eight, on the history of comets, were attempts to prove that their appearance always portended remarkable or calamitous events. Mather was familiar with the work of Hooke and Kepler, and the latest publications of the Royal Society; he admitted that comets proceeded from natural causes, but insisted that their appearance could not be predicted. For he had as yet no knowledge of Halley's identification of the Comet of 1683 with those that had appeared in 1531 and 1607. And although Increase still clung to the portentous aspect of comets, his point of view was worlds apart from that of the ecclesiastics who had condemned Galileo in 1633, for an hypothesis that was contrary to Holy Writ. Mather accepted what the scientists had observed; but as the facts of history seemed to prove a time correlation between the appearance of comets and disasters in human affairs, it was

---

[17] The two were printed together in the second edition of *Heaven's Alarm* in 1682. T. J. Holmes, *Increase Mather: A Bibliography*, p. 295.

still reasonable to suppose that there was some connection.[18]

Those were busy years in Increase Mather's study. In 1683 he and a number of Boston gentlemen, including Samuel Willard, formed a scientific club: the Philosophical Society they called it. This was the first child of the Royal Society of London; the Dublin Philosophical Society, founded the following year, being the second. The Boston group met fortnightly 'for conference upon improvements in philosophy and additions to the stores of natural history.' But it only lasted about ten years.

WITCHCRAFT[19]

It seems probable that Mather hoped that through this club there might be compiled a natural history of New England, according to the 'rules and method described by that learned and excellent person Robert Boyle, Esq.';[20] and he might even have tried it himself, had he not already

[18] 'The interesting feature' of Mather's *Kometographia*, says Preserved Smith (*History of Modern Culture*, I, 430), 'is its erudition.' And on p. 439 he shows that Mather's position was exactly that of the humane and cultivated John Evelyn.

[19] The literature of witchcraft in New England is vast. George Lyman Kittredge, *Witchcraft in Old and New England* (Harvard University Press, 1929), places the Salem outburst in its proper setting, and is completely documented, but has little detail. G. L. Burr, *Narratives of Witchcraft* (Original Narratives Series, 1914), reprints some of the essential documents and narratives, with an introduction that differs in several important points from Kittredge. For witchcraft in Boston, and the part played by the Mathers, there is an excellent account by W. F. Poole in Justin Winsor, *The Memorial History of Boston*, 1630-1880 (Boston, 1880-1881), II, 131-71. Perry Miller has thrown new light on the subject in *The New England Mind: From Colony to Province* (Cambridge, 1953); and both events and literature are discussed in T. J. Holmes, *Increase Mather: A Bibliography* (Cleveland, 1931) I, 106-38.

[20] Preface to *Illustrious Providences*, last page.

begun a more congenial compilation, *Illustrious Providences*. That book begins the history of the Salem witchcraft delusion, which provides a tragic anticlimax to the scientific advance that we have been chronicling so far.

The Mathers and their learned contemporaries were not only interested in witchcraft as clergy, but as scientists. Witchcraft was one of the numerous classes of phenomena, such as light, heat, comets, growth of plants, and human anatomy, that men of science were investigating; only it had a more immediate and emotional appeal because of the terror that it aroused and its supposed connection with the devil, whom it was the particular business of parsons to fight. As George Lyman Kittredge has shown, almost every English scientific contemporary of the Mathers who has left his opinion on record believed in witchcraft; and if examples are wanted of men of science taking a particular interest in demonology and witchcraft, we have not far to seek. 'It was typical of the seventeenth century situation that . . . Henry More, the Cambridge rationalist and neo-Platonist, after proving his faith in the language of loftiest Metaphysics, should proceed to buttress it by stories of "Coskinomancy" or of the "vomiting of Cloth stuck with Pins, Nails, and Needles."' [21] And Joseph Glanvil, F.R.S. and skeptic, after delivering a devastating blow to the Aristotelian tradition, and eloquently defending modern philosophy and the experimental method in his *Vanity of Dogmatizing*, proceeded to open a Pandora-box of witchcraft and apparitions in his *Sadducismus Triumphatus* (1681). The recording of remarkable providences had

[21] Basil Willey, *The Seventeenth Century Background* (London, 1934), p. 168.

been, as we have seen, a leading motive of the early New England chroniclers, and of historians like Morton and Hubbard. Acting on a suggestion of Matthew Poole, an English divine for whom the New Englanders had great respect, a meeting of ministers of the Massachusetts Colony issued and circulated in 1681 "Some Proposals concerning the Recording of Illustrious Providences," the results of which Increase Mather was asked to collect and work up in a book.[22]

The result, which was very different from the Natural History of New England suggested by Robert Boyle, was published as an *Essay for the Recording of Illustrious Providences* at Boston in 1684. Three of the twelve chapters concerned 'Things Preternatural which have hapned in New England,' mostly witchcrafts; and other tales of demons, wizards, and witches; the rest of the book was devoted to shipwrecks, thunderstorms, tempests, remarkable escapes in the Indian wars, stories of people being struck blind and dumb, 'the woful end of drunkards,' and the like. Much the same material is to be found in the early *Philosophical Transactions* of the Royal Society, in the *Ephemerides Medico-Physicae,* a German scientific annual, and in Renaudot's *Conférences du Bureau d'Adresse,* from which Mather frequently quotes. Mather had read and considered the arguments of antiwitchcraft writers, like Scot, Ady, and Webster; but, as Kittredge has shown, these early skeptics admitted so much in the way of demons and spooks that their position was far less logical than that of scientists like Glanvil who went the whole way with the witch-hunters.

[22] Printed in preface to Increase Mather, *Illustrious Providences* (1684).

In 1688 there occurred a witchcraft case in Boston. Four children of one of the Mathers' parishioners went into fits and accused an old woman with whom they had had an altercation about the family wash of having bewitched them. The poor creature confessed she had made a compact with the devil, and was discovered to have the traditional witch apparatus of rag dolls representing the victims, which she stroked or pinched to torment them.[23] The woman was tried, found guilty, and executed for witchcraft, but the children's convulsions, ranting, and riding invisible horses, continued. Cotton Mather took the oldest girl, aged thirteen, into his family, soothed her and prayed with her as a Christian psychiatrist might do in a similar case of nerves today, kept secret the names of the persons she accused, and cured her, completely. If the girls who started the trouble at Salem had been similarly dealt with, that frenzy would not have gone so far as it did.[24] Unfortunately Mather's vanity at this favorable outcome of his efforts was such that he rushed into print with *Memorable Providences Relating to Witchcrafts* (Boston, 1689), describing the Goodwin case, with all its symptoms in detail; and just as newspaper stories of crime seem to stimulate more people to become criminals, so *Memorable Providences* may well have had a pernicious power of suggestion in that troubled era. That it had any such purpose cannot honestly be maintained by anyone who takes the trouble to read the book; but it is always convenient

---

[23] Dr. Alice Hamilton in *American Mercury*, X, 71-75, tells of the same apparatus being used by Italian witch-doctors in Chicago, in the present century.

[24] Mather, to his credit, proposed to do this; but the local magistrates refused to accept his advice. *Memorial History of Boston*, II, 145-46.

to have a scapegoat to take the guilt of a community after it has gone mad. Robert Calef, who had it in for Cotton Mather, tied a tin can to him after the frenzy was over; and it has rattled and banged through the pages of superficial and popular historians. Even today the generally accepted version of the Salem tragedy is that Cotton Mather worked it up, aided and abetted by his fellow parsons, in order to drive people back to church.

Yet the terrible outbreak at Salem Village in 1692 needed no clerical belief in witchcraft to bring it about. It arose, as witchcraft epidemics had usually arisen in Europe, during a troubled period, the *Decennium Luctuosum* of New England history when the people were uneasy with rebellions, changes of government, and Indian attacks; and in a community that had for several years been torn by factions. Salem Village, now Danvers, was an outlying parish of Salem township. It had no school, the people were poor, and their ministers had been of rather low grade. A group of girls aged from nine to nineteen began early in 1692 to simulate the physical jerks and shrieks that had been manifested by the Goodwin girls in Boston a few years before. They accused Tituba, a half-breed slave in the minister's family, and two poor old women of having bewitched them. At this point a good spanking administered to the younger girls, and lovers provided for the older ones, might have stopped the whole thing. Instead, the slave was flogged by her master into confessing witchcraft; and to save herself accused two ancient goodwives of being her confederates. The vicious circle was started. The 'afflicted children,' finding themselves the object of unusual attention, and with the exhibitionism natural to young girls, persisted in their accusations for fear of being found out; and a state of neurosis developed similar to that of the shell-shocked soldier torn between fear of death and fear of disgrace. Those accused implicated others to escape the gallows, and confessed broomstick rides, witches' sabbaths, copulation with the devil, and anything that was expected of them. Honest folk who declared the whole thing hokum were cried out upon for witches; and in May, 1692, when Governor Sir William Phips arrived in Boston, several dozen alleged witches were in jail awaiting trial.

The Governor appointed a special court composed of worthy magistrates, some of them college graduates, and presided over by William Stoughton, who had also been a fellow of New College, Oxford. This panel of learned magistrates became infected with the panic; they declined to follow the best rules for detecting witches laid down by professional English witch-hunters, and urged on them, collectively and individually, by the ministers.[25] Before they adjourned in September, 1692, nineteen persons and two dogs had been hanged for witches, and one, the brave Giles Corey, was pressed to death according to the English common law, for refusing to plead guilty or not guilty in order to save his property for his family.

In the face of this terrible frenzy, the intellectual class as a whole kept a cowardly silence. They all believed in witchcraft, to be sure; but those who had given the matter any thought knew that the rules of the game were not be-

[25] Cotton Mather's letter to one of the judges, John Richards, 'most humbly' begging him not to 'lay more stresse upon pure Spectre testimony than it will bear' is printed in 4 *Coll. M.H.S.*, VIII, 392. The date is May 31, 1692. Cf. C. K. Shipton, in *The American Historical Review*, XL (1935), 464-66.

ing observed by the court; that people were being condemned on 'spectral evidence' alone, on accusations by
alleged victims, of whom the devil was supposed to have
taken possession. Yet they kept silent, until twenty persons
had been done to death. For, as Palfrey the historian observed, New Englanders have an 'ingrained reverence for
law as such.' Hence, many who knew perfectly well that
the court was condemning innocent people held their
tongues, lest they bring the judges and the government into
contempt.[26] How true that analysis is, and how it recalls
the actions of wise and good people in the same commonwealth, in the Sacco and Vanzetti case! Cotton Mather
wrote letters to the judges, but he did not speak loudly
enough. After the Salem frenzy had subsided, he recorded
in his diary:

> I was always afraid of proceeding to convict and condemn any
> Person, as a Confoederate with afflicting Daemons, upon so feeble
> an Evidence as a spectral Representation. Accordingly, I ever testi-
> fied against it, both publickly and privately: and in my letters to
> the Judges, I particularly besought them that they would by no
> means admit it. . . . Nevertheless, on the other side, I saw in most
> of the Judges, a most charming Instance of Prudence and Patience,
> and I knew their exemplary Piety . . .[27]

So he could not bring himself to denounce such wise and
good men publicly, as they deserved.

Reticence or cowardice on the part of men who knew
better, and to whom (if to anyone) a frenzied public might
listen, has been so common in the eras of mass madness
through which we have recently passed as to compel us to

---

[26] J. G. Palfrey, *History of New England*, IV (1875), 130-31.
[27] Cotton Mather, *Diary*, I, 150-51.

be charitable to the Mathers. And Increase Mather, who had a good share of that wisdom of the serpent denied to his son, took effective measures to stay the frenzy before it destroyed the community. When the court adjourned in September, 1692, twenty persons had been executed, seven had been condemned but not executed, fifty or more persons were in prison awaiting trial, and at least two hundred more had been accused.[28] Following the history of the delusion in England, there was every reason to expect that the vicious circle would widen, until the victims were numbered by the hundreds, and not a mere score. In August, 1692, a group of seven ministers met with Increase Mather at Cambridge to discuss the trials. They decided to make an effort to rule out spectral evidence, and sent to New York to ask the opinion of the ministers there. The New York parsons, French Protestant and Dutch Reformed, replied urging circumspection. Mather then drew up a treatise to guide the court if and when it reassembled; and the book later printed as *Cases of Conscience concerning evil Spirits* was the result. In this treatise, written with a care and caution that may deceive a hasty reader, they spoke so firmly and conclusively against the use that the court had made of spectral evidence that those in power had to listen. While still in manuscript the treatise was laid before a ministers' meeting in October, and then, signed by Mather and thirteen other ministers, sent up to Governor Phips. The Governor, anxious to do what was right, then dissolved the special court, and ordered spectral evidence to be ruled out by Massachusetts courts in future. Without spectral evidence, there were no more condemnations. As

28 Palfrey, *op. cit.*, IV, 110.

the Governor wrote to the home government, 'The stop put to the first method of proceedings hath dissipated the blak cloud that threatened this Province with destruccion.' [29] Nor did Increase Mather consider his work finished until he had visited in prison some of the persons who under terror had confessed witchcraft, and obtained recantation from eight of them. No more people were executed or even tried as witches in New England; although one was condemned to death in England as late as 1712, and executions went on in Continental countries until the end of the eighteenth century.

Cotton Mather would have come off unscathed in reputation but for his vanity, and his desire to pose as the official champion of Massachusetts justice. At the request of Governor Phips, and moved by his own passion for publicity, he hastily compiled, during the first three weeks after the witch trials ended (October, 1692), what purported to be an objective account of the whole affair. *The Wonders of the Invisible World: being an Account of the Tryals of Several Witches Lately Executed in New-England* (Boston, postdated 1693), by wrapping a mantle of sanctity about the foul and dreadful doings of the Salem court, exposed Mather to the charge of hypocrisy, and, as it were, proffered the tail to which Calef fastened the tin can.[30]

Nevertheless, the younger Mather made partial reparation by preventing a witchcraft outbreak in Boston. Two serving wenches in Boston, who appear to have resented the

[29] Quoted in T. J. Holmes, *op. cit.*, I, 128, where (pp. 115-34) the whole question of Mather's influence on the proceedings is ably discussed.

[30] Calef's satirical and devastating *More Wonders of the Invisible World* (London, 1700) reprinted in *Narratives of Witchcraft*, pp. 291-393.

fact that Salem girls were getting all the publicity, tried to put Boston on the witchcraft map in 1692 and 1693 by simulating the same symptoms. Cotton Mather never gave them a chance to get a following, or to bring the case before the courts. First one and then the other were taken home with him for treatment; and after they had become bored with being prayed over by a married minister, who was interested only in their souls, they consented to be cured. As in the Goodwin case, Cotton Mather was careful not to divulge the names of those whom the girls accused of bewitching them, lest Boston catch the madness.[31]

So ended this terrible scourge. Relatively speaking, the Salem witchcraft frenzy was but a small incident in the history of a great superstition. It will always be a blot upon New England because the members of her governing class, especially the judges, did not earlier take a firm stand that would have prevented a mischief. Yet we cannot close even this brief account of the affair unless we relate the sequel, without precedent in the annals of witchcraft. Almost everyone concerned in the accusations and the prosecution, including the ringleaders of the 'afflicted children,' but with the notable exception of Lieutenant-Governor Stoughton, afterwards confessed their error, begged forgiveness of their neighbors, and, so far as in them lay, made reparation. Twenty years after, in consequence of a movement begun by the aged Michael Wigglesworth, the legis-

[31] *The Memorial History of Boston*, II, 148-57; and see Cotton Mather's *Diary*, index under Margaret Rule, and *Narratives of Witchcraft*, pp. 255-87. Professor Burr, in his introduction and notes to the Rule case, puts on Mather's actions, the (it seems to me) totally unwarranted construction that he was moved solely by a desire for notoriety, and to save his own skin, in case the wench accused him of witchcraft.

lature annulled the convictions, reversed the attainders, and granted indemnities to the victims' heirs.[32] The story of this tragedy, in which science joined hands with superstition, may close with mention of that memorable winter's day of 1697, in the Old South Meeting-house, Boston, when Samuel Sewall, former member of the witchcraft court, rose in his pew and stood with bowed head while the minister read his retraction and confession of sin:

> Samuel Sewall . . . being sensible, that as to the Guilt contracted upon the opening of the late Commission of Oyer and Terminer at Salem, . . . he is, upon many accounts, more concerned than any that he knows of Desires to take the Blame and shame of it, asking pardon of men, and especially desiring prayers that God . . . would pardon that sin and all other his sins; and . . . Not Visit the sin of him, or of any other, upon himself, or any of his, nor upon the Land.[33]

THE GROWTH OF SCIENTIFIC KNOWLEDGE

The storm of witchcraft passed, and left New England much as it had been before. Nobody connected with it, except the obscure village witch-hunters, appears to have been discredited. The Mathers still dominated the intellectual scene from their stronghold in the Second Church in Boston, and appear to have been no less respected and unpopular after 1692 than before. Even Stoughton, dying unrepentant in 1701, had no stones cast on his grave. Robert Calef's witty and scurrilous attack on Cotton Mather appeared eight years after the tragic events, and failed notably to revive the dying embers. The ministers, by common con-

[32] Palfrey, IV, 116-17; cf. Sibley, *Harvard Graduates*, IV, 231, for the work of a very young minister, Joseph Green, in bringing peace to Salem Village. Wigglesworth's letter is in 4 *Coll. M.H.S.*, VIII, 645-46.

[33] Sewall, *Diary*, I, 445.

sent, renewed their struggle with the devil by preaching good morals and sound religion, and wisely left God to handle his satanic adversary in the 'invisible world,' whose wonders some of them had unwisely attempted to probe.

The ministers who were concerned with absorbing the scientific discoveries of the 'century of genius' and passing them on to the people in such a form and manner as to enhance love of God through knowledge of his wondrous works, were ably reinforced in 1686 through the arrival in New England of two eminent English dissenters, Charles Morton and Samuel Lee. Both had been students at Wadham College, Oxford, at a time when that little society was the centre of English science; when Wallis, Ward, Christopher Wren, William Petty, Robert Boyle, and Robert Hooke formed the nucleus of the Royal Society in the lodgings of Warden Wilkins. Both became dissenting clergymen, suffering the usual vicissitudes of that group after the restoration of the monarchy; Morton became head of one of the most successful of those academies for higher education where dissenters sent their boys from the grammar schools, when excluded from the universities by the new oaths and tests designed by a timid government to maintain hundred-per-cent conformity in politics and religion. Morton's academy at Newington Green near London numbered among its pupils Samuel Wesley and Daniel Defoe, both of whom gave him great praise as a schoolmaster, much as they disliked his religion. The persecution at the end of Charles II's reign determined Morton to give up his academy and emigrate to New England in 1686; and Samuel Lee came over the same year. Morton had been slated for president of Harvard in place of Mather, but political complications prevented, and instead he took the vacant pulpit at Charlestown near Boston, and received the somewhat empty honor of vice-president of the college. Lee tarried in Boston a few months and became minister of Bristol, Rhode Island (then a part of Massachusetts), for a few years.

Lee was the author of a number of popular treatises, in which the new scientific discoveries were improved to the glory of God. Pious New Englanders bought Lee's *Joy of Faith* (Boston, 1687) or *Day of Judgement* (Boston, 1692), thinking they were purchasing a devotional manual, and obtained a good bit of modern science before they got through. Morton worked through students, not through the press. He had compiled for the use of his English pupils, and largely from the *Philosophical Transactions* of the Royal Society, a manuscript textbook of science entitled *Compendium Physicae*, or, in some copies, *Natural Philosophy*. Although lacking in originality and occasionally in understanding, this manuscript textbook of some forty thousand words was superior to any printed manual of modern science in the English language. It was promptly 'adopted' at Harvard, replacing Heereboord's *Meletemata*, and continued to be used as the scientific text, both there and at Yale, until about the year 1725. Every student was supposed to make his own copy of a standard one given to the college by Morton, and five or six copies of the full text, with at least a dozen digests, are now found in our older libraries.[34]

---

[34] Morton's *Compendium Physicae* has been reprinted as *C.S.M.*, XXXIII, with an introduction by Dr. Theodore Hornberger, and a brief biography of Morton by S. E. Morison.

The impact of Morton's *Compendium* in the adolescent mind is perceived in the bachelors' commencement theses of 1687 and subsequent years. Instead of propositions from Aristotelian science, we have such theses as

> *Heat consists in motion, cold in rest*
> *The less dense body is the colder, the more dense the warmer*
> *All motion tends to a straight line*
> *Rarefaction is not augmentation, nor condensation, diminution*
> *Gravity is the attractive force of the Earth*
> *Rays of light are corpuscular*
> *The Magnet acts not by occult power, but by actual effluvia*
> *Sight, hearing, taste, and smell are methods of feeling*
> *Fish breathe by attraction and emission of air* [35]

And in 1689 we get the curious though natural mixture of science and superstition:

> *The Nature of cold consists in quiet*
> *Fluids are those bodies whose tiny particles are in motion*
> *Matter is neither generated nor corrupted*
> *Diversity of senses depends on diversity of nerves*
> *Variety of sounds depends on diversity of motion*
> *Witches exist*
> *Witchcraft is effected through an impious compact of men with demons*

Nathaniel Mather, even more precocious than his older brother Cotton, argued at his master's commencement in

---

[35] Harvard College, Commencement Broadside, 1687. *Theses Physicae,* Nos. 7, 10, 14, 15, 17, 21, 30, 33, 36. All the extant theses to 1708 are in Morison, *Harvard College in the Seventeenth Century.*

1688, 'There *is* a vacuum.' The same year, shortly after his nineteenth birthday, he died; and Cotton Mather, in a brief biography of the promising lad, declared that in this discourse, 'as well as by other Memorials and Experiments left behind him in Manuscripts' Nathaniel 'gave a Specimen of his Intimate acquaintance with the *Corpuscularian* (and only right) Philosophy.' [36] This meant that both Mathers had gone the whole way with Robert Boyle, a position by no means attained by the generality of English clergymen at that time; Ralph Cudworth, the Cambridge neo-Platonist, had lately denounced 'corpuscularianism' as akin to atheism.

Robert Boyle in 1663 struck the keynote of what later became known as natural theology in his *Usefulness of Experimental Natural Philosophy*. Probing into the secrets of nature, far from being an impious attempt to substitute materialism for a divinely ordered cosmos, unfolded the wonder, beauty, and symmetry of the universe created by God for the use of his errant children. Cotton Mather echoed this note in his Thanksgiving Day sermon of 1690 entitled *Wonderful Works of God Commemorated* incorporating some of Boyle's remarks about the bewildering number of new species discovered by naturalists. In 1691, John Ray, the father of natural theology, published his *The Wisdom of God Manifested in the Works of the Creation;* and only two years later, the year after the witchcraft affair, Cotton Mather echoed this in his *Winter-Meditations. Directions How to employ the Leisure of the Winter For the Glory of God*. In both his works, Mather spoke of the wonders revealed by the microscope. 'There

[36] Quoted in Sibley, *Harvard Graduates*, III, 323.

is not a Fly, but what would confute an Atheist,' he declares. 'And the *Little* things which our Naked Eyes cannot penetrate into, have in them a *Greatness* not to be seen without Astonishment. By the Assistance of *Microscopes*, have I seen *Animals* of which many Hundreds would not Aequal a Grain of Sand. How exquisite . . . must the Structure of them be!' [37]

Obviously, Cotton Mather is anticipating the eighteenth century, and moving fast toward the stand that he later takes in his *Christian Philosopher* (1721), that the world is completely planned and ordered, as well as geared and oiled to impeccable performance, by an all-wise Creator. Hence our wonder and love of God should increase with our knowledge of nature. But Mather could never eradicate from his mind the earlier conception, which the seventeenth-century puritans inherited from medieval theology, that there was no natural law that God could not and did not frequently set aside according to His good pleasure. Mather's *Magnalia Christi*, completed around 1700 and published in 1702, is a chronicle of violent interventions of the Deity in the affairs of New England and the lives of New Englanders. We should not hold this dualism against Mather, because it still exists. We still pray for prosperity and rain, and to be delivered from 'plague, pestilence, and famine; from earthquake, fire and flood; from battle and murder, and from sudden death.'

New England suffered for want of amateur scientists;

[37] Quoted by Dr. Hornberger in "Cotton Mather's Interest in Science," *American Literature*, VI (1935), 413-20. 'Hundreds' was stepped up to 'Thousands' in *Winter-Meditations*.

John Winthrop, Jr., Thomas Brattle, and the Mathers stand alone in that category until the eighteenth century. Increase Mather's Philosophical Society died before 1700. Paul Dudley, who was in college when Morton's *Compendium* was introduced, and later became a Fellow of the Royal Society and a frequent contributor to the *Philosophical Transactions*, reported sadly, 'as to more Experiments, our People don't much care for making them.' [38] Throughout Anglo-America there was a lamentable lack of curiosity as to fauna and flora, mineralogy, meteorological data, and the manners and customs of the Indians, compared with the interest shown by the French in Canada, the Dutch in Brazil, and the Spaniards in Mexico and Peru.

But we are not yet through with Cotton Mather, who has lately been hailed by two Johns Hopkins medical historians as the 'first significant figure in American medicine,' [39] His interest in medicine, which began at an early age, was stimulated by the discoveries of the microscope; he imported and read the leading medical works published in England, and became a pioneer advocate of the animalcular or germ theory of transmitting contagious diseases. In 1720 he began to write a general treatise on medicine called *The Angel of Bethesda* for which, greatly to his disappointment, he was never able to find a publisher. 'It is imbued with a modernity of feeling, . . . and is characterized throughout by the natural freshness that derives

[38] Sibley, *op. cit.*, IV, 51.
[39] Otho T. Beale, Jr., and Richard H. Shryock, *Cotton Mather, First Significant Figure in American Medicine* (Baltimore, 1954).

specifically from the fact that Mather intended to present the "best discoveries" and actually did so.' [40] His belief in the germ theory led, in time, to his courageous championing of Zabdiel Boylston in the great controversy over inoculation for smallpox in the Boston epidemic of 1721. In so doing, Mather championed an unpopular cause; he and Boylston were violently opposed by most of the populace and the politicians, by the newspaper edited by Benjamin Franklin's brother, and by the only M.D. in the colony, the Scots Dr. William Douglass, who charged that inoculation was in a class with witchcraft. But for the evidence produced in the Boston epidemic—a mortality of ten per cent for inoculated cases as against seventeen per cent for noninoculated cases—the case for inoculation could hardly have been sustained or the practice of it extended, in the British Isles.

Thus, our seventeenth-century men of science, few and poorly equipped though they were, contributed to the thin stream of scientific experiment and observation which fed the mighty rivers of the twentieth century.

The English puritans who emigrated to New England in the 1630's intended, and in a great measure succeeded, in transmitting European civilization to the New World. Realizing that all aspects of human life not directly useful or necessary were apt to be dissolved in the struggle for existence, anticipating that intellectual degeneracy would lead to spiritual decay, they made great sacrifices to trans-

---

[40] I. Bernard Cohen in *Isis*, XXXIII, 659; quoted by Drs. Beale and Shryock in *A.A.S.*, LXIII (1953), 165, where (pp. 167-274), *The Angel of Bethesda* is for the first time printed.

plant the apparatus of civilized life and learning. A university college, grammar schools, elementary schools, a printing press, and libraries they formed. The puritan creed, an intellectualized form of Christianity, stimulated mental activity on the part of those who professed it. The ministers, the most learned class in the colony, maintained an open mind and a receptive attitude toward the scientific discoveries of their century, and young college graduates made some attempt to dispel superstition by their popular essays in the almanacs. The 'warfare between science and theology' found no battleground in New England, where the clergy were leaders in liberalism and enlightenment, purveyors of new learning to the people.[41] Although the clergy did attempt to canalize the popular mind into religious channels, and to a remarkable degree succeeded, their conception of religion was sufficiently broad and stimulating to provide a dynamic motive for the intellectual movement in New England, and to give colonial literature a certain unity and dignity. They neither made, nor intended to make a breach with English and classical culture. The best of the ancient classics were included in the school and college curricula; contemporary English literature was imported and read; young men showed an appreciation of the humane poetry of the Elizabethan era, and wrote imitations of it as best they could.

In providing a framework and setting up values that later generations could use and respect, the New Englanders were more successful than in actual intellectual production. Three institutions of lasting significance for

[41] See facts marshaled by C. K. Shipton in *The American Historical Review*, XL, (1935), 460-67.

American life were firmly established: the college, the public-school system, and the Congregational Church. A veneration for learning, a respect for the humanities, and a habit of considering values other than material had been so firmly established among the New England people by 1701, that they were as well prepared as any people in the world to be quickened by new ideas, and to play their part in the coming drama of the Rights of Man.

Thus, the story of the intellectual life of New England in the seventeenth century is not merely that of a people bravely and successfully endeavoring to keep up the standards of civilization in the New World; it is one of the principal approaches to the social and intellectual history of the United States. Primitive New England is the porch to the temple; a puritan *pronaos* as it were to the American mind of the nineteenth century, and of today.

NOTE

*Inhabitants of the Thirteen Colonies Elected Fellows of
the Royal Society of London*

I am indebted to Mr. Frederick E. Brasch and Dr. Raymond P. Stearns for help in compiling the list. Although a Chronological Register of Fellows was printed in *The Records of the Royal Society of London* (3d ed., London, 1912), other elections of colonists have been found in the records. A man did not become a complete Fellow until he visited London and signed the constitution, hence some of the colonists elected (such as Cotton Mather) were never able to qualify; and William Brattle modestly declined his election on account of his personal insufficiency. But I have included all that were elected in this list. Fellows from the West Indies are not included, nor is Governor Fauquier of Virginia, who was elected before he went to America.

Name	Born	Died	Elected Fellow	Colony
John Winthrop	1606	1676	1663	Connecticut
William Byrd	1674	1744	1696	Virginia
Cotton Mather	1663	1728	1713?	Massachusetts
William Brattle	1662	1717	1714	Massachusetts
John Leverett	1662	1724	1714	Massachusetts
Paul Dudley	1675	1751	1721	Massachusetts
Thomas Robie	1689	1729	1725	Massachusetts
Zabdiel Boylston	1679	1766	1726	Massachusetts
John Winthrop	1681	1747	1734	Connecticut
John Mitchell	?	1768	1748	Virginia
Benjamin Franklin	1706	1790	1756	Pennsylvania
John Morgan	1735	1789	1765	Pennsylvania
John Tennent	?	c.1770	1765	Virginia
John Winthrop	1714	1779	1766	Massachusetts
Alexander Garden	1730?	1791	1773	South Carolina
Benjamin Thompson (Count Rumford)	1753	1814	1779	Massachusetts
James Bowdoin	1726	1790	1788	Massachusetts
David Rittenhouse	1732	1796	1795	Pennsylvania

INDEX